Dedication

This book is dedicated to the students, teachers, and professors
we have worked with in Africa and in the United States.

Volumes in This Series:

VOICES FROM THE CONTINENT

A Curriculum Guide to
Selected North and East African Literature

Sara Talis O'Brien
Saint Peter's College

Renée T. Schatteman
Georgia State University

Africa World Press, Inc.

P.O. Box 1892
Trenton, NJ 08607

P.O. Box 48
Asmara, ERITREA

Africa World Press, Inc.

P.O. Box 1892
Trenton, NJ 08607

P.O. Box 48
Asmara, ERITREA

Copyright © 2004 Sara Talis O'Brien and Renée T. Schatteman

First Printing 2004

Cover Design: Roger Dormann
Illustrations: Ann T. Ball

Library of Congress Cataloging-in-Publication Data

O'Brien, Sara Talis.
  Voices from the continent : a curriculum guide to selected North and East African literature / Sara Talis O'Brien, Renée T. Schatteman.
      p. cm.
  Includes bibliographical references.
  ISBN 1-59221-194-1 (cloth) — ISBN 1-59221-195-X (pbk.)
1. African literature—History and criticism. I. Schatteman, Renée. II. Title.

PL8010.O325 2004
809'.896—dc22

                    2004006267

CONTENTS

———

INTRODUCTION

Literature reflects the persistent and tenacious nature of culture, and tales passed on for generations in Africa form an extensive and pervasive base of knowledge and shared experience for particular ethnic groups. Modern African writers spring from the oral traditions of their people and write in indigenous and European languages. These artists paint vivid descriptions of life in Africa, dramatize the profound effect of change, and in many cases, chronicle the historical highlights of particular segments of society and ethnic groups. *Voices from the Continent: A Curriculum Guide to Selected North and East African Literature* is an invitation for college and university professors as well as teachers of English and social studies on the high school level to integrate multi-cultural themes and to diversify the standard curriculum by introducing students to modern North and East African literature written or translated into English.

This guide strives to synthesize anthropological and historical research as well as literary criticism and offers lesson plan ideas, reproducible student handouts, teacher resources, and reading resources on five narratives from North and East Africa. These works are accessible in the United States and appropriate for use in a variety of courses with students at different reading levels. The literature introduces a variety of universal themes, which raise complex issues and present the experiences of particular ethnic groups in various regions of Africa. The lessons are tools that instructors may adjust in order to fit particular teaching styles and address the needs of various groups of students meeting in a variety of time patterns. The lessons are elastic and may be taught in forty-five minute time periods, divided up into smaller time frames, or taught in longer segments in the block schedule. The units may be used in whole or in part, and they may be integrated into larger units on world literature, cultural diversity, psychology, social studies, African history, sociology, and women's studies. The texts presented in this guide may be also be taught together as a semester course focusing on the peoples, cultures, history, and literature of North and East Africa.

The peoples of Algeria, Egypt, Uganda, and Kenya are represented in this guide, and the authors include Assia Djebar, Naguib Mahfouz, Nawal El Saadawi, Okot p'Bitek, and Ngugi wa Thiong'o. Assia Djebar's *A Sister to Scheherazade* is a novel about women's solidarity in Algeria, and Naguib Mahfouz's *Fountain and Tomb* depicts a young boy's reflections on the daily life of the residents in a back alley of Cairo. Nawal El Saadawi's novel *Woman at Point Zero* highlights the violence and oppression faced by women, and Okot p'Bitek's *Song of Lawino* and *Song of Ocol* raise issues concerning the conflict of western and African cultures. Finally, Ngugi wa Thiong'o's *A Grain of Wheat* is a powerful psychological novel about personal and political revolution.

Each chapter of this guide focuses on one text and begins with suggested lesson plans. Instructors may choose to incorporate as much of the historical spine provided within each unit as seems appropriate. The lessons also include a study of the author's life and work as well as background on the cultural context of the work. For example, a focus on the image of women in the classic tales of the *Arabian Nights* illustrates how women need one another to escape oppression in a male dominated society in *A Sister to Scheherazade,* and a study of the Gikuyus' belief in the cycle of life illuminates the experience of revolution in *A Grain of Wheat.* Each unit also includes an analysis of the characters and plot development and suggested assessment tools, which again, the instructor may adjust. The reading resource in each chapter provides a detailed summary of the text and synthesis of the basic literary criticism. The resource is an efficient way for instructors to review new texts and pinpoint the content of specific chapters assigned to students during particular lessons. This resource may assist absent students or be provided to aids working with individual students. Finally, the student handouts in each chapter may be reproduced as class sets.

Needless to say, this guide is neither an attempt to review all North and East African texts suitable for study at the college, university, and high school levels, nor is it an effort to set a canon of North and East African literature. Indeed, instructors may wish to consider texts that reflect pre-colonial Africa more explicitly, such as Grace Ogot's short stories *Land without Thunder* and her romantic novel *The Promised Land*. Other popular texts include award-winning *The Gunny Sack* by M.G. Vassanji and *The Trial of Christopher Okigbo* by Ali Mazuri. Additional teachable texts by authors represented in this collection include Assia Djebar's *Women of Algiers in Their Apartment* and *Fantasia*, Naguib Mahfouz's *Midaq Alley*, and Ngugi wa Thiongo's *The River Between, Weep Not Child*, and *Matigari*. Proficient readers will also enjoy Ngugi's political novels *Petals of Blood* and *Devil on the Cross*.

Finally, as peoples of the world become increasingly interconnected, more and more college and university professors and teachers of English and social studies at the high school level are responding to demands to diversify the curriculum and foster global awareness. By learning about peoples of various cultures, students will better understand the world around them, develop a sensitivity to the nature and complexity of ethnic diversity, and be better equipped to function in a multi-cultural society. We believe that literature is both a window on the world and a probe into the minds and hearts of others. Literature not only provides a unique window through which readers may travel the world and meet people of many cultures, but it also brings the dry bones of history to life. We hope *Voices from the Continent: A Curriculum Guide to Selected North and East African Literature* contributes to this profound truth.

Sara Talis O'Brien
Saint Peter's College

Renée T. Schatteman
Georgia State University

List of Works Cited

p'Bitek, Okot. *Song of Lawino*. 1966. Published with *Song of Ocol*. Portsmouth, NH: Heinemann, 1984.

---. *Song of Ocol* .1970. Published with *Song of Lawino*. Portsmouth, NH: Heinemann, 1984.

Djebar, Assia. *A Sister to Scheherazade*. Trans. Dorothy S. Blair. London: Quartet, 1987.

---. *Fantasia: An Algerian Cavalcade*. Trans. Dorothy S. Blair. London: Quartet, 1988.

---. *Women of Algiers in Their Apartment*. Trans. Marjolijn de Jager. Charlottesville: University Press of Virginia, 1992.

Mahfouz, Naguib. *Fountain and Tomb*. Trans. Soad Sobhy, Essam Fattouh, and James Kenneson. Washington, D.C.: Three Continents Press, 1988.

---. *Midaq Alley*. Trans. Trevor Le Gassick. 1966. Washington, D.C.: Three Continents Press, 1990.

Mazuri, Ali. *The Trial of Christopher Okigbo*. London: Heinemann, 1971.

Ngugi, wa Thiong'o. *Weep Not Child*. 1964. Portsmouth, NH: Heinemann, 1988.

---. *The River Between*. 1965. Portsmouth, NH: Heinemann, 1990.

---. *A Grain of Wheat*. 1967. Portsmouth, NH: Heinmann, 1994.

---. *Petals of Blood*. 1977. Portsmouth, NH: Heinemann, 1991.

---. *Devil on the Cross*. Trans. Ngugi wa Thiong'o. 1982. Portsmouth, NH: Heinemann, 1987.

---. *Matigari*. Trans. Wangui wa Goro. Portsmouth, NH: Heinemann, 1987.

O'Brien, Sara Talis. *A Teacher's Guide to African Narratives*. Portsmouth, NH: Heinemann, 1998.

Ogot, Grace. *Land without Thunder*. Nairobi, Kenya: East Africa Publishing House, 1968.

---. *The Promised Land*. Nairobi, Kenya: East Africa Publishing House, 1966.

Saadawi, Nawal El. *Woman at Point Zero*. Trans. Sherif Hetata. London: Zed Books Ltd., 1983.

Vassanji, M. G. *The Gunny Sack*. Portsmouth, NH: Heinemann, 1989.

CHAPTER ONE

———

African Literature:
An Introduction

To the teacher:
The discussion of African literature may precede a unit or be woven into a unit. The student handouts in this chapter provide background information that may be helpful in introducing African literature. Suggested lesson ideas include the following:

Objectives:
1. Students will be able to distinguish between traditional African oral literature passed on in indigenous languages and modern African literature written in indigenous languages and European languages or translated into European languages.
2. Students will be able to explain the language issue in modern African literature.
3. Students will be able to identify the language link between traditional African literature and modern African literature.
4. Students will be able to discuss the sociological perspective on African literature.
5. Students will be able to compare and contrast some of the prominent themes in modern African literature with prominent themes in modern British and American literature.

Materials:
1. Student Handout: What is African Literature?
2. Student Handout: Location of Language Families in Africa
3. Student Handout: Linguistic Classification of Some African Languages
4. Student Handout: The Language Issue
5. Student Handout: The Beginnings of Modern African Literature
6. Student Handout: The Sociological Perspective on African Literature
7. Student Handout: Prominent Themes in Modern African Literature

Procedure:
1. Ask students to define African literature. African literature basically includes:
   - oral literature including songs, dances, and rituals passed on in indigenous languages for centuries within specific ethnic groups;
   - modern African literature written in indigenous languages, which may have been translated into European languages;
   - modern African literature written in European languages.
2. Distribute Student Handout: What is African Literature? and review the background of traditional African literature and the definition of modern African literature.
3. Ask students how many languages are spoken in Africa and to name a few. Linguists believe over 1,000 languages are spoken in Africa; over 250 languages are spoken in Nigeria alone. Some African languages include Luo, Maasai, Swahili, Zulu, and Shona, which are all spoken in East and southern Africa; Yoruba, Igbo, and Hausa, which are spoken in West Africa, and Arabic, which is spoken in northern Africa.
4. Distribute Student Handout: Location of Language Families in Africa and highlight the language families of the various regions of the continent.

5. Distribute <u>Student Handout: Linguistic Classification of Some African Languages</u> and ask students to locate the regions where various languages are spoken.

6. Distribute <u>Student Handout: The Language Issue</u>. Review the basic difficulties posed by language for modern African writers.

7. Distribute <u>Student Handout: The Beginnings of Modern African Literature</u> and ask students to identify the language link between traditional and modern African literature. Explain that the first published works in African literature were written in English and indigenous languages and that some works have been translated into English.

8. Distribute <u>Student Handout: The Sociological Perspective on African Literature</u> and ask students to define the sociological perspective. Emphasize that this perspective is not in opposition to formal analysis.

9. Distribute <u>Student Handout: Prominent Themes in Modern African Literature</u>. Ask students to compare and contrast some of the prominent themes in modern African literature with the themes in modern British and American literature.

Assessment:

The depth of analysis of traditional and modern African literature and the issues involved depend upon the level of the students and the requirements of individual teachers.

Student Handout
What is African Literature?

Background

Few students in western nations of the world have had the opportunity to study the history of the vast continent of Africa, meet her people, and explore her cultures. Many are unaware that ancient Egypt, which developed a complex system of hieroglyphics and built massive pyramids commemorating the pharaohs, is in fact located in Africa. Likewise, the stories of leaders like Sundiata and Mansa Musa, who built the powerful Mali Empire of the Sahara and developed the Islamic center of learning at Timbuktu in West Africa, are virtually unknown.

Literature reflects the persistent and tenacious nature of culture, and tales passed on for generations form an extensive and pervasive base of knowledge and shared experience for particular ethnic groups. African literature includes a variety of different types of narratives including creation myths, stories about heroes, explanations of social and political development, didactic lessons, and stories designed purely to entertain. For example, an East African creation myth explains how the Gikuyu people sprang from the ten daughters of Gikuyu and Mumbi and recounts how God gave these people the land surrounding Mt. Kenya. Likewise, an Acholi myth about a spear and a bead explains the historical migrations of heroes and the social divisions in Uganda. Tswana tales also recount heroes' deeds and teach the value of maintaining traditional society in southern Africa. Finally, in many entertaining vignettes, humorous animals personify human characteristics and embark on hilarious journeys through life. The hare and the hornbill of East Africa are classic comics, and Anasi, the trickster spider of West Africa, is so clever that he has traveled into the folklore of the Caribbean through the Diaspora.

What is African Literature?

African literature is basically divided into two sections:
- traditional oral literature including songs, dances, and rituals passed on in indigenous languages for centuries within specific ethnic groups;
- modern literature written in indigenous languages, which have been translated into European languages or modern literature written in European languages.

African literature, therefore, ranges from orature and oral performance in indigenous languages to complex novels written in indigenous languages and/or European languages. The literature available to students in the United States is obviously that which has been written or translated into English. In general terms, African literature is written by men and women of Africa; it does not include Caribbean literature or African American literature.

The critic Simon Gikandi indicates that "it is often said that modern African literature originates with Achebe" even though writers such as Thomas Mofolo in southern Africa and Amos Tutuola in Nigeria recorded African oral traditions before Chinua Achebe wrote *Things Fall Apart* (p. 2). Gikandi states that Achebe's seminal status lays "precisely in his ability to have realized that the novel provided a new way of reorganizing African culture" (p. 3). In his article entitled "The Role of the Writer in a New Nation," Achebe indicates that fiction may serve as a "validation of the African culture denied by colonial historiography" (p.7). In fact, understanding the relationship between literature and history is crucial in the study of African literature.

Source: Gikandi, Simon. *Reading Chinua Achebe*. Portsmouth, NH: Heinemann, 1991.

Student Handout: Location of Language Families in Africa

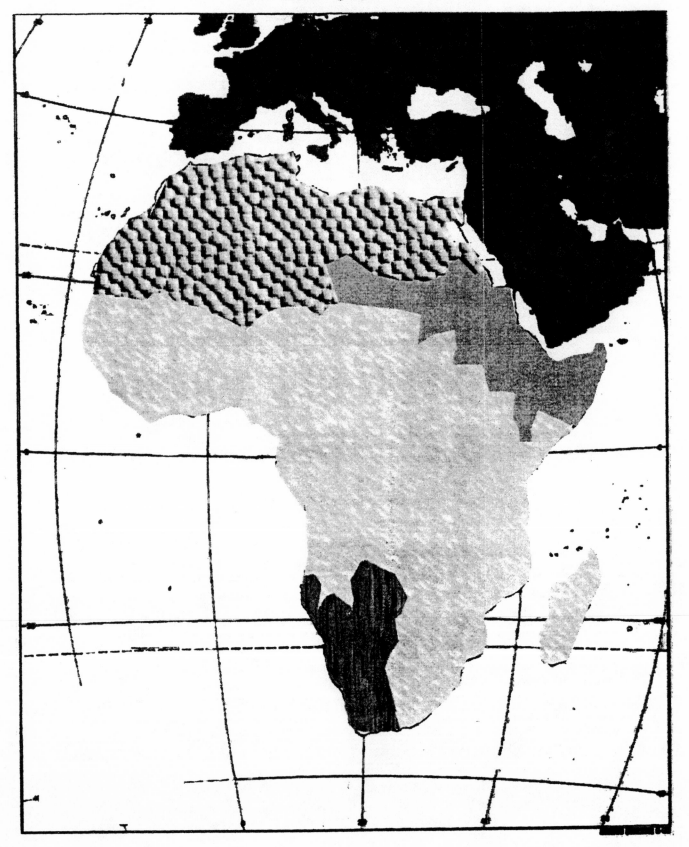

Student Handout
Linguistic Classification of Some African Languages

Legend
Language Family

- Sub-Family

Afro-Asiatic

- Chadic
  - Hausa
- African-Semitic
  - Arabic
  - Amharic

Niger-Kordofanian

- Atlantic
  - Fula
- Benue-Congo
  - Yoruba
- Bantu
  - Swahili
  - Zulu
  - Kikuyu
  - Shona

Nilo-Saharan

- Chari-Nile
  - Maasai
  - Luo

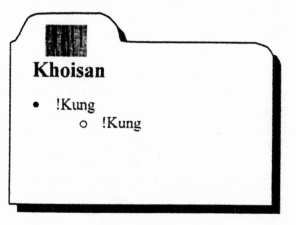

Khoisan

- !Kung
  - !Kung

Source: Leslie Belay, Priscilla Hinckley, and Aida Levi. "What Do We Know About Africa?" The African Outreach Program. Boston, MA: Boston University, 1985.

Student Handout
The Language Issue

The language issue is at the heart of modern African literature and poses a paradox for the African author who writes in a language of the oppressor. The audience for African literature written in a European language is problematic since only educated elite Africans can read European languages.

Some writers like Chinua Achebe "Africanize" English. For example, Igbo words are sprinkled throughout *Things Fall Apart* and complex Igbo concepts are defined in the novel's glossary. The novel is also peppered with Igbo proverbs. For instance, the author says, "Among the Igbo the art of conversation is regarded very highly, and proverbs are the palm-oil with which words are eaten" (*Things Fall Apart*, p. 5).

Like Achebe, Ama Ata Aidoo of Ghana, also writes in English. In an interview with Adeola James, she states, "I think that the whole question of the writer's relationship to her society has to do with language….here we are, writing in a language that is not even accessible to our people and one does worry about that, you know. For instance, writing in English makes it possible for me or any African writer to communicate with other people throughout the continent who share that colonial language. On the other hand, one's relationship to one's own immediate environment is fairly non-existent or rather controversial. These are some of the ideas that one comes up with. I have not pretended to myself that I have an answer. I have thought also that, whilst one is aware of the language issue as a big issue, it is better for a writer to *write*, in English, than not to write at all" (Adeola James, *In Their Own Voices*. Portsmouth: Heinemann, 1990, p. 9).

On the other hand, Ousmane Sembene of Senegal writes in French, Wolof, and Diola; many of his works are also translated into English. In order to reach a wider African audience, Sembene has extended his art to film. His films in French and indigenous languages include "Mandabi" (1968), based on a story about a money order, "Emitai" (1971), which focuses on the clash between the French and the Diola after World War II, "Xala" (1974), a biting satire on post-colonial Senegal, and "Ceddo" (1976), a controversial interpretation of the Wolof warriors' resistance to Islam in the 19th century. By breaking through the language barrier and visually telling his tales not only in French, but in indigenous languages, Sembene acts like the *griot*, or the traditional storyteller with a responsibility to his society.

Ngugi wa Thiong'o of East Africa is another example of an African writer who initially wrote in English, but now writes in an indigenous African language. When Ngugi wrote *Ngaahika Ndeenda*, or *I Will Marry when I Want*, in the Kikuyu language in 1977, the overwhelmingly popular response convinced him of the importance of writing in a language Kenyans could understand. In 1980, he published *Caitaani Mutharaba-ini* in Kikuyu, which came out as *Devil on the Cross* in English in 1982. The powerful oral reading of the novel in Kikuyu in Kenyan villages made Ngugi realize that the common people could not read any of the other works he published in English. His latest novels include *Matigari*, which was published in Kikuyu in 1986 and translated into English in 1987, and *Murogi wa Kagoog*, which is written in Kikuyu.

Ngugi's theoretical works include *Writers in Politics* (1981), *Decolonizing the Mind* (1986), *Moving the Center* (1993), and *Penpoints, Gunpoints and Dreams* (1998), all of which challenge artists to seek freedom from western cultural dominance. In January 2000, Ngugi organized an international conference in Asmara, Eritrea, which focused on African language and literature.

Note: See author chapters for references on Sembene and Ngugi's work.

Student Handout
The Beginnings of Modern African Literature

Readers and critics alike often hail Chinua Achebe as the "father" of modern African literature because his novel *Things Fall Apart*, published in 1958, has been so widely read and paints such a vivid portrait of life in colonial Nigeria. However, many other African writers contributed to the beginning of modern African literature by expressing the oral traditions of particular ethnic groups.

The Nigerian writer Amos Tutuola returns to the roots of Yoruba folklore and bases his myths in monstrous magic and incredible fantasy. Tutuola's fantastic stories are linked by the single device of a journey. Heroes and heroines participate in mythical quests and travel in cosmic territories inhabited by spirits; they are confronted with malevolent forces bent on destruction. Through confrontation and conquest, each main character grows in knowledge and through suffering, begins to understand life and to acquire a perception that enables him or her to help others. Tutuola published the following works in English between the years 1952 and 1958 in London and New York: *The Brave African Huntress, My Life in the Bush of Ghosts, The Palm-Wine Drinkard*, and *Simbi and the Satyr of the Dark Jungle*.

In East Africa, Okot p'Bitek published his first novel in the Acholi language titled *Lak Tar Miyo Kinyero Wi Lobo*, or *Are Your Teeth White? Then Laugh!* in 1953. This novel recounts the hopeless spiral of poverty that affected the Acholi people of Uganda in the 1950s. In 1963, he wrote a song titled "Wer pa Lawino," also in Acholi. This song was performed and discussed throughout the Gulu area of Uganda, and in 1965, p'Bitek read a small section of the piece at the East African Cultural Heritage conference held in Nairobi. His song about Lawino was an explosion that opened up the East African literary scene, for the traditional Acholi oral song was uniquely African and not structured after European models. Lawino's message about the value of African culture also challenged writers who looked to Europe for inspiration. Shortly after p'Bitek published *Song of Lawino* in English in 1966 with the East African Publishing House, it became an East African classic.

Thomas Mofolo, born in the mountain kingdom of Lesotho in 1876, wrote his first novel, *Moeti oa Bochabela*, or *Traveler to the East*, in 1907. This was the first creative work by a Mosotho writer and was published by Paris Evangelical Morija Press in the indigenous language of Sesotho in September 1907. The following year, Mofolo presented "L'Ange Dechu," or "The Fallen Angel," which was rejected by the publisher, and in 1909, he submitted the first draft of *Chaka*, which received brief but negative comments from the Lesotho missionary press. In January of the same year, the *Leselinyana*, a newspaper that encouraged writing among literate Basotho, began to serialize another novel titled *Pitseng*, which was also published by Morija Press in 1910. Finally, *Chaka* was published by Morija Press in Lesotho in 1925. In this classic of African literature, Mofolo selects historical events, retells oral histories, and embellishes the *Book of the Chronicles of Zulu* collected by Sekese, as he retells the tragic demise of Shaka, the mighty military strategist who amalgamated the powerful Zulu nation in southern Africa. *Chaka* has been translated from the original Sesotho into English, French, German, Zulu, Swahili, and Afrikaans; Mofolo's other novels have not been translated from Sesotho into English.

Source: Kunene, Daniel P. *Thomas Mofolo and the Emergence of Written Sesotho Prose*. Johannesburg: Ravan Press, 1989.

Student Handout
The Sociological Perspective on African Literature

African literature holds a certain historical and sociological significance. Traditional African literature exists in indigenous languages and is related to indigenous society and cultures. Modern African literature has grown out of the rupture created by the colonial experience. The two different phases of African history and literature reflect two different phases in the collective experience and consciousness of the African people.

Abiola Irele states that critics must recognize the uniqueness of African literature and its reference to the living context of African life. He explains that the major significance of modern African writing is the comprehensive testimony it offers of the drama of Africa. Irele states, "That drama has its source of course in our relation to the Western world, which has crossed our historical path and modified the realities of our life as well as our entire perspective upon the world. The imaginative writing in particular stands both as a direct representation of the concrete facts of our collective experience and as a reconstruction" (p. 2). Irele, like Chinua Achebe, recognizes the profound human implication of art. The question of artistic achievement in modern African literature is complicated, however, because writers express the African experience in European languages and foreign literary structures. This forces comparison with the established figures of the Western literary tradition when in fact, modern African literature is really a testimony to a certain state of incoherence in African society.

Irele emphasizes the significance of literature's reference to the lived world and explains that the essential force of African literature is "its reference to the historical and experiential" (p. 11). He discusses formal and sociological approaches to understanding African literature and acknowledges that formal analysis is intrinsic to literary study. On the other hand, the sociological approach correlates a work with the social background and explores an author's theme in the wider social context. Through the sociological approach, the reader is aware of how a writer captures a "moment of the historical consciousness of the society" (p. 34).

Irele sees no opposition between the formal approach and the sociological approach to literature, but he does acknowledge that African literature is often regarded merely as social documentary and too many commentaries are concerned with tracing and elucidating cultural references. Nevertheless, Irele feels that the sociological approach can provide a context of interest and substance to the abstract preoccupation with presentation in form and adds that content analysis will necessarily view African works through a sociological perspective.

In conclusion, Irele maintains that African literature has a significance for human experience beyond Africa. He believes that the fundamental question "... is not simply one of understanding African literature but of apprehending it in its complex resonances–of each individual text related, even in its uniqueness, to a common framework of consciousness and in that way integrated into a cultural whole which situates the aesthetic event within the living context of the historical" (p. 24). He feels that no single approach to studying African literature is adequate, " ... for we are dealing with a phenomenon which, by its nature, is irreducible to any sort of common measure" (p. 23-24).

Source: Irele, Abiola. *The African Experience in Literature and Ideology.* Bloomington: Indiana University Press, 1990.

Student Handout
Prominent Themes in African Literature

African literature reflects the African experience. Some prominent themes are listed below:

Conflict
- African peoples vs. the colonial oppressor
- traditional life vs. modern life
- informal traditional education vs. formal western education
- myth and divination vs. reality

Selfhood
- articulating self
- understanding self within indigenous cultures
- situating self amid currents of social change
- writing back to the empire

Resistance
- liberation movements
- revolution
- Marxist politics

Individual Responsibility
- heroism and courage
- solidarity with the collective
- complicity with the colonial oppressor
- guilt and ambiguity

Complaint
- neocolonialism
- hypocrisy
- corruption

Means of regeneration
- rediscovery of roots
- adopting a hybrid position*
- creating new traditions

Gender Relations
- role of women
- the patriarchy

*The concept of "hybridity" in the African novel is complex and more than simply combining cultural perspectives and aesthetics to form a hybrid of form and content. Hybridity often involves complex dialogues and confrontations between African and European cultures.

List of Works Consulted

Achebe, Chinua. *Morning Yet on Creation Day*. Portsmouth, NH: Heinemann, 1975.

Amuta, Chidi. *The Theory of African Literature: Implications for Practical Criticism*. London: Zed Books, Ltd., 1989.

Austen, Ralph. "Teaching Africa Through Culture Areas and Literary Texts." *Great Ideas for Teaching about Africa*. Ed. Misty Bastian. Boulder, CO: Lynne Rienner Publishers, 1999. 193-202.

Azevedo, Mario and Gwendolyn Prater. *Africa and Its People: An Interdisciplinary Survey of the Continent*. Dubuque, Iowa: Kendall/Hunt Publishing Co., 1982.

Belay, Leslie, Priscilla Hinkley and Aida Lewis. "What Do We Know about Africa?" The African Outreach Program. Boston, MA: Boston University, 1985.

Bjornson, Richard, ed. *Research in African Literatures: The Language Question* 23.1 (1992).

Booker, Keith. *The African Novel in English*. Portsmouth, NH: Heinemann, 1998.

Courlander, Harold. *The Cow-Tail Switch and Other West African Stories*. 1947. New York, NY: Henry Holt, 1986.

Courlander, Harold. *A Treasury of African Folklore: The Oral Literature, Traditions, Myths, Legends, Epics, Tales, Recollections, Wisdom, Sayings, and Humor of Africa*. New York, NY: Crown Publishers, Inc., 1975.

Gakuo, Kariuji. *Nyumba ya Mumbi: The Gikuyu Creation Myth*. Nairobi, Kenya: Jacaranda Designs, Ltd., 1992.

Gikandi, Simon. "Ngugi's Conversion: Writing and the Politics of Language." *Research in African Literatures* 23.1 (1992): 131-144.

---. *Reading the African Novel*. Portsmouth, NH: Heinemann, 1987.

---. *Reading Chinua Achebe*. Portsmouth, NH: Heinemann, 1991.

Gugelberger, George, ed. *Marxism & African Literature*. London: James Currey Ltd., 1985.

Hay, Margaret, ed. *African Novels in the Classroom*. Boulder, CO: Lynne Rienner Publishers, 2000.

Heywood, Christopher ed. *Perspectives on African Literature*. London: Heinemann, 1979.

Irele, Abiola. *The African Experience in Literature and Ideology*. Bloomington: Indiana University Press, 1990.

James, Adeola. *In Their Own Voices: African Women Writers Talk*. Portsmouth, NH: Heinemann, 1990.

Kunene, Daniel P. *Thomas Mofolo and the Emergence of Written Sesotho Prose*. Johannesburg: Ravan Press, 1989.

---. *Thomas Mofolo's* Chaka: *A New Translation by Daniel Kunene of the Famous Novel*. London: Heinemann, 1981.

Lindfors, Bernth, ed. *Critical Perspectives on Amos Tutuola*. Washington, D. C.: Three Continents Press, 1975.

Lo Liyong, Taban. *Eating Chiefs: Lwo Culture from Lolwe to Malkal*. London: Heinemann, 1970.

Mofolo, Thomas. *Moeti oa Bochabela*. 1907. Lesotho: Morija Press, 1961.

---. *The Traveler of the East*. Trans. H. Ashton. London: Society for Promoting Christian Knowledge, 1934.

---. *Pitseng*. 1910. Lesotho: Morija Press, 1960.

---. *Chaka*. 1925. Lesotho: Morija Press, 1962.

Niane, D.T. *Sundiata: An Epic of Old Mali*. Trans. G. D. Pickett. 1960. New York: Longman African Classic, 1987.

O'Brien, Sara Talis. *A Teacher's Guide to African Narratives*. Portsmouth, NH: Heinemann, 1998.

Obiechina, Emmanuel N. *Language and Theme: Essays on African Literature*. Washington, D.C.: Howard University Press, 1990.

Okpewho, Isidore. *African Oral Literature: Backgrounds, Character, and Continuity*. Bloomington: Indiana University Press, 1992.

p'Bitek, Okot. *Hare and Hornbill*. London: Heinemann, 1978.

---. *Song of Lawino*. Nairobi: East African Publishing House, 1966; published with *Song of Ocol* Portsmouth: Heinemann, 1984.

---. *Lak Tar. White Teeth*. Nairobi: Heinemann, 1989.

Rubadiri, David. "The Development of Writing in East Africa." *Perspectives on African Literature*. Ed. Christopher Heywood. London: Heinemann, 1979.

Sandomirsky, Natalie. "Teaching Africa Through Literature." *Great Ideas for Teaching about Africa*. Ed. Misty Bastian. Boulder, CO: Lynne Rienner Publishers, 1999. 59-66.

Schapera, Isaac and John Comaroff. *The Tswana*. London, New York: Paul Kegan International in Association with International African Institute, 1991.

Scheub, Harold. *The African Storyteller: Stories from African Oral Traditions*. Dubuque, IA: Kendall/Hunt Publishing Company, 1990.

Tutuola, Amos. *The Brave African Huntress*. London: Faber and Faber, 1958.

---. *My Life in the Bush of Ghosts*. London: Faber and Faber, n.d.

---. *The Palm-Wine Drinkard*. New York, NY: Grove Press, 1953.

---. *Simbi and the Satyr of the Dark Jungle*. London: Faber and Faber, n.d.

Wilkinson, Jane, ed. *Talking with African Writers: Interviews with African Poets Playwrights & Novelists*. London: Heinemann, 1992.

CHAPTER TWO

———

Africa: An Overview of the Continent

To the teacher:

The maps in this chapter provide background information that may be helpful in teaching the various units in this curriculum. Suggested lesson ideas for introducing the maps include the following:

Objectives:

1. Students will be able to locate African countries on Student Handout: Map of Africa.
2. Students will be able to identify the countries in West, East, Central, Southern, and North Africa by filling in Student Handout: Blank Map of Africa.
3. Students will be able to identify the countries in West, East, Central, Southern, and North Africa by referring to Student Handout: Map of Africa Quiz and writing the name of the country on the line provided next to the corresponding number on Student Handout: Map of Africa Quiz Answer Sheet. Teachers may wish to refer to Teacher Resource: Map of Africa Quiz Answer Sheet.
4. Students will be able to identify the predominantly Muslim countries in Africa by referring to Student Handout: Map of Islam in Africa.

Materials:

1. Student Handout: Map of Africa
2. Student Handout: Blank Map of Africa
3. Student Handout: Map of Africa Quiz
4. Student Handout: Map of Africa Quiz Answer Sheet
5. Teacher Resource: Map of Africa Answer Sheet
6. Student Handout: Map of Islam in Africa

Procedure:

1. Introduce the narrative by referring to the country of the author's origin on a classroom wall map and Student Handout: Map of Africa.
2. Ask students to list the various countries in the regions of Africa such as West, East, Central, Southern, and North Africa by referring to Student Handout: Map of Africa and filling in Student Handout: Blank Map of Africa, or have students identify countries on the blank map from memory.
3. If desired, ask students to complete the map of Africa quiz by referring to Student Handout: Map of Africa Quiz and completing Student Handout: Map of Africa Quiz Answer Sheet. Refer to Teacher Resource: Map of Africa Answer Sheet.
4. Ask students to identify the various countries that are predominantly Muslim in Africa by referring to Student Handout: Map of Islam in Africa.

Assessment:

The level of knowledge, detail, and accuracy in locating African countries on the maps depends upon the level of the students and the requirements of individual teachers.

Student Handout
Map of Africa

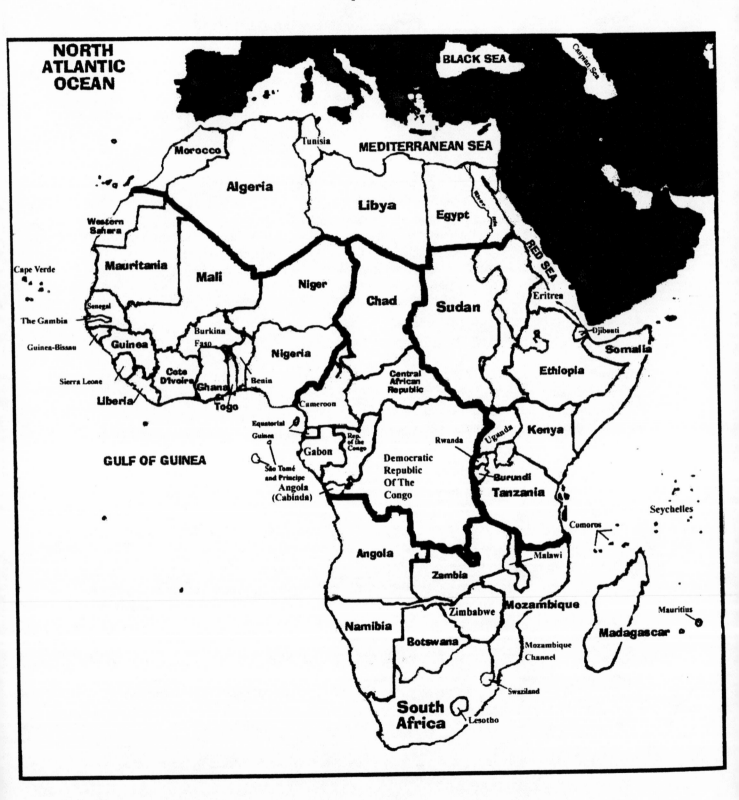

Student Handout
Blank Map of Africa

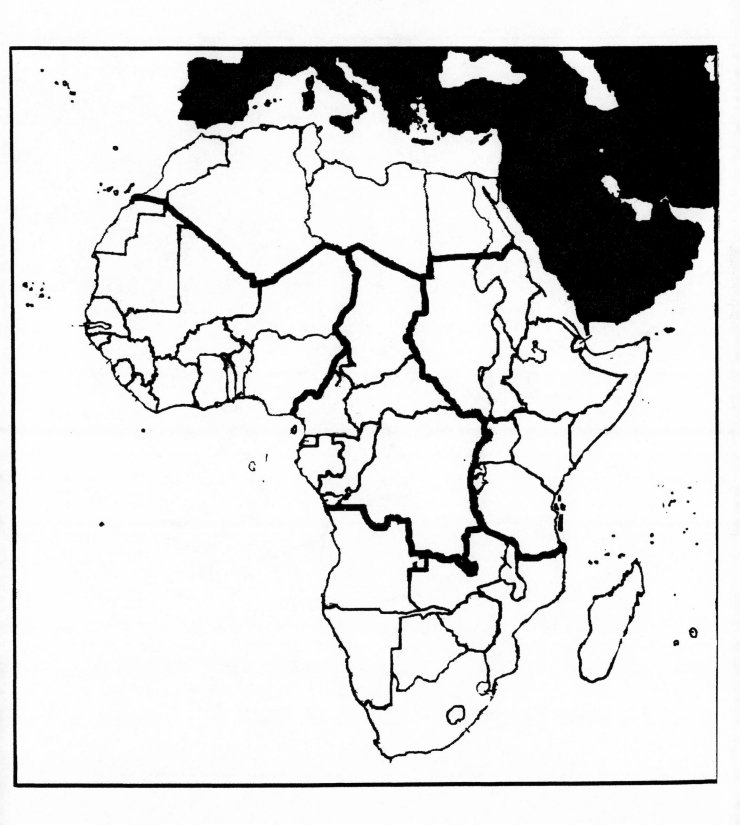

Student Handout
Map of Africa Quiz

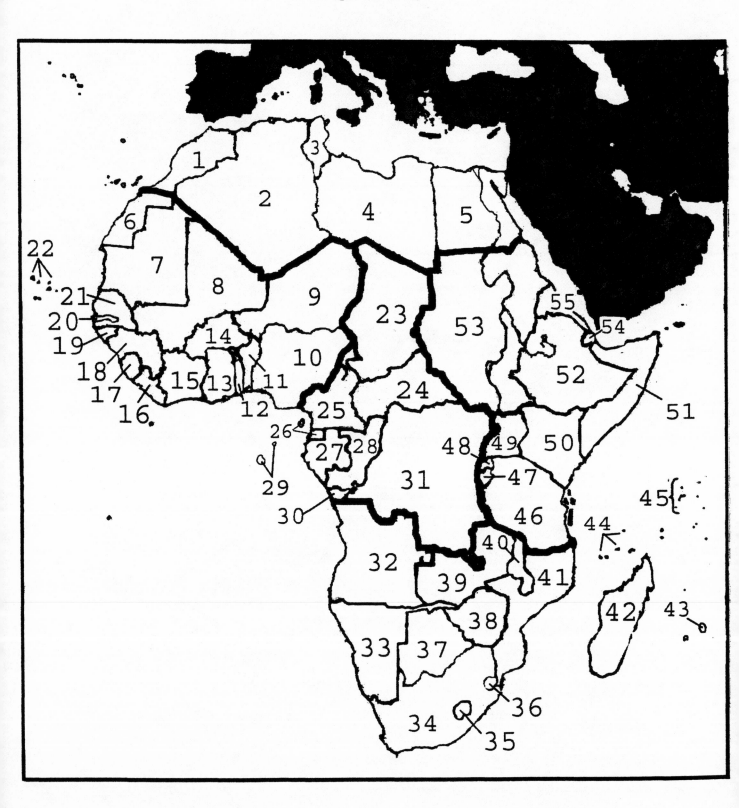

Student Handout
Map of Africa Quiz
Answer Sheet

Your Name _____

Northern Africa

1. _____

2. _____

3. _____

4. _____

5. _____

Western Africa

6. _____

7. _____

8. _____

9. _____

10. _____

11. _____

12. _____

13. _____

14. _____

15. _____

16. _____

17. _____

18. _____

19. _____

20. _____

21. _____

22. _____

Central Africa

23. _____

24. _____

25. _____

26. _____

27. _____

28. _____

29. _____

30. _____

31. _____

Southern Africa

32. _____

33. _____

34. _____

35. _____

36. _____

37. _____

38. _____

39. _____

40. _____

41. _____

42. _____

43. _____

Eastern Africa

44. _____

45. _____

46. _____

47. _____

48. _____

49. _____

50. _____

51. _____

52. _____

53. _____

54. _____

55. _____

Teacher Resource
Map of Africa Quiz
Answer Sheet

Northern Africa

1. Morocco

2. Algeria

3. Tunisia

4. Libya

5. Egypt

Western Africa

6. West Sahara

7. Mauritania

8. Mali

9. Niger

10. Nigeria

11. Benin

12. Togo

13. Ghana

14. Burkina Faso

15. Côte D'Ivoire

16. Liberia

17. Sierra Leone

18. Guinea

19. Guinea-Bissau

20. The Gambia

21. Senegal

22. Cape Verde

Central Africa

23. Chad

24. Central African Rep.

25. Cameroon

26. Equatorial Guinea

27. Gabon

28. Rep. of Congo

29. São Tomé & Principe

30. Angola (Cabinda)

31. Dem. Rep. Congo

Southern Africa

32. Angola

33. Namibia

34. South Africa

35. Lesotho

36. Swaziland

37. Botswana

38. Zimbabwe

39. Zambia

40. Malawi

41. Mozambique

42. Madagascar

43. Mauritius

Eastern Africa

44. Comoros

45. Seychelles

46. Tanzania

47. Burundi

48. Rwanda

49. Uganda

50. Kenya

51. Somalia

52. Ethiopia

53. Sudan

54. Djibouti

55. Eritrea

Student Handout
Islam In Africa

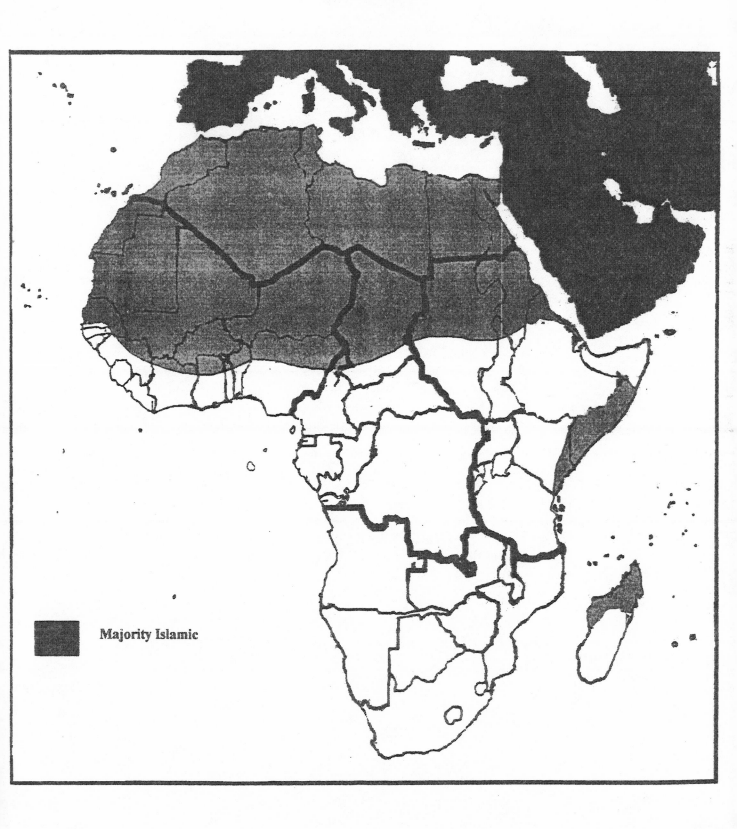

Majority Islamic

CHAPTER THREE

———

A Sister to Scheherazade
A Novel about Women's Solidarity in Algeria
by Assia Djebar

Assia Djebar, internationally celebrated as one of northern Africa's most important writers, explores women's struggle for liberation in *A Sister to Scheherazade*. Djebar seeks to liberate the odalisques, the female slaves or concubines in the Oriental harems of old, and their present-day representatives, Isma and Hajila. Isma is the vibrant, articulate, and seemingly emancipated woman who has divorced her husband and selected the passive, quiet, and traditional Hajila as his second wife. Isma tells her own story in the first person narrative; she also tells Hajila's story in the second person narrative as she addresses Hajila. Isma knows Hajila's story intimately; Hajila does not know Isma until the end of the novel. Isma moves through the past of her childhood and early years of marriage in order to understand the present; Hajila moves through public places in order to escape the traditional life of the sequestered Muslim woman. Isma seems to break through the psychological prison walls constructed by the patriarchy and then seeks to reintegrate tradition into her life. However, Isma both condemns Hajila to a life of oppression and offers her the key to her own freedom. Throughout the novel, Isma and Hajila are "ghost and mirror-image of each other" (p. 158) and need one another in order to emancipate themselves from the male dominated Muslim society. Isma and Hajila are compared to Scheherazade, the bride of the bloodthirsty sultan, and her sister, Dinarzade, in the tales of the *Arabian Nights*. Like Isma and Hajila, these sisters need one another to escape death at the sultan's hands. The novel criticizes the oppression of women around the world; it does not target Islam or Muslim people in general.

Note: This provocative novel includes graphic sexuality. Teachers are encouraged to seek parental and/or school administrative permission before introducing this unit. Students who will not read the novel may focus on the tales of the *Arabian Nights* and thus participate fully.

Lessons

Lesson One   Introduction: Background The *Arabian Nights* and the Myth of Scheherazade
                   The Harem, the Veil, and the Turkish Baths
                   Reading Assignment: Part I, Chapters 1-7, pages 1-48
                   Research Assignment: The Tales of the *Arabian Nights*

Lesson Two   Islam in Africa History of the Islamic Peoples of Algeria
                   Reading Assignment: Part I, Chapters 8-14, pages 49-91
                   Research Assignment: The Tales of the *Arabian Nights*

Lesson Three   The Author, Characters, and Plot Development
                   Reading Assignment: Part II, Chapters 1-9, pages 94-138
                   Research Assignment: The Tales of the *Arabian Nights*

Lesson Four   Tales of Women
                   Reading Assignment: Part III, Chapters 1-3, pages 141-160
                   Research Assignment: The Tales of the *Arabian Nights*

Lesson Five   The Sultan's Bride: Is the Odalisque in Flight?
                   Research Assignment: The Tales of the *Arabian Nights*

Lesson One
Introduction
The *Arabian Nights* and the Myth of Scheherazade
The Harem, the Veil, and the Turkish Baths

Objectives:
1. Students will become familiar with the tales of the *Arabian Nights* and read the myth of Scheherazade.
2. Students will identify northern Africa by locating Algeria and her neighbors.
3. Students will become familiar with the concepts of the harem, the veil, and the Turkish baths.
4. Students will identify the relationship between Isma and Hajila, the two main characters in the novel, and become familiar with the narrative structure.
5. Some students will begin to research the tales of the *Arabian Nights*.

Materials:
1. Classroom World Map
2. Student Handout: Map of Africa, Chapter Two: Africa Overview of the Continent
3. Student Handout: Scheherazade and the Tales of the *Arabian Nights*
4. Student Handout: The Harem, the Veil, and the Turkish Baths
5. Student Handout: Research on the Tales of the *Arabian Nights*
6. Optional: Several copies of different versions tales of the *Arabian Nights*

Procedure:
1. Explain that *A Sister to Scheherazade* is a complex novel by an Algerian writer that uses the Arabian myth of a beautiful woman named Scheherazade and her sister Dinarzade as its inspiration.
2. Explain that the tales of the *Arabian Nights* and the myth of Scheherazade originated in Egypt, India, and ancient Persia; these are the areas around the Arabian Sea and include the modern-day nations of Pakistan and Afghanistan. Ask students to locate the Arabian Sea and the areas that surround it on a classroom wall map.
3. Distribute Student Handout: Scheherazade and the Tales of the *Arabian Nights*. Read the handout orally and ask the students to explain the significance of Scheherazade's triumph over the bloodthirsty sultan.
4. Ask the students to locate Algeria in Northern Africa on a wall map. Distribute Student Handout: Map of Africa. Have students identify Algeria, Morocco, Tunisia, Libya, and Egypt as the countries that comprise North Africa. Explain that the tales of the *Arabian Nights* were part of the culture that the Islamic people of the East brought with them as they migrated into northern Africa.
5. Introduce the novel by explaining that two women, Isma and Hajila, are wives of the same man. Isma is the narrator and tells both her story and the story of Hajila. As Isma tells Hajila's story, she speaks directly to Hajila although Hajila is unaware of Isma's presence in the beginning of the novel. These two women are modern day representatives of Scheherazade and her sister Dinarzade in the frame story of the tales of the *Arabian Nights*.
6. Distribute Student Handout: The Harem, the Veil, and the Turkish Baths. Discuss these concepts and explain that these ideas will help the students understand the novel.
7. Read through the introduction, Chapter 1, "Hajila," and Chapter 2, "Isma."
8. Explain that in these preliminary chapters and throughout Part I the narrator will focus on concepts such as movement out of doors, the activities of the bedroom, and relationships with others. These topics will be addressed from the perspective of both women, Isma and Hajila.
9. Some students may not have permission to read *A Sister to Scheherazade* based on its symbolic and in some cases explicit references to sexuality. Explain that these students will

form the Research Group will research selected tales of the *Arabian Nights* and present their findings to the class.

10. Distribute <u>Student Handout: Research on the Tales of the *Arabian Nights*</u> to the students in the Research Group.

Assessment:
Ask students to compare Isma and Scheherazade in both the novel and the tales of the *Arabian Nights*. In a very basic way, students should understand that both women are storytellers.

Reading Assignment:
A Sister to Scheherazade, Part I, "Every Woman's Name is Wound," Chapters 1-7, pages 1-48.

Thought Questions:
1. In what way does Hajila's kitchen resemble the enclosure of the harem? (Chapter 1)
2. Compare Isma's freedom of movement with Hajila's situation. (Chapter 2)
3. Explain why Hajila wears the veil as she leaves her apartment and then why she removes the veil when she is out of doors. (Chapter 3)
4. Compare Isma and Hajila's experiences in the bedroom with their husband. (Chapter 4)
5. Why does Hajila feel like she is stripped naked as she walks in the garden? (Chapter 5)
6. Compare and contrast Isma and Hajila's attitudes toward the traditional veil. (Chapter 6)
7. Explain Touma's attitude toward Hajila's marriage? (Chapter 7)

Research Assignment:
1. Each of the students in the Research Group should borrow any version of the tales of the *Arabian Nights* from the teacher or the local or school library. Students should bring the tales of the *Arabian Nights* to the next class.
2. Students in the Research Group should select and read one tale and complete "Part I, Introduction," on <u>Student Handout: Research on the Tales of the *Arabian Nights*</u>.

Lesson Two
Islam in Africa
History of the Islamic Peoples of Algeria

Objectives:
1. Students will outline the history of the African people featured in this novel by identifying the historical highlights of the Islamic peoples of Algeria.
2. Students will begin to define the religious dogma of Islam.
3. Students will identify the area of Islamic influence in Africa.
4. Students in the Research Group will retell one tale as narrated by Scheherazade to the bloodthirsty sultan in the tales of the *Arabian Nights*.

Materials:
1. Student Handout: The Dogma of Islam
2. Student Handout: Islam in Africa
3. Student Handout: Map of Islam in Africa, Chapter Two: Overview of the Continent
4. Teacher Resource: Historical Highlights of the Islamic Peoples of Algeria
5. Reading Resource: Summary and Analysis: Part I, "Every Woman's Name is Wound," Chapters 1-7

Procedure:
1. Discuss the thought questions for Part I, Chapters 1-7. Refer to Summary and Analysis: Part I, Chapters 1-7. Again, ask students to clarify the relationship between Isma and Hajila and the role of Isma the narrator.
2. During this discussion, ask students in the Research Group to briefly describe to one another the tale of the *Arabian Nights* they read for homework.
3. Reconvene the entire class. Distribute Student Handout: The Dogma of Islam. Discuss Islam as a religion that focuses on one God, Allah, and his prophet Muhammad. Discuss the relationship of Islam to other major world religions.
4. Distribute Student Handout: Islam in Africa. Ask students to identify the reasons why the Islamic faith spread so rapidly in North Africa.
5. Distribute Student Handout: Map of Islam in Africa. Ask students to identify the major areas of Islamic influence in Africa.
6. Inform students of important events and periods in the history of the Islamic Peoples of Algeria. Refer to Teacher Resource: Historical Highlights of the Islamic Peoples of Algeria.

Assessment:
1. Ask students who are reading the novel to compare and contrast Isma and Hajila in terms of their relationships to the outside world.

2. Ask students in the Research Group if any of the stories they have read so far focus on the relationships between individuals and the outside world. If so, and if time permits, ask one or two of these students to retell the story as Scheherazade would have told it to the sultan.

Reading Assignment:
A Sister to Scheherazade, Part I, "Every Woman's Name is Wound," Chapters 8-14, pages 49-91.

Thought Questions:
1. As Hajila grows in self-discovery in her relationship with others in Chapter 7, Isma attempts to understand herself by reflecting upon her relationship with her ex-husband. Describe that relationship. (Chapter 8)
2. Contrast Isma and Hajila's relationship with "the man." (Chapter 9)

3. Why do Isma's feelings for her husband change? (Chapter 10)
4. Why has Isma returned to Hajila's household? (Chapter 11)
5. Compare the patios of Isma's past with the ancient concept of the harem. (Chapter 12)
6. Why is "the man" so upset when he learns that Hajila has been moving freely around the city despite the fact that his first wife Isma always moved freely about the city? (Chapter 13)
7. Explain the significance of the Arabic word *derra*. (Chapter 14)

Research Assignment:
Students in the Research Group should complete "Part II, Scheherazade and the Sultan," on Student Handout: Research on the Tales of the *Arabian Nights*.

Lesson Three
The Author, Characters, and Plot Development

Objectives:
1. Students will become familiar with the author Assia Djebar by reviewing her life and work.
2. Students will identify the major characters in *A Sister to Scheherazade*.
3. Students in the Research Group will report on the history of their version of the tales of the *Arabian Nights* and illustrate and retell one tale as narrated by Scheherazade to the bloodthirsty sultan.

Materials:
1. Construction paper and magic markers
2. Student Handout: The Author and Her Work
3. Student Handout: A Selected Bibliography of Assia Djebar's work
4. Student Handout: Characters in *A Sister to Scheherazade*
5. Teacher Resource: Characters in *A Sister to Scheherazade*
6. Student Handout: Research on the Tales of the *Arabian Nights*
7. Reading Resource: Summary and Analysis: Part I, "Every Woman's Name is Wound," Chapters 8-14

Procedure:
1. Ask students in the Research Group to review Part I of their homework on the background of the tales of the *Arabian Nights*. Provide construction paper and magic markers and ask each student to draw a sketch of the second tale he or she read. Ask the students to title and sign their sketch and be prepared to retell the tale to the class.
2. While students in the Research Group are completing their sketches, discuss the thought questions for Part I Chapters 8-14. Refer to Summary and Analysis: Part I, Chapters 8-14. Again, ask students to clarify the relationship between Isma, Hajila, and their husband. Note that "the man" is husband to both women. Isma is divorced from "the man," and Hajila is married to "the man."
3. Reconvene the large group. Distribute Student Handout: The Author and Her Work and Student Handout: A Selected Bibliography of Assia Djebar's Work. Discuss the background of the author and ask the students if they see any traces of Assia Djebar in the character of Isma in the novel.
4. Distribute Student Handout: Characters in *A Sister to Scheherazade* and ask students to identify the characters. Refer to Teacher Resource: Characters in *A Sister to Scheherazade*.
5. Explain that Isma will focus on two themes in "Part II, Destruction at Dawn." The first focus in the myth of Scheherazade and her sister Dinarzade; the second focus is her own childhood.
6. Ask students in the Research Group to show their books of the tales of the *Arabian Nights* to the class and to briefly explain the history of their version of the tales. Students should refer to Part I Background on Student Handout: Research on the Tales of the *Arabian Nights*.
7. Ask students in the Research Group to display and explain the sketch they have drawn about the second tale they read in tales of the *Arabian Nights*.

Assessment:
Ask students in the entire class if they can make connections between the author Assia Djebar, the narrator Isma in *A Sister to Scheherazade* and Scheherazade in the tales of the *Arabian Nights*. Students should realize that all these women are storytellers.

Reading Assignment:
A Sister to Scheherazade, Part II, "Destruction at Dawn," Chapters 1-9, pages 94-138.

Thought Questions:
1. Review the story of Scheherazade and her sister Dinarzade. (Introduction)
2. How is the child under the bed like Dinarzade? (Chapter1)
3. How does Dinarzade in the story of the *Arabian Nights* relate to Hajila in the novel? (Chapter 2)
4. Describe the woman's bitter complaint in Isma's childhood home. (Chapter 3)
5. Why was the beggar's kiss so important to Isma? (Chapter 4)
6. Why does Isma feel so connected to "the outcast"? (Chapter 5)
7. How does Isma feel about traditional Muslim marriages? (Chapter 6)
8. According to Isma, what is the final relief for Muslim women? (Chapter 7)
9. Explain why Isma is so shocked by Houria's behavior. (Chapter 8)
10. Why does the swing remain such an important symbol of Isma's childhood? (Chapter 9)

Research Assignment:
Students in the Research Group should complete "Part III, Tales about Women," on Student Handout: Research on the Tales of the *Arabian Nights*.

Lesson Four
Tales of Women:
A Sister to Scheherazade and the Tales of the *Arabian Nights*

Objectives:
1. Students will retell the stories Isma tells about women in her reflection on childhood in Part II "Destruction at Dawn" in *A Sister to Scheherazade*.
2. Students will retell various stories involving women in the tales of the *Arabian Nights*.
3. Students will analyze the themes of the stories and the attitudes of Assia Djebar and the authors of the tales of the *Arabian Nights* toward women.

Materials:
1. Student Handout: Tales of Women: *A Sister to Scheherazade* and
                       the Tales of the *Arabian Nights*
2. Reading Resource: Summary and Analysis: Part II, "Destruction at Dawn," Chapters 1-9

Procedure:
1. Review the frame story of Scheherazade and her sister Dinarzade in the tales of the *Arabian Nights* and the introduction and first two chapters of Part II, "Destruction at Dawn," of the novel. Emphasize again that the story of Scheherazade and her sister Dinarzade in *A Sister to Scheherazade* is the same as the frame story in the tales of the *Arabian Nights*.
2. Ask students in the Research Group if they can add any more details to the story of the two sisters. For example, in some versions of the tales of the *Arabian Nights*, the narrator ends each night's story by saying, "But morning overtook Scheherazade, and she lapsed into silence. Then Dinarzade said, "Sister, what an amazing and entertaining story! Scheherazade replied, "Ah, but this is nothing compared to the story I will tell you tomorrow night if the Sultan lets me live!"
3. Divide students who have read *A Sister to Scheherazade* into six groups or more. Ask students in the Research Group to work together.
4. Assign each group of students who have read the novel one of the stories Isma tells about herself or other Muslim women in Part II "Destruction at Dawn." Suggested chapters include the following: Chapter 4, "The Kiss," Chapter 5, "The Outcast," Chapter 6, "Nuptials on a Straw Mat," Chapter 8, "A Young Girl's Anger," and Chapter 9, "The Swing." If necessary, assign two groups the same chapter.
5. Distribute <u>Student Handout: Tales of Women: *A Sister to Scheherazade* and the Tales of the *Arabian Nights*</u> and ask students to follow the directions.
6. Ask one student in each group who read the novel to retell the story they have been assigned. As each story is completed, relate the story to the rest of the novel and the situation of women.
7. Ask each student in the Research Group to tell his or her story.
8. Encourage students to act as Dinarzade and egg on the next storyteller as each story is completed.

Assessment:
At the end of the storytelling session, ask the students to analyze the themes of the stories and the attitudes of Assia Djebar and the authors of the tales of the *Arabian Nights* toward women.

Reading Assignment:
A Sister to Scheherazade, Part III, "The Sultan's Bride Looks On," Chapters 1-End, pages 141-160.

Thought Questions:
1. What do you think would happen if Dinarzade did not wake Scheherazade? (Introduction)
2. Why does Isma compare Touma to the eunuchs that guarded harems of ancient times? (Chapter 1)
3. Compare and contrast the harem with the Turkish bath. (Chapter 2)
4. Do you think Hajila has attempted suicide or has she attempted to abort her fetus at the end of the novel? Explain your position. (Chapter 3)
5. The odalisque is the female slaves or concubines of the Oriental harems of the past. Is the author implying that this odalisque is in flight or not? Explain your position. (The Lute)

Research Assignment:
Students in the Research Group should complete "Part IV, Tales about Hope and Freedom from Oppression," on Student Handout: Research on the Tales of the *Arabian Nights*.

Lesson Five
The Sultan's Bride: Is the Odalisque in Flight?

Objectives:
1. Students will define the term odalisque literally and figuratively.
2. Students will evaluate whether or not the odalisque is in flight according to Assia Djebar and the writers of the tales of the *Arabian Nights*.
3. Students will determine the role of Scheherazade and her sister Dinarzade in propelling or obstructing the flight of the odalisque in both *A Sister to Scheherazade* and the tales of the *Arabian Nights*.
4. Students will determine the overall message of Assia Djebar's *A Sister to Scheherazade* and the tales of the *Arabian Nights*.
5. Students will write about the odalisque, the role of Scheherazade and her sister Dinarzade, or the role of Isma and Hajila in propelling or obstructing the odalisque.

Materials:
1. Student Handout: The Sultan's Bride: Is the Odalisque in Flight?
2. Reading Resource: Summary and Analysis: Part III, "The Sultan's Bride Looks On,"
                                       Chapters 1-End

Procedure:
1. Ask students in the Research Group to review Part IV of their research on the tales of the *Arabian Nights*. Ask students to analyze the final tale they read in terms of the questions listed on the handout.
3. While students in the Research Group are completing their analysis, discuss the thought questions numbers 1-4 for Part III, Chapters 1-3, with the students who read the novel. Refer to Summary and Analysis: Part III, "The Sultan's Bride Looks On," Chapters 1-End.
2. As a whole class, refer to thought question number 5 and define the term odalisque literally and figuratively. Literally, the odalisque is the female slaves or concubines of the Oriental harems of the past; symbolically, the odalisque may refer to the oppression of women by men.
3. Ask students to decide whether or not the odalisque is in flight according to Assia Djebar and the writers of the tales of the *Arabian Nights*. Ask students to refer to passages in the texts to prove their points.
4. Ask students to define the roles that Scheherazade and her sister play in propelling or obstructing the odalisque in *A Sister to Scheherazade* and the tales of the *Arabian Nights*. Ask students to refer to passages in the texts to prove their points.
5. Ask students to compare Isma and Hajila and discuss the role these women play in propelling or obstructing the odalisque in *A Sister to Scheherazade*. Ask students to refer to passages in the texts to prove their points.
6. Ask students to explain the overall message of Assia Djebar's *A Sister to Scheherazade* and the tales of the *Arabian Nights*. Ask students to refer to passages in the texts to prove their points.

Assessment:
Distribute Student Handout: The Sultan's Bride: Is the Odalisque in Flight? Ask students to write a response to one of the questions on the handout.

Student Handout
Scheherazade and the Tales of the *Arabian Nights*

The tales of the *Arabian Nights* originated in ancient India, Egypt, and Persia, areas that include modern day Pakistan and Afghanistan. The stories were passed down orally by merchants and tribesmen until finally, in the second half of the 13th century, they were recorded either in Syria or Egypt. The original version of the *Arabian Nights* included eleven nucleus tales; as various translations were made over the years, other stories were added to the original collection. Each time the tales were told, storytellers embellished the details.

Scholars believe that the archetype for the *Arabian Nights* was a Persian work titled the *Thousand Tales*. This collection provides the frame story of Scheherazade and Dinarzade who entertain the bloodthirsty sultan or king with tales that continue for a thousand and one nights. Some of the tales Scheherazade tells in various collections include "The Voyages of Sinbad the Sailor," "Ali Baba and the Forty Thieves," and "Alladin and his Wonderful Lamp."

The frame story goes like this. Once upon a time, there were two brothers, Shahrayar and Shahzaman, who were very just and kind kings. One day before visiting his older brother, Shahzaman discovers his beloved wife sleeping with a slave. He is enraged, slaughters his wife and her lover, and hurls their bodies from the top of the palace. Just after hearing the distressing news of Shahzaman, his brother Shahrayar discovers that his own wife has also been unfaithful. Distraught, the two sultans travel through the countryside until they hear of a tragedy more terrible than their own.

As the sultans are grieving their misfortune, a genie appears carrying a glass chest. He pulls out a beautiful woman, makes love with her, and then falls asleep with his head in her lap. Then the woman insists that the sultans also make love to her and add their rings to the rings of the hundred men she has slept with under the demon's nose.

Shahrayar is enraged by the actions of this woman and his own misfortune. After the brothers return to the palace, he orders his highest official to put his wife to death and to slaughter his slave girls. He swears to marry a virgin every night and murder her the following morning in order to save himself from the wickedness of women. He believes there are no chaste and faithful women on the face of the earth. Shahrayar continues his cruel practice for three years.

Now, the highest official who put Shahrayar's brides to death every morning had two daughters named Scheherazade and Dinarzade. These women are destined to break the bloody cycle. It happened like this: the beautiful, well-read, and wise Scheherazade insisted on marrying King Shahrayar so that she could deliver her people from his violence. On her wedding night, Scheherazade asks the sultan if her sister may sleep under their bed. He agrees. Dinarzade waits until he is finished with her sister and then says, "Sister, if you are not too sleepy, tell us one of your wonderful stories." Scheherazade tells a story, and at daybreak the sultan is burning with curiosity to hear the ending. Scheherazade agrees to finish the story the next night if he spares her life.

The sultan loves the first story and Scheherazade promises to tell him an even more wonderful story the next night if he again spares her life. Tradition has it that at Dinarzade's prompting, Scheherazade tells the sultan stories for a thousand and one Arabian nights. Finally, her treasure trove is exhausted, and she asks the sultan to spare her life for the sake of the three children she has borne him. The sultan realizes Scheherazade is an intelligent, ingenuous, pious, and chaste woman, and he repents his past crimes. Together, Dinarzade and Scheherazade break the bloody cycle of violence against women symbolized by the sultan's senseless murder of his unfortunate, voiceless brides.

Student Handout
The Harem, the Veil, and the Turkish Baths

The Harem:

The word "harem" is derived from the Arabian words *harama,* which means to forbid and *harim,* which literally means prohibited place. The harem includes the wives, concubines, and women servants in a Muslim household. Some women are restricted from moving out of the cloister into public places.

In 1832, a painter by the name of Delacroix was allowed a brief look at the women in a Muslim harem. He painted a picture entitled "Women of Algiers in Their Apartment" from his memory. The cloistered Arab women in the painting seem to be exotic, mysterious, decorated, and mute objects in the secrecy of the harem. The women seem to be lost in their own world as they gaze silently at one another. One woman looks out of the painting and appears to be lost in silent reverie.

Assia Djebar views this painting not only as an image of the women of the harem in 1832, but as a valid representation of modern Algerian women. She borrowed the title of the painting for the title of her collection of short stories, which features stories about women and was published in 1980.

The Veil:

The word for veil in Arabic is *haik,* which is derived from the word *haka,* which means to weave. However, this veil is not simply a head covering; it refers to the heavy woolen cloth with which Middle Easter women cover themselves when they go out of doors. This veil is like an all-enveloping sheet, and it is worn as an outer garment leaving only one eye visible.

In her collection of short stories entitled *Women of Algiers in Their Apartment,* Assia Djebar explains that veiled women are free to circulate in public. According to Koranic law, a man may not prevent his veiled wife from leaving the harem and visiting the baths or the *hammam* at least once a week. However, wealthy men could build a *hammam* for his harem within the household and thereby restrict their movement.

Djebar states, "The veiled woman who circulates during the day in the city streets is, therefore, a woman in the first stage of so-called progressive behavior. Since, furthermore, the veil signifies oppression of the body, I have known young women who, when they reached adolescence, refused the principle of having to be veiled when circulating. The result was that they had to remain cloistered behind windows and bars, and so see the exterior world only from afar. . . ."

The Turkish Baths:

In *A Sister to Scheherazade*, Djebar describes the *hammam* as a "place of respite or amaranthine garden. The sound of water obliterates the walls, bodies are liberated under the wet marble. Every night the Turkish bath serves as a dormitory for country-folk in transit and so becomes a harem in reverse, accessible to all—as if, in the melting-pot of sweat, odours and dead skin, the liquid prison becomes a place of nocturnal rebirth. And of transfusion. Here, women can communicate by signs; here, a split-second glance, a barely perceptible touch, will seal their secret collusion" (p. 148).

Sources:
The Harem: Mildred Mortimer. "The Evolution of Assia Djebar's Feminist Conscience." *Contemporary African Literature.* Ed. H. Wylie. Washington, D.C.: Three Continents Press, 1983. 7-14.

The Veil: Assia Djebar. *Women of Algiers in Their Apartment.* Charlottesville: University Press of Virginia, 1980. 153.

Student Handout
The Dogma of Islam

There are many similarities among Judaism, Christianity, and Islam. Moses, Jesus, and Muhammad taught many of the same concepts about God, human destiny, sin, death, heaven, and hell.

Islam holds that the main figures of the Bible were sent to the specific people to whom they belonged and whose language they spoke. Therefore, Abraham was sent to the people at Mecca; Moses was a political prophet for the Israelites in Egypt, and Jesus was sent to the children of Israel. The prophet Muhammad is an exception because he received a universal mission valid for the whole world for the final period of history. Muslims believe that Muhammad reformed Judaism and Christianity.

The basic dogma of Islam is two fold: there is no God but God, or Allah, and Muhammad is his prophet. This is the first of the Five Pillars of Islam. The Second Pillar requires five ritual prayers daily; the Third Pillar requires a social taxation, which is used to care for the poor. The Fourth Pillar of Islam requires the believer to fast for the month of Ramadan, and the Fifth Pillar obliges every free adult male to make a pilgrimage to Mecca once in a lifetime.

Like Jews and Christians, Muslims believe that God is the creator of the world; he is eternal, omnipotent, infinitely good, and merciful. He is both forgiving and punishing. Muslims have at least ninety-nine names for God including "The Oft-Forgiving," "The Prodigal," and "The Equitable." A Muslim entrusts his or her free will to God's will with complete confidence. Muslims believe there is a divine decree for everything—basically, God has already decided everything in life.

Muslims also maintain a lively faith in the invisible world. For example, it was the angel Gabriel who brought the texts of the Koran, the sacred book of Islam, from God to Muhammad. Muslims also believe in *jinns,* or genies who are akin to spirits and who are organized into communities that include Muslims and non-believers.

Muslims believe that revelation, or the sacred books, are more important than the prophets because the prophets only transmit the sacred scripture. These books are the sum total of the interventions of divine grace in human history. Muslims believe that the great messengers of God, Moses, David, Jesus, Muhammad, literally transmitted the books which were dictated to them resulting in the Torah, the Psalms, the Gospel and the Koran. Although the Koran is the basis of all Muslim law, the *hadith*, or interpretations of the word and the traditions of Muslim groups play a major role in Muslim law and spirituality.

Like Judaism and Christianity, Islam predicts the end of the world when the faithful will face judgment; the good will enjoy paradise, and the evil will descend into hell. The dogma of Islam relates to the upheavals at the end of the world and the resurrection of the body when the dead will emerge from the tombs at the final trumpet blast. A person's actions will be weighed, and for some, the intercession of Muhammad may secure release from small and great sins.

Finally, Islam is a religion of law, holding a believer to legislation on ritual prayer, marriage, and inheritance. It is a grave sin to kill a Muslim, a person who commits adultery is put to death, and the hand of a thief is cut off. It is a serious sin to corrupt a virtuous Muslim or to run away from a *jihad* or a holy war. According to Islamic law, it is also sinful to drink alcohol or provide loan at interest.

Source: Jomier, Jacques. "The Dogma of Islam." *How to Understand Islam*. New York: Crossroad, 1989. 38-48.

Student Handout
Islam in Africa

Student Handout Islam in Africa Centuries of interaction between the Arabs and the Berbers, people of northern Africa, as well as common adherence to Islam have promoted a certain sense of cultural unity in northern Africa. By the time of the Crusades in the eastern Mediterranean, most northern African societies were incorporated into the Muslim world, even though the area had been the home of many early Christian scholars such as Tertullian, the first Christian theologian to write in Latin (230 AD), and Saint Augustine, whose writing set the theological traditions of the Roman church (430 AD).

The Muslim world expanded through trade. As the faith of the Arab conquerors took root in northern Africa, Islam spread persistently as leading towns and market cities became Islamic. Eventually, Muslims conducted the trans-Saharan trade along with various indigenous African groups. Gradually, Muslim influence was felt in commerce and the techniques of local government. The Arab African Islamic civilizations also evolved in parts of Western and Eastern Africa as well.

African Islamic cultures developed rapidly because the community, or the *umma*, was based on religious belief, not on ethnic or national allegiance. The promise of membership in a new and broad community of Islam beyond the community of a specific ethnic group was attractive. The cultural roots and the perspective of the *umma* were non-African.

In terms of spiritual influence, African and Arabian settlers alike accepted Islam and valued their membership in the Muslim world. However, Islam did not take the place of traditional African religions, nor did Islam replace African cultures. Islam did not supersede indigenous African religious rites but merely added new rituals, which provided a broader cultural and spiritual link. Furthermore, the indigenous African groups maintained their own ethnic identities by retaining their own languages and customs, evolving their own oral literature, and building their own urban civilizations.

Many elements of African life were consistent with or absorbed into Islam. For example, the interpretation of the Koran, which allowed a Muslim man to marry up to four wives if he could treat them all equally was consistent with the African practice of polygamy, whereas the Christian view of monogamy was not. The Sufi brotherhoods in particular made compromises with the local ideas and existing spiritual and cultural practices of the African people. This acceptance and flexibility contributed to the rapid growth of African Islamic communities. Furthermore, elements of African life that could not be absorbed into Islam were allowed to exist in parallel. Thus, the dynamic tension between Islam and African culture resulted in a remarkable unity of African Islamic culture.

Today, Islam is one of the major religions of Africa practiced by the peoples of Algeria, Tunisia, Libya, Egypt, the Sudan, Chad, Niger, Nigeria, Mali, Burkina Faso, Mauritania, Senegal, Western Sahara, and Morocco. Arabic, which is the language of the Koran, is spoken almost exclusively in Libya and Egypt. In Algeria, Morocco, and Tunisia, Arabic coexists with various indigenous African languages, which are collectively known as Berber.

Sources:

Bravmann, Rene. *African Islam*. Washington, DC: Smithsonian Institution Press, 1983.

Rahman, Fazlur. *Islam*. Chicago: University of Chicago Press, 1979.

Teacher Resource
Historical Highlights of the Islamic Peoples of Algeria

Phase I   **Arab Islamic Unity**

1. 632 AD - Prophet Muhammad dies after uniting all Arabs of Arabia under Islam
2. 642 AD - Arabs conquer lower Nile region and expel Byzantine power from Egypt
3. 690 AD - Arabs defeat the Byzantine fleet, destroy Carthage, and build the city of Tunis
4. 732 AD - Islam rule extends from Atlantic coast of Morocco and Spain to River Indus

Phase I I   **Discord in the Arab World**

1. 750 AD - Conflict over succession; Oyyamad and Abbasyd dynasties vie for control
2. 950 AD - Fatimids move into central Maghrib*
3. 950 AD - Fatimids conquer most of Maghrib region of northern Tunisia and Algeria
4. 969 AD - Fatimids seize control of Egypt; declare Egypt independent from rule of Bagdhad

Phase III   **Arab Migration into Northern Africa**

1. 900's - Arab pastoral nomads, or Bedouin, migrate from Arabia into northern Africa
2. 1050-1070 - 250,000 Bedouin move westward from Egypt into the Maghrib
3. 1200's - Berber nomads move eastwards from the Maghrib into Egypt
4. 1300's - Local populations of the Maghrib and Egypt speak Arabic

Phase IV   **Ottoman Empire**

1. 1453 - Ottoman Turks conquer Constantinople; change name to Istanbul
2. 1500 - Ottoman Empire stretches over northern Africa
3. 1565 - Turks are defeated at Battle of Malta; lose dominance in Mediterranean
4. 1600's - 1700's - Tunis and Algiers become major Turkish bases for raiding trading ships

Phase V   **French Invasion**

1. 1800 - Algeria's Turkish ruler has little effect over independent Berber towns
2. 1830 - French occupy coastal towns of Algiers and Oran; Turkish ruler exiled
3. 1830 - Jihad or Holy War of African resistance against French
4. 1840 - 'Abd al-Qadir unites Arab-Berbers and Muslims into powerful Islamic state
5. 1879 - French conquer Algeria after 50 years of war

Phase VI   **Independence**

1. 1945 - Colonial police open fire upon peaceful Muslim demonstration
2. 1954 - Front de Liberation Nationale (FLN) resistance movement founded
3. 1962 - Algeria achieves independence; FLN Leader becomes president
4. 1965 - Coup d'etat by FLN's armed forces

*Arabs refer to the whole coastal region of North Africa west of Egypt as al-Maghrib, Maghrib, or Maghreb meaning "the West."

Student Handout
Research on the Tales of the *Arabian Nights*

Part I: Introduction
   A. Background
      1. On a separate piece of paper, list the title, editor or translator, and publication information, including date, of your version of the *Arabian Nights*.
      2. Read the introduction to the text and write a paragraph explaining the history of your particular version.
   B. The First Tale
      1. Read one tale of the *Arabian Nights* and summarize the tale in your own words. Write your summary on a separate piece of paper. Be sure to include the title of the tale.
      2. Be prepared to comment on the tale in class.

Part II: Scheherazade and the Sultan
   A. The Frame Story
      1. Look through all the tales of the *Arabian Nights* focusing on Scheherazade.
      2. In a brief paragraph, explain how Scheherazade introduces each tale and maintains the sultan's interest at the end of each tale. Use direct quotes from the tales of the *Arabian Nights* and cite at least one page number as a reference.
   B. The Second Tale
      1. Read a second tale of the *Arabian Nights* and summarize the tale in your own words. Write your summary on a separate piece of paper. Be sure to include the title of the tale.
      2. What is the moral or message? Analyze the tale in a separate paragraph.
      3. Be prepared to comment on the tale in class.

Part III: Tales about Women
   A. Review
      1. Look through the entire *Arabian Nights* for tales focusing on women or the relationships between men and women.
      2. Write the titles of three of these tales.
   B. The Third Tale
      1. Read one of the tales that focuses on women or the relationships between men and women.
      2. Summarize the tale and analyze its meaning in terms of women.
      3. Be prepared to retell the story in class.

Part IV: Tales about Hope and Freedom from Oppression
   A. Review
      1. Look through all the tales of the *Arabian Nights* and find a tale that focuses on hope and freedom from oppression.
      2. Write the title of this tale.
   B. The Third Tale
      1. Read the tale you have selected that focuses on hope.
      2. Summarize the tale and analyze its meaning in terms of hope.
      3. Be prepared to retell the story in class.

Student Handout
The Author and Her Work

Fatima Zohra Imalayen was born in Cherchell, Algeria in 1936. Her father was a teacher in the French colonial education system, and as a child, she learned both French and Arabic. Educated in Algeria and later in France at the Lycée de Slidia and the Sorbonne, she was admitted to the elite Superior Normal School at Sèvres in 1955 but expelled three years later. Her brother was in prison, and her husband, Ahmed Ould-Rouis, was a freedom fighter wanted by the French police. In 1956 she published her first novel *La Soif* in French; it was published in English as *The Mischief* in 1958. However, fearful of displeasing her father, Fatima Zohra Imalayen took the pen name Assia Djebar; she returned to Algeria to teach history at the University of Algiers.

During the war of independence, Djebar taught at the Universities of Rabat and Tunis and worked as a journalist. She also published three more novels and a documentary: *Les Impatients* (*The Impatient Ones*, 1958), *Women of Islam*, a collection of photographs with commentary (1961) *Les enfants du nouveau monde* (*Children of the New World*, 1962), and *Les alouettes naïves* (*The Naïve Larks*, 1967).

She also produced two films: *La Nouba des femmes du Mont Chenoua* (*The Nouba of the women of Mount Chenoua*, 1979), a documentary about women, which won the International Critics' Prize at the 1979 Film Festival in Venice, and *La Zerda ou les chants de l'oubli*, (*The Zerda and Songs of Forgetting*, 1982), a chronicle of life in the Maghreb in the early twentieth century.

In 1980, Djebar published *Les femmes d'Alger dans leur appartement*, a collection of short stories which was translated as *Women of Algiers in their Apartment* in 1992. She also translated Nawal El Saadawi's *The Hidden Face of Eve* from Arabic into French in 1980. In 1985, Djebar published *L'Amour, la fantasia*, the first volume of a proposed quartet, which was translated as *Fantasia: An Algerian*

Cavalcade in 1988. This work interlaces her own autobiography with the history of French colonialism in Algeria from 1830 to independence in 1962. In 1987, she published *Ombre sultane*, the second novel in the quartet, which was translated as *A Sister to Scheherazade* in the same year. This novel focuses on the spaces of confinement and liberation for women under Islamic law.

In 1991, Djebar returned to historical themes and tackled Islamic fundamentalism in *Loin de Medine*, which was translated as *Far from Madina* in 1994. Her autobiographical novel *Vaste est la prison* (*Vast is the Prison*) appeared in 1995 followed by *Le blanc de l'Algerie* (*The Whites of Algeria*) in the same year. In 1997, Djebar published *Oran, langue morte*, which focuses on Algerian women at home and abroad who have suffered through some of the worst times in Algerian history.

Assia Djebar has lived and worked in Algeria, France, Tunisia, and Morocco teaching theatre, film, and history. She lectures throughout the world and has held a research appointment at the Algerian Cultural Center in Paris. Overall, her work portrays the quandary Muslim women face as victims of a double colonization by the French regime and the Islamic patriarchy. Djebar retells Algerian history and illustrates women's struggles to redefine their role in post-colonial Algerian society. Finally, Assia Djebar is one of North Africa's most widely acclaimed writers; however, none of her novels have been translated into Arabic in her native Algeria for political reasons.

Source: Vogl, Mary. "Assia Djebar." *Postcolonial African Writers: A Bio-Biographical Critical Sourcebook.* Ed. P. N. Parekh. Westport, CT: Greenwood Press, 1998. 135-143.

Student Handout
A Selected Bibliography of Assia Djebar's Works

L'Amour, la fantasia. Paris: Lattès, 1985. *Fantasia: An Algerian Cavalcade*. Trans. Dorothy S. Blair. London: Quartet, 1988.

La Nouba des femmes du Mont Chenoua. (film) 1978.

La Soif. Paris: Julliard, 1957. *The Mischief*. Trans. Frances Frenaye. New York: Simon and Schuster, 1958.

La Zerda ou les chants de l'oubli. (film) 1982.

Le blanc de l'Algerie. Paris: Albin Michel, 1995.

Les alouettes naïves. Paris: Julliard, 1967.

Les enfants du nouveau monde. Paris: Julliard, 1962.

Les femmes d'Alger dans leur appartement. Paris: Editions des Femmes, 1980. *Women of Algiers In Their Apartment*. Trans. Marjolijn de Jager. Charlottesville: University Press of Virginia, 1992.

Les Impatients. Paris: Julliard, 1958.

Loin de Medine. Paris: Albin Michel, 1991. *Far from Madina*. Trans. Dorothy S. Blair. London: Quartet, 1994.

Ombre sultane. Paris: Lattès, 1987. *A Sister to Scheherazade*. Trans. Dorothy S. Blair. London: Quartet, 1987.

Oran, langue morte. Paris: Sud, 1997.

Vaste est la prison. Paris: Albin Michel, 1995.

Women of Islam. London: Deutsch, 1961.

Student Handout
Characters in *A Sister to Scheherazade*

Hajila   _____

Isma   _____

Man   _____

Meriem   _____

Nazim   _____

Old Touma   _____

Kenza   _____

Nasser   _____

Scheherazade   _____

Dinarzade   _____

Lla Hadja   _____

Houria   _____

Teacher Resource
Characters in *A Sister to Scheherazade*

Hajila	co-wife of Isma
Isma	narrator; matchmaker to her own husband
Man	husband to Hajila and Isma
Meriem	Isma's daughter
Nazim	Man's nine year old son
Old Touma	Hajila's mother
Kenza	Touma's daughter
Nasser	Touma's son
Scheherazade	Sultan's bride
Dinarzade	Scheherazade's sister
Lla Hadja	rich widow and gossip
Houria	woman about to be married

Student Handout
Tales of Women:
A Sister to Scheherazade and the Tales of the *Arabian Nights*

Novel Groups

1. You will be assigned one of the stories that Isma tells about herself or other Muslim women in Part II, "Destruction at Dawn," of *A Sister to Scheherazade*. Suggested chapters include the following: Chapter 4, "The Kiss," Chapter 5, "The Outcast," Chapter 6, "Nuptials on a Straw Mat," Chapter 8, "A Young Girl's Anger," and Chapter 9, "The Swing."

2. Review the content of the story you have been assigned, and choose a storyteller who will retell the story to the class. The storyteller may embellish some of the details of the story if he or she wishes.

3. After each story is told in class, any one may feel free to play the part of Dinarzade and encourage the next storyteller.

Research Group

1. Briefly review the stories you have read about women in the tales of the *Arabian Nights*. Each one of you should be prepared to tell your story to the rest of the class. As the storyteller, you may embellish some of the details if you wish.

2. After each story is told in class, any one may feel free to play the part of Dinarzade and encourage the next storyteller.

Student Handout
The Sultan's Bride: Is the Odalisque in Flight?

Reflect upon the following questions and respond to one in a well-organized essay:

1. What does the odalisque represent in *A Sister to Scheherazade* and/or the tales of the *Arabian Nights*? Is the odalisque in flight? Why or why not? Use at least three direct quotes and other references in the text you read in order to support your points. Cite the page numbers.

2. What role do Scheherazade and her sister Dinarzade play in propelling or obstructing the odalisque in *A Sister to Scheherazade* and/or the tales of the *Arabian Nights*? Use at least three direct quotes and other references in the text you read in order to support your points. Cite the page numbers.

3. What role do Isma and her sister Hajila play in propelling or obstructing the odalisque in *A Sister to Scheherazade*? Use at least three direct quotes and other references in the text in order to support your points. Cite the page numbers.

4. Select a story from the tales of the *Arabian Nights*.
   A. Write the title of the tale and briefly summarize the tale in your own words.
   B. Analyze the tale in terms of the following questions:
      - What does the tale teach the reader about human nature?
      - What does the tale reveal in terms of man or woman's relationship to God and nature?
      - What does the tale reveal about human relationships? i.e. man's relationship to man or the relationships between men and women.
      - Use at least three direct quotes and other references in the text in order to support your points. Cite the page numbers.
   C. Explain how the tale connects with other stories in the tales of the *Arabian Nights*.

Reading Resource
Summary and Analysis

Part I: Every Woman's Name is Wound
Introduction

Summary: Isma, the narrator introduces Hajila and herself as wives of the same man. Isma is aware of the situation; Hajila is unaware. Isma addresses Hajila and herself as a younger woman. Isma has matched Hajila with her husband in order to free herself from the bond of passionate love. She denies any feeling of remorse even though Hajila seems to be like a hopeless beggar. Isma questions whether she offered Hajila as a sacrifice, if she liberated herself, or if she reaffirmed her power at Hajila's expense. Her answer is "No, I was cutting myself adrift" (p. 1). Meanwhile, Meriem, Isma's daughter, calls out to Hajila. Hajila ignores Meriem's cries and is shaking with spasmodic laughter as if she is in pain. Isma and Meriem leave the city and return to Isma's childhood home. There has been no real communication between Isma and Hajila even though they sat side by side in the Turkish bath or the *hammam*. Their relationship is like flowing water—a symbol of truce or disappearance. Isma cannot tell whether or not they have reversed their roles, and she wonders if the legacy of Muslim oppression of women will finally pass. Hajila laughs hopelessly at dawn. Meriem continues to call her name, and the harbor is filled with sound of men.

Analysis: *A Sister to Scheherazade* is the second volume of a quartet. The first volume is *Fantasia: An Algerian Cavalcade*, which features the loosely autobiographical story of the author character against the backdrop of Algerian history. Isma is the narrator in both volumes. The projected third and fourth volumes of the quartet will focus on the problems of Algerian women who supported the liberation movement and then were expected to return to the confines of a patriarchal society. It is not necessary to have read the first volume in the quartet in order to understand the second.

A Sister to Scheherazade opens with Isma, the narrator, speaking intimately to the reader. She begins the narrative saying: "A shadow and a sultan's bride; a shadow behind the sultan's bride" (p.1). Isma refers to the tales of the *Arabian Nights* in which the princess bride Scheherazade is married to a bloodthirsty sultan who plans to kill her at dawn. However, Scheherazade intrigues her husband with interesting stories and thereby saves her life. Her success depends on her sister, Dinarzade, who is hiding under the bed and wakes Scheherazade each morning so she can continue to weave her tales. Isma, the narrator, refers to herself and Hajila as "an arabesque of intertwining names" (p.1). Isma's name means "listen"in Arabic, and Hajila's name means "little quail"[1] (p.8). When the names are conjoined, the message reads, "Listen, little quail." Isma is not sure if she and Hajila have reversed roles. She does not analyze the question but leaves it for the reader to ponder throughout the novel. She indicates that the older generation, Hajila's mother, and the younger generation, Isma's daughter, are waiting and crying for the answer amid the sounds of men in the outside world. The reader will discover later in the novel that Isma has divorced her husband and Hajila is his second wife.

Chapter 1: Hajila

Summary: The introductory quote indicates that the harem cannot be violated without violating honor. Isma addresses Hajila, the housewife, in the kitchen. Hajila is overcome by grief. She prays, but she is feverish and depressed. Her husband, who is referred to only as the "man" leaves the house (p. 7). Hajila is imprisoned in her apartment. She hits the pane of glass and cries herself to sleep in the smallest bedroom after her husband leaves. Finally, the "man's" daughter,

---

[1] Mildred Mortimer. *Journeys through the French African Novel*. Portsmouth, N.H.: Heinemann, 1990.

Meriem, and his son, Nazim, arrive. Both children speak French, and Hajila wonders about the children's mother. Nazim tells her it is not nice to cry.

Analysis: Hajila is trapped in the prison of her apartment. As her name indicates, she sees herself as a shivering "dirty-white bird" (p. 8). The narrator refers to her husband as the "man" in respect for Islamic tradition. His name is never actually revealed in the novel, and he seems to symbolize all Islamic men in the patriarchal society of Algeria. Hajila envies her husband because he has gone out into the world. The author sets up a binary structure whereby interior spaces are female and exterior spaces are male.[2] Isma speaks of and for Hajila in the second person singular. As in *Fantasia*, Isma becomes the translator and scribe for women who can neither speak nor write in French.[3]

Chapter 2: Isma

Summary: In this chapter, Isma focuses on her own life. She begins, "O memory!" (p. 1). In her memory's eye, Isma is slim; the eyes of the man are on her as she moves through the city. A taxi driver whistles at her; coffee scalds her throat, and she is late to meet a friend. Isma remembers her life in both excruciating detail and in general phases. At twenty, Isma travels through the city. At thirty, she spends rich, fertile time with her friend. At forty, she is aware of her aging face and welcomes her love.

Analysis: Isma is a young attractive woman who dances through the city experiencing life outside the kitchen and the home. She is not veiled by anything including make-up. She says she no longer has a face or possesses a veil. She seems to want to recreate her past and the past of all women. The reader can easily contrast the free-spirited Isma who moves about the city with the depressed Hajila who is trapped in her apartment. In fact, the first two chapters set up the structure of the alternating narrative about two women. The novel juxtaposes both first and second person narratives that represent Isma, the emancipated Algerian woman, and Hajila, the traditional Algerian woman. The narrator alternates Hajila's story with her own.[4]

Chapter 3: Out of Doors

Summary: Hajila has been in her seventh floor apartment for six months. When she saw it the first time with her mother, Touma, they both avoided the windows. The glass partition dividing the living room seems silly to Touma; the kitchen, however, is beautiful even though she thinks it needs a traditional low table. The whole extended family wonders about the marriage. At night, Hajila lies carefully in the bed avoiding contact with her husband. She has never had intercourse with him, so she is not pregnant. Hajila dreams of being spirited away to some dark cavern. One day three months ago, she actually did leave the house secretly for the first time. She draped herself in an everyday veil of unbleached wool and wore slippers like an old woman. Once out of doors, she was intoxicated. Then she realized that she may not be able to find her way home. She was ashamed as she passed the concierge unveiled and returned to her apartment.

---

[2] In the afterword to *Women of Algiers in Their Apartment* by Assia Djebar, Clarisse Zimra indicates that Djebar has presented the binary inside/outside structure as an ideological topography of her work. Critics have followed her lead including Mildred Mortimer in *Journeys through the French African Novel*. Portsmouth, N.H.: Heinemann, 1990.

[3] Mildred Mortimer. *Journeys through the French African Novel*. Portsmouth, N.H.: Heinemann, 1990.

[4] Mildred Mortimer. *Journeys through the French African Novel*. Portsmouth, N.H.: Heinemann, 1990.

Analysis: When she arrives in her new home, Hajila places her veil as if she is about to go out again. In Islamic society, only veiled women are free to circulate in public places. The veil or the *haik*, is "the all-enveloping, heavy, woolen square of cloth with which Middle Eastern women cover themselves out of doors, leaving only one eye visible" (see glossary). As Hajila looks out of the balcony on to the world, she no longer feels like a grain of dust in a dungeon or vermin lurking in a corner. She wonders about the children's mother and seems to be tentative and afraid. In this chapter, Hajila leaves the enclosure of her apartment for the great outdoors and begins her journey of self-discovery. When she returns, her face is unveiled as a clear sign of freedom, yet she feels it is wrong to return the concierge's greeting. Hajila's freedom out of doors is contrasted to her oppression within the confines of her apartment. She is free outside; inside she is a slave expected to wait on her husband.

Chapter 4: The Bedroom

Summary: Isma, the narrator, returns to her own story and remembers a scene in her marital bedroom with "the man." She describes their erotic relationship saying "a peal of laughter rings out—convulsing the whole body, rippling through outstretched arms down through bare legs to nymph's feet with wide-spread toes—and the whole body dissolves invading the four corners of the room" (p. 21). Isma reminiscences about her wedding night and many other nights. The "man" explains that the bridal chamber is the room where he was born. Because they will be moving, Isma is not interested in furniture; however, his mother insists that the couple will use the mattresses only until the furniture arrives. A storm causes the light to swing wildly.

Analysis: Isma's bridal chamber and marriage is in sharp contrast to Hajila's. Isma's marriage is erotic, and Hajila's is lifeless. Isma's passionate lovemaking requires little furniture; Hajila lies motionless on a huge mahogany bed that is like a throne. Sometimes she sleeps on the carpet. The "man" loses himself in erotic love with Isma, but only fondles Hajila's breasts as she shrinks away. One might suggest that the bedroom is a haven for Isma and shelter from the storm of the outside world. This is not true for Hajila. In her analysis, Mildred Mortimer explains that throughout this text, Hajila steps out of the harem into the great outdoors on a journey of self discovery. Isma, on the other hand, returns to the interior spaces or the enclosures of her past including her marital bedroom.[5]

Chapter 5: Naked in the Wild Outdoors

Summary: Hajila's husband takes her to see her family; he speaks Arabic with an accent that is different from hers, and everything seems to be expressed in the masculine form. He speaks to his daughter in French, but there are things he does not seem to understand. Nazim wants to stay with Hajila because he loves her; Meriem, however, never speaks to her. Hajila realizes she has been married to act as a governess. During the ride, Hajila sees a red-headed Arabian woman radiant with joy and without a veil playing with her child out of doors. She makes an irrevocable decision to go out to the public garden again. Hajila describes her fearful walk; as she crosses the street, a car screeches, and a man swears at her. She removes her veil and feels as if she wants either to disappear or explode. Her hair falls down, and she realizes she is out of doors! She appreciates the smells around her and folds up her veil. She is Hajila stripped naked, and she is fearful that someone will recognize her. Hajila travels excitedly through a maze of narrow alleys and encounters a beautiful, veiled girl with her lover. Hajila sits down, and an old man passes by; she feels men looking at her. Finally, she returns home and puts the veil on again. She curses everyone and wonders what the concierge thinks of her – perhaps she is meeting someone or selling herself. Then Hajila takes a bath and imagines the people who were

---

[5] Mildred Mortimer. *Journeys through the French African Novel*. Portsmouth, N.H.: Heinemann, 1990.

out of doors accompanying her—the naked Hajila. A new Hajila stares back at her coldly in the mirror.

Analysis: Hajila is filled with the excitement and joy of the young Arabic woman playing with her child in the garden. The women in unveiled and so is Hajila. The veil is a symbol of death, and it is compared to "the wool of a shroud" (p. 31). Hajila is transformed from an unfeeling ghost inside her apartment to another person as she moves out of doors without the veil, and she is surprised to be walking so easily. She evokes God as the "Sweet Messenger of the Lord" (p. 30). This is a breakthrough, and Hajila feels naked without the veil out of doors. The veil is a shroud that masks the woman, for no one recognizes her under the veil. Although the veil gives Hajila the freedom to speak in Islamic society, the narrator explains, "under the white veil grey anger folds up its wings" (p. 34). As Hajila she is figuratively naked as she travels to and from the garden without her veil, she is literally naked taking her bath and looking at herself in the mirror. The new Hajila emerges with the help of the images of other people in the community out of doors.

Chapter 6: Veils

Summary: Isma switches from narrating Hajila's story back to narrating her own story in this chapter. Both Isma and her husband veil themselves in clothes they have chosen for each other as they enter the great outdoors. She talks about preening herself and wearing a new red dress. Isma takes a shower and thinks about being a nun just so that she could stand before the mirror and let the veil suddenly slip down her naked body. She says, "I wallow in unashamed sensuality" (p. 37). Isma continuously releases her body to the night's activities. Isma and her husband reminisce about traveling and sleeping everywhere together, including in an abandoned hut. Isma had a child in February, and she explains that she never calls her "my daughter" (p. 38). Her body grows slack, and she feels hollow and weak when her husband plays with Meriem. The family moves several times; the baby is very good, and Isma and her husband reminisce about their past together.

Analysis: Isma continues her journey of self discovery in her reminisce of her early years of marriage. Her journey takes her within the interior of the many bedrooms she shared with her husband and then to the birth of her child. The chapter is titled "Veils" and focuses on the veils of the two women, Isma and Hajila. Unlike Hajila who leaves the house shrouded in the traditional veil, Isma leaves the house veiled in a new red dress. Unlike Hajila who, after walking outside unveiled, sees herself naked after her bath surrounded by images of the people of the great outdoors, Isma imagines her veil falling off her naked body. Isma is extremely sensual; she is like a courtesan dallying in foreplay in the bedroom, and she does not seem particularly well suited for motherhood. Although her daughter is good, Isma seems to feel sick or perhaps jealous when her husband plays with the baby.

Chapter 7: The Others

Summary: Hajila roams around the apartment, and Nazim is concerned. She ignores the "man" when he calls for his ashtray, and she swears she will burn her woolen veil. On the third day, she goes out again, and she goes out every day after that. She always finds her way, but she never sees the joyful woman with the red hair again. Hajila convinces herself that she too has a story. While she is sitting in the public gardens, a man asks her a question, but she does not respond. Unveiled, she has lost the power of speech whereas she can easily shout insults when she is wearing the veil. Now that she is out of doors, the narrator indicates that the next phase for Hajila is to remember aspects of the other people she encounters. She is aware of these people and all the sounds around her. Specifically, she holds the memory of the red headed woman laughing with her child out of doors. Hajila wonders about the women who venture outside and wishes she could talk to women who own several dresses and jewels. She always wears the same dress out of doors; it is her second skin. When Touma realizes that Hajila leaves the house, she is very upset and says Hajila will disgrace the family. Touma recounts the family history explaining their evacuation from the Dunes, and the death of Hajila's father. Hajila's husband was supposed to be a sign of justice for the family, and Touma hopes he will assist them find housing. Hajila loves Touma, but she cries bitterly because she has been told never to go out again.

Analysis: After three days in her prison, Hajila goes out again. Her flight from her apartment is like resurrection from death after three days in the tomb. However, she seems unable to speak when the stranger in the garden approaches her. She can only speak when she is wearing the veil, but then she speaks with the voice of anger and revenge. Hajila has not yet found another voice. Out of doors, she tries to convince herself that she has a history, which she in fact does. However, her history is retold in her mother's voice, and it connects the pain of the past with hope in the future. Touma does not understand Hajila's marriage or her journey of self-discovery and new life out of doors. Touma is an example of an Algerian matron who seeks to improve her family's economic position through the loveless marriage of her daughter. The title of this chapter is "Others." The ever-instructing narrator tells Hajila that she must proceed in her journey of self-discovery by remembering aspects of other people she encounters out of doors.

Chapter 8: The Other

Summary: Isma returns to the narration of her own story in this chapter. She explains how she learns about the body of "the other," her husband. She reminisces about the past and conjures up the images of four women for him. The first is his elder sister; she has the face of virtuous virgin, and she has a good nature even though she always takes a back seat to him. Then, there is the sickly, melancholy sister who is one year younger than her husband. The third sister is also sad even though she had wedding gifts and a wedding. Finally, the fourth sister is shy and loves childish games. Isma is haunted by powerful images of her husband's sisters and mother. Isma and her husband move to another city, but she reminisces about the holidays spent in her husband's childhood home. Isma's mother-in-law is hard to understand. She breast-fed her son for three years during the war, and now she seems to interfere with their lovemaking. One morning, her husband has a violent nightmare. Isma throws off her nightgown, clings to him, and makes love to him. Nevertheless, he needs to find his way back to his mother's womb. Although Isma and her husband live in his mother's home, Isma believes she has expelled his nightmares and separated him from his mother.

Analysis: Isma instructs Hajila to focus on public people or "others" in the great outdoors in the last chapter, while she herself focuses on the intimate or the "other," her husband, in this chapter. Isma seems interested in her husband's sisters in order to better understand him. She says, "So, in the solitude of our bedroom, I talk to my husband at length about his sisters. I conjure up their presence. Night after night, I piece together the body of the man I love, with eyes that speak for me and groping hands that take the place of sight" (p. 50). It seems as if Isma is both united with and haunted by her husband's family. She says, "This obsession with his origins is a sword thrust into the man, wounding him . . ." (p. 51). Perhaps her husband's family is in fact the nightmare that controls him. In any event, in spite of their travels, Isma and her husband seem to return to his family's home. Isma seems to be growing in her understanding of herself through her reflection upon her life within the confines of her extended family and home.

Chapter 9: The Man

Summary: At home, Hajila easily conjures up pictures of the people outside such as women and children crossing streets and crowds of people at bus stops. As Hajila listens to the noises outside the house, it seems as though Meriem is suspicious about something. Later, Nazim takes a coin to a beggar, and his father reprimands him. Hajila says, "A stranger's blessing can protect us all" (p. 55). Her husband is astonished, and Hajila would like to tell him that she does more than speak; she actually goes out of the house. The "man" pinches Nazim's ears until they bleed and then calls Hajila to bed. He forces himself upon her, and she thinks of the streets as she bleeds after intercourse. He tosses her a towel and changes into clean pajamas. She lies on a mattress on the floor while he lies on the high bed. He seems to want to talk, but she is not interested. He asks her to sleep with him, but she ignores him. Finally, she performs the ritual of ablutions and reminisces about her family history. Thereafter, Hajila clenches her teeth every night and waits for the male to finish. She beats against the walls of the bathroom and finally refuses intercourse with him until she cleanses herself in the Turkish bath. Hajila is no longer afraid of her husband, and he is no longer impotent. However, intercourse is violent. While at the baths, she does not converse with the young brides who boast about their wonderful wedding nights because she knows they are lying.

Analysis: While Hajila is inside, she is filled with sounds from the outside even though she is trapped in her apartment. She has achieved some degree of freedom, but she worries about Touma's curse that she will bring destruction on the family. Hajila would like her stepdaughter Meriem to be spared the veil, and she cannot stop thinking about her sister Kenza, who is living in poverty while she is living in luxury like a doll. The tragic history of her family keeps reverberating as Hajila attempts to adjust to married life. Hajila wonders if her violent experience of sexual intercourse with her husband is rape. As she attempts to resist intercourse, she thinks of the streets where she is free. Hajila has gained strength through the freedom she experienced strolling through the sunlit town, and she is filled with confidence in herself. Obviously this chapter presents two conflicting portraits of the "man" with his two wives: Isma and Hajila. Night after night of erotic intercourse with Isma is contrasted with six months of celibacy with Hajila culminating in a violent experience of rape.

Chapter 10: Words

Summary: Isma continues to talk about her relationship with her husband. He speaks in his sleep, and his words are needle-sharp. She abandons herself to sensuality; then suddenly, she resists intercourse and thrashes about biting and scratching him. Her husband is perplexed by Isma's violence. She seems indolent and silent; then they seem to reconcile and resume their lovemaking as usual sometimes amid a tangle of passionate words

Analysis: Isma focuses on words as she narrates her own story. Words seem to be part of her confusion in this phase of her self-discovery. She says, "Our words throw light on neither pain nor joy; they are snares. Their tintinnabulation wells from springs of passion. The half-darkness inveigles them into our bed, just as our transports approach flash point" (p. 65). Isma seems to be confused; it seems as if words get in the way of making love and then encourage making love. In any event, the consistent eroticism of Isma's relationship with her husband seems to be faltering. The reason for this shift is unclear. The reader seems to be as confused as Isma is about her changing feelings.

Chapter 11: The Return

Summary: In this chapter, Isma continues to tell her own story, and she also addresses Hajila. Hajila knows nothing about Isma. At eighteen, Isma was a rebellious adolescent who visited her lover secretly. In an uncontrollable fit of madness, she attempted suicide the day before her engagement. She has returned to the city now after being away for many years. Isma has visited many women in her family—they are all withering from being indoors. She has been living abroad and now seeks a job in her hometown in order to look after her daughter. Meriem has not been able to adjust to living with Hajila; she tells Isma that Hajila is pregnant. Isma takes a position at an infant's school teaching the mother tongue again; she says it doesn't matter if she is enclosed in the veil of tradition because she will be near her daughter. Her ex-husband has started drinking. Hajila resumes walking outside, but she wonders how long she will be able to walk since she is pregnant. She decides to wait until Touma and Kenza are moved into subsidized housing before she aborts the fetus. Her husband falls through the window on the balcony calling Isma's name; Hajila pulls him in. Nazim tells Hajila that his mother is French, and she left him with her parents a long time ago. Then, he lived with Isma and the "man" for a few months. Hajila holds Nazim and tells him that she is his mother. Isma asks herself why she did not face this tragedy.

Analysis: Isma's return brings both parts of her narrative together. Isma knows Hajila intimately because she has set Hajila up in the marriage to her ex-husband, and she has narrated every detail of Hajila's story for the reader. In contrast, Hajila does not even know that Isma exists. As the pregnant Hajila becomes stronger walking around in public places, Isma seems to seek the enclosure of an infant school and is even willing to wrap herself up in a traditional veil. Isma's return may be provoking her ex-husband to drink. As Hajila had once been imprisoned in the kitchen of her apartment, now her husband is imprisoned, drinking in the kitchen and throwing up in the bathroom. The disorder in the house seems to bring Nazim and Hajila together. Isma apparently never faced the issue of Nazim. She realizes that she is condemned to provoking separation and discord and is unable to foster any kind of unity in the family.

Chapter 12: Patios

Summary: Isma continues to tell her story; the patios of her childhood home provide the setting for this chapter. Women who are related by marriage are sitting around a Moorish house. Three different branches of family live there—the patriarch and his three wives. The youngest wife is Isma's grandmother who became his bride at puberty. She is actually the same age as her husband's grandchildren. Women talk about the complex marriage relationships within the family—there is really nothing else for them to talk about. They are confined to their home, and the house is like their city. Blood ties and social roles identify the men in the family. One of the men, Isma's father, is a widower. Although he sent her away to boarding school, she felt permanently linked to those women prisoners on the patio. As an adult, the bitterness of these women overtakes Isma. Light streams into the patio where the women seek solidarity with one another. Isma loved her husband, and he became her alter ego. She has returned to live with an aunt. After Isma was divorced, she stayed away on foreign soil because she needed to be out of doors to reflect. She believes Algeria annihilates women by shutting them up away from view. She thought her ex-husband would find a child bride and laughter, or he would want a woman who would look after the house and children. Isma thought Meriem would be happy with her father's new wife, so she ran away. She tried to keep her distance in order to break up the past, but she returned for Meriem because she could not free herself on her own.

Analysis: According to critic Mildred Mortimer, Isma attempts to understand the present by examining her past. She therefore enters the maternal world of her ancestors by returning to the patios of her childhood. Only women gather here—the patios are the enclosures of the veiled and sequestered and in fact suggest the sealed-off chamber of the harem.[6] In assigning Hajila to her ex-husband in an arranged marriage, Isma has assigned two possible roles to Hajila—the role of a governess to children or the role of a companion to an unhappy and impotent man. Isma addresses Hajila as a concubine who belongs to the kingdom of the patio. She draws strength from addressing Hajila and assumes that Hajila is familiar with periods of waiting. Perhaps she is referring to the time that is required to grow in self-understanding. In any event, Isma has decided to return and claim her daughter, an interest that seems to be self-serving.

Chapter 13: The Drama

Summary: Isma speaks to Hajila, who is actually a phantom that Isma's voice has brought to life. She is concerned with the imminent drama of their story, for although their husband is a wall separating them, they share a common secret. When her husband discovers that

---

[6] Mildred Mortimer. *Journeys through the French African Novel*. Portsmouth, N.H.: Heinemann, 1990.

Hajila leaves the house everyday, she assumes he will take her back to her mother's shantytown. It won't take long for her to pack her clothes—she was really only in transit in the marriage. He is drinking heavily and calls Hajila "Isma." He interrogates her, and Hajila admits she enjoys walking naked without the veil. Isma interjects and says that she used to walk naked with her husband, but she asks herself, " . . . how was I to walk like this beside the man I loved? There was no tradition to serve me as a beacon" (p. 86). Isma says, "I left him for myself" (p. 86). The "man" strikes Hajila and threatens to put her eyes out with a broken bottle. He says, "I'll break your legs and then you'll never go out again, you'll be nailed to a bed and . . ." (p. 87). Nazim runs to neighbors for help. Isma concludes her narrative stating that "A man has a right to go off the rails when he is drunk, but what punishment will the Apostles of the Revealed Law—that unwritten law—mete out to a woman who goes about 'naked', without her master's knowledge?" (p. 88).

    <u>Analysis</u>: This chapter is the fulcrum of the novel. As the lives of Isma and Hajila merge, Isma wonders if women find sisters only in prisons, and she refers to the fortress of ecstasy that she erected around herself. Isma walked freely with the man she loved, but there was no tradition in place to show her how to maintain a sense of self. Therefore, Isma left her husband in order to find herself; she needed some sense of independence. Hajila, on the other hand, has emerged from her confinement. The kitchen, which was once Hajila's prison, is now the "man's" tomb. He can do nothing. The wife he loves has abandoned him, and the wife he does not love has humiliated him. Isma implies that the unwritten Islamic law is unjust in forgiving a drunk, abusive Muslim man but not allowing a Muslim woman to walk freely in public. However, because the narrative is told only from the perspective of Isma, the reader must wonder if her husband feels wronged.

Chapter 14: The Wound

    <u>Summary</u>: The "man" strikes Hajila, and she takes the blow; she does not step aside. Isma tells Hajila, "It is the moment after the pain that you have to face. The real wound that cannot be healed" (p. 89). Isma also says Hajila was too hasty in her move for freedom, and she was not prepared for the harsh sun of the outside world. Nevertheless, Hajila leaves the house. She walks at random, free to look around her. In the concluding page of Part I, "Every Woman's Name is Wound," Djebar provides the etymology of the word *derra*, which is translated into English as "wound" (p. 91). She says, "*Derra*: the word used in Arabic to denote the new bride of the same man, the first wife's rival; this word means 'wound'—the one who hurts, who cuts open the flesh, or the one who feels hurt, it's the same thing!" (p. 91). Therefore, the first wife retreats when the second wife appears, as the second wife retreats for the third wife, and the third wife retreats for the fourth wife. Under Islamic law, a man may marry as many as four wives provided he bestows upon each and every co-wife an equal share of conjugal love. Djebar says, " . . . in our land, a man has a right to four wives simultaneously, as much as to say, four . . . wounds" (p. 91).

    <u>Analysis</u>: Hajila does not avoid her husband's blow; she symbolizes the concept of "wound." Isma claims that the wound or pain of being a woman cannot be cured. She then accuses Hajila of being hasty and unprepared in her quest for freedom in the outside world, just as she herself was unprepared to walk freely with her husband and still maintain her sense of self-worth. The meaning of the word "wound" here includes inflicting and feeling hurt. Djebar says a man is entitled to four wounds. The title of Part I of the novel is "Every Woman's Name is Wound," so the author seems to imply that all women are wounds; they hurt just by virtue of being women; they are also capable of inflicting and receiving pain.

Part II: Destruction at Dawn
Introduction
Summary: Scheherazade is about to become the sultan's bride; it would be taboo for the sultan to marry Scheherazade's sister, Dinarzade, as well. The sultan is bloodthirsty, and Scheherazade must save herself from being murdered by him at dawn. She does this by telling wonderful stories that intrigue her husband. She asks her sister to sleep in the bridal chamber and keep watch during the night; she must wake Scheherazade one hour before daybreak so that she can spin more interesting stories. Dinarzade's voice under the bed coaxes her sister above. Scheherazade wakes as if she had never slept and continues her story. Dinarzade listens to the carnal feast above. The narrator explains that the fears haunting women today are dispelled because of the two faces of the sultan's bride.

Analysis: This introduction gives the reader background on the story of Scheherazade and Dinarzade as recorded in the tales of the *Arabian Nights*. Djebar seems to indicate that the two faces of the sultan's bride—the storyteller, Scheherazade, and her sister and companion, Dinarzade, will dispel women's fears today. The reader is challenged to relate this information to Isma and Hajila as the novel continues to unfold. Is Isma the storyteller, Scheherazade, and is Hajila her sister, Dinarzade, who inspires the story and supports Isma the storyteller?

Chapter 1: The Child
Summary: The child under its parents' bed hears its mother's song throughout the night; it gradually falls asleep. The mother's song rejoices and laments; it isolates "the faceless father, whose oppressive weight on the bed makes the night indecent . . ." (p. 96). The child rejoices; one day she will become a woman. Her voice will ring out, and memory will transport her back to that place under her parents' bed. The young woman will hear the voice beneath her own bed. In the warmth of this ignorance, the harem closes in on all women.

Analysis: The mother's song and the movement of the bed are like ocean waves that lull the child to sleep. The image connects to the waters of the womb. The child under the bed reminds the reader of Dinarzade, the sister who supports Scheherazade. Dinarzade is likened to a child in the womb, while Scheherazade is liken to a woman and a mother. The implication is that someday the child Dinarzade will become a woman like Scheherazade.

Chapter 2: The Sister
Summary: The voice under the bed is once again the sister who must wake the sleeping bride before dawn; she is the hope of her sister's salvation. The sultan's bride knows she will be sacrificed at sunrise if she does not continue to tell her stories, for "with every word she utters, she hovers between extinction and the throne" (p. 98). The man is interposed between one woman listening to another woman, as the current flows from the woman below to the storyteller above. He suspends the death sentence for twelve hours at a time. The sister below is taboo to the sultan; the lovemaking above her is like deadly flood waters. She hears everything and shields her sister from death. As the wife above spins her tales fighting for her life, the sister below rallies past victims.

Analysis: Perhaps Dinarzade, the sister below the bed, is Hajila in the novel. She does not speak clearly, but she provides the inspiration and the story for Scheherazade. Perhaps Scheherazade is Isma, the storyteller. Whether or not the author lines the sisters in the tales of the *Arabian Nights* up with Hajila and Isma, the implication is that all women are sisters, and it is the story or the spoken word that saves the sisters from destruction at the hands of the sultan. The women's voices and the word symbolize life not execution. The tale is like a tapestry, and one sister will pick up a lost stitch for another.

Chapter 3: The Complaint

Summary: Isma continues her narration of her own life. She returns to her childhood home by the sea and remembers that here, girls are not allowed to go into the city; they perch on the low wall of the terrace looking out toward the ocean. The boys, on the other hand, go out with their fathers, enjoy activities such as Boy Scouts, and swim in the sea. They return showing off their shells and describing the taste of delicious spicy foods that are taboo for girls. Isma hears the vain complaints and the anger among the women. For example, the women cook as the men parade in for special occasions such as her cousin's circumcision, her uncle's engagement, and her father's second marriage. As a child, she hears the complaint of one woman who cries, "How long must I endure this life of drudgery, cursed that I am? " (p. 102). She cries louder, "At night no respite for us wretched women! We still have to suffer them, our masters, and in what attitude . . . with our bare legs stuck in the air!" (p. 102). The women want the motherless Isma to leave. Twenty years later Isma tries to suppress their tenacious curses. She imagines herself beneath the bed waking a concubine on the bed above. She holds the image of the bare legs and women who are slaves by day and lovers at night. She wonders if the tale of the sultan's bride will save one of those oppressed women stepping over the fire. Isma, like other women, holds the scars of the wound of being a woman; these scars make it impossible for her to find love.

Analysis: The first two chapters of Part II "Destruction at Dawn" explain the story of Scheherazade and her sister Dinarzade. The remainder of Part II focuses on Isma's life story. As this chapter begins, Isma describes the Arabian girls in her hometown as "little quails" (p. 100). She may be implying that traditional women like Hajila are in fact adolescents like these girls who are restricted from enjoying activities out of the home. As Isma hears the complaints of the women, who are described as concubine/slaves, she wonders if she can be Dinarzade, the sister under the bed in the tales of the *Arabian Nights*, and through her story save some of these women. Perhaps her story will awaken some of her other sisters and begin to help Arabian women move out of the oppression they suffer. Nevertheless, whether she inspires stories or tells the stories of other women, Isma can never escape the wound of being a woman. She cannot not find and sustain love. She refers to herself when she says, "And the motherless child preserves them, the scars of the wound, to intone them on the pillow of an impossible love . . ." (p. 104).

Chapter 4: The Kiss

Summary: Isma's family lives in poverty in the scorched olive groves. Here, gypsy women dance in the night, and local leaders view them with lustful eyes. Later in her life, Isma realizes that the gypsies are prostitutes. She sees them both as "disfigured victims" and "pagan princesses" (p. 106). Isma continues the story of her childhood. She visited her mother's family's mountain retreat every summer. In this rural society, girls eleven, twelve, or thirteen years old would be restricted in the harem. The relationships in her home were complex, for her grandfather had two wives. The women in the country seemed to be open to laughter in their youth, and then suddenly, they became old and authoritarian. As a child, an old man once kissed her hands and called her the bearer of the ancestor's blessing. Isma's ancestors were Sufi saints in the hills who bequeathed their spiritual powers to the men in the family for four or five centuries. The old man told Isma that she must uphold the "tradition of the Word and prophesy" by becoming a priestess (p. 108). The women in the family were upset because Isma was sitting with the men, but Isma made much of old man's blessing, and her father's smile sanctioned it. Yet, as an adolescent, Isma rushed to modernize herself, and she disparaged the superstitions of the peasants. She believes that she as she "passed through the tunnel of enforced silence," her hands were protected by the beggar's kiss. Isma believes that this link attached her hands "to the spiral of the past" (p. 109).

Analysis: As a child, the gypsies of the forest appeared like goddesses in the night to Isma. She seems to be attracted by their freedom of movement. Isma is linked to the past, which she describes as a spiral, by the beggar's kiss and blessing. This kiss breaks with tradition in seeming to designate a woman as the ancient saints' priestess, but it also seems to connect Isma with the downward spiral of oppression against women in the past. Isma is asked to uphold the "Word." Is this what Isma is doing as she tells the story of Hajila and herself? Is the "Word" Isma upholds the story of women in Algeria?

Chapter 5: The Outcast

Summary: Lla Hadja is a rich woman who had been to Mecca. She presided over the street ritual in Isma's hometown. Some people suggested Lla Hadja kept her eye on the women of the community in order to pay for her past sins. She was especially interested in the twelve-year-old girls who entered the first stage of close confinement in the harem and only went out to the bath once a week. One young wife in particular was the victim of Lla Hadja's venom; she was known only as "the outcast"; the nickname itself veiled the veil of the unknown woman. After Isma left her childhood home, she met "the outcast" in a prison waiting room in the capitol. The woman's brother and Lla Hadja had driven her out of her home fifteen years before. Isma believes she was exiled for the crime of having wished to love and retells her story. One day, a young man who had been "the outcast's" childhood friend returned to the city and bought the family house for his widowed mother. He bathed in the sea everyday and passed Lla Hadja's window on his way home. The "outcast" was a young, childless wife with an ailing husband; she saw the young man pass her window every day. Lla Hadja spread rumors that the young wife called to the man one day. As a result, the woman's brother exiled her with her ailing husband and bought her out of the house. Finally, the woman's husband died, and she spent her days visiting prisoners. She has become like a saint to Isma.

Analysis: The only love story Isma ever heard during her childhood was the story of the young wife who was cast out of town for her desire to love. The story illustrates the restrictions of young women in society and the power of the patriarchy. It was actually the woman's brother who exiled her, but his actions were fueled by the gossip of the community watchdog Lla Hadja. Isma seems to indicate that older women in the society support the patriarchy of the Muslim world. These women, like Lla Hadja, are on the lookout and will report anyone who does not obey society's restrictive mandates. Djebar criticizes women like Lla Hadja who refuse to recognize other women as sisters and destroy people like "the outcast." In addition to attacking the patriarchy, throughout the novel, Djebar appeals for solidarity among women. Lla Hadja works against "the outcast"; she is the antithesis of Dinarzade who helps her sister Scheherazade.

Chapter 6: Nuptials on a Straw Mat

Summary: Isma's story of her childhood now focuses on a family who lived next door. The eldest daughter was "given" to a cousin in marriage (p. 119). The second daughter hoped to marry for love. She was a wonderful dressmaker and had created a "trousseau fit for a princess" (p. 120). She was a beautiful, modest girl, and her mother rejected many suitors before she finally accepted a young man from a neighboring village. However according to his family's tradition, the bride had to be married beneath "Sisi Naamar's Bough"; otherwise the children would be handicapped (p. 121). The custom required the bride to be wed in humility; she could not wear any adornments. The ceremony was just as Saint Maawa declared it should be four hundred years ago. The virgin bride was shrouded in a seamless veil as if she were to be buried. Only her husband saw her on the wedding night. The next day, the bride's womenfolk traveled to her new home carrying the trousseau and the wedding feast. They arrived to find "convulsive sobs coming from a white-shrouded heap huddled up against the wall . . ." (p. 124). The bride's mother was angry, and the bride's sister console her in her misery by huddling with her under her veil. The marriage had been consummated on a straw mat. Although the bride's eyes were swollen with crying, she appeared in her finery in the afternoon. The gossiping townspeople claimed that the marriage would be miserable. As Isma recalls the details of the wedding—including the copulation on a straw mat, the boorish bridegroom, and the tearful bride—she believes that there is no hope in these marriages, whether they are blessed by a saint or filled with music.

Analysis: With this event, the child Isma understands that a traditional Muslim marriage can be a death experience for many young women. She says, "I became aware of what heavy destructive footsteps had crushed the tender shoots in the dream garden" (p. 125). Although the bride combined the local Andalusian tradition with European style in the creation of her trousseau, and her mother carefully chose her husband, she was still trapped by tradition. Instead of wearing her elegant wedding gown, she was shrouded in a traditional veil that symbolized death. Her mother's anger did not help the young bride; only the bride's sister could console her as they huddled together under the death veil of traditional marriage. The reader is again reminded of the two sisters, Scheherazade and Dinarzade, who together survive the night in the sultan's bridal chamber. The reaction of the bride's community is mixed. Many feel that the her new in-laws are like barbarians and that she was offered as a "sacrificial lamb to the herdsmen!" (p. 122). However, one woman defends the traditional custom saying, "Islam is one, Islam is pure and unadorned! . . . The law cannot change, it is the same, everywhere from our town to faraway Medina . . ." (p. 122).

Chapter 7: Rest by the Wayside

Summary: Isma does not know why she is "conveying this cascade of misery" as she tells the story of women's struggles (p. 127). Women nurture men and children tirelessly all day long, and the men alone enjoy the daylight. At night, women must submit their weary bodies to their men when they long for rest. As women age, they get some respite. For example, if a husband takes a co-wife, the first wife is free to pray five times a day before Allah. Older women may move about the streets, and their veils become items of adornment. Death is the final release for women.

Analysis: Isma indicates that women are exhausted as they continually give birth, nurture children, and meet their husband's sexual demands. As a woman ages, she may get some relief if her husband marries a second, third, or fourth wife. However, Isma implies that working with co-wives and praying to Allah five times a day is not much of a rest for Muslim women. She believes that women long for death, for in their graves, they may finally find "rest by the wayside" (p. 127).

Chapter 8: A Young Girl's Anger

Summary: Isma says that traditional Muslim women who are confined on their patios think they are "queens of the harem," but they really only have "walk-on parts" (p. 130). Isma tells the story of a young girl named Houria. Houria's mother was called "the broody hen" because she had eight children in fifteen years and she was expecting again (p. 131). This woman and her husband slept with their eight children between them. He called his wife for sex as the eldest daughter listened. Isma can still hear Houria describing her parents' copulation. Houria challenged her mother in public and claimed her mother should refuse to go to the man when he called her for sex by banging his slippers on the floor. The women were shocked; Houria called her father "the man," and ran away (p. 133). Isma cannot remember the rest of the scene because she was so upset by Houria's "blazing outburst of stark hatred, expressed towards the too-submissive mother" (p. 133).

Analysis: Isma provides much detail in the story of Houria's anger about her mother's relationship with her father, but then she says, "Total amnesia has swallowed up the rest of the scene for me" (p. 133). Isma is not shocked at Houria's lack of modesty in attacking her mother in public or the image of all the children sleeping between Houria's copulating mother and father. Rather, Isma is shocked by Houria's vehement anger at her mother. Isma may feel that Houria's mother does not deserve Houria's wrath because she is simply following the dictates of her role as a woman in Muslim society. Houria herself is just about to become engaged. If she is fertile—

as her mother is fertile—one wonders how she will escape the plight of her mother. The reader might also wonder if Houria will call her own husband "the man" (p. 133). Finally, as the reader holds the story of Scheherazade and Dinarzade in mind, Houria is like Dinarzade who hears her sister copulating with the sultan on the bed above her; she may also be like Scheherazade who tells quite an intriguing story.

Chapter 9: The Swing
Summary: As an adolescent, Isma always reminded herself that she was saved from the harem by her father. She had an "insatiable appetite for the wind" and seemed as if she "was in danger of taking off" as a young woman (p. 134). She later left the man she loved in order to "disburden" herself and explore a "primal injury" that "risked reappearing" (p. 134). Isma returns to the experience of the swing in her childhood. One day, one of her boy cousins lured her to a fun fair in town. She climbed into a huge metal swing opposite her cousin. She says, "I felt my body rise and dance to the regular rhythm, nothing else existed, neither the town, nor the crowds, nor my cousin, only the motion of space and myself swinging to and fro" (p. 135). Isma reveled in the freedom and "exhilaration of being so high up in the air" (p. 136). She was intoxicated with the feeling of weightless in the high altitude. However, upon returning to the ground, Isma's angry father grabbed her by the arm and steered her home. He was angry because she had been swinging in a short skirt that exposed her legs to all the men who were staring up at her from the ground below. Isma was punished; however, she kept telling herself that she loved her father and that he had saved her from the harem. But Isma says, "It was with difficulty that I discovered the truth: my father was at the best only the organizer of premature funerals" (p. 137).

Analysis: Isma begins to explain why she left her husband in this chapter. As a young woman, she had been exposed to "too much sun" or freedom (p. 134). She was like the child intoxicated by the wind and the freedom of movement on the swing. Like the little girl swinging on the swing, the young woman Isma is the object of men's lustful eyes. Although Isma's father protected her from the harem, he actually set her up for a premature death. The reader may understand this death as the failure of her first marriage to "the man."

Childhood, O Hajila!
Summary: Isma addresses Hajila again in a lyrical invocation to childhood. She says, "Childhood, O Hajila! I must unearth you from this mouldering heap under which you have been buried" (p. 139). She struggles for a way to introduce herself to Hajila and says, "Before continuing our story, I must find the source of all these sighs, I must discover the lacerations hidden in the depths of the soul" (p. 139). Isma calls herself the "impossible rival, haphazardly weaving a story to free the concubine" (p. 139). She also questions whether the storyteller is really herself or if it is "some ghost within me, who steals in, sandals in hand, and mouth gagged? To waken her sister to what disillusionment . . . " (p. 139). This invocation completes Part II, "Destruction at Dawn."

Analysis: In this invocation, Isma seems to indicate that by reflecting upon her childhood she has gained some understanding and strength and is now in a position to introduce herself to Hajila. Isma seems to liken herself to Dinarzade, for she weaves a haphazard tale like the sister under the sultan's bed in order to free the concubine above. Perhaps Isma suggests that the tale of her childhood as well as the tale of Scheherazade and his sister Dinarzade will free Hajila and all other Muslim women like her. However, Isma is not sure if she really is the inspiration for the storyteller, and she is unclear of her mission. She indicates that she wakens her sister, Hajila, only to disillusionment. In conclusion, Part II, "Destruction at Dawn," has elaborated the story of the sultan's bride in the tales of the *Arabian Nights* and retold the story of Isma's childhood with a focus on the plight of traditional women.

Part III: The Sultan's Bride Looks On
Introduction
Summary: The narrator asks the reader to imagine what would happen if the sister under the bed did not wake Scheherazade, and if she were continually sacrificed every morning only to be reborn. Furthermore, what would happen if none of Scheherazade's sisters supported her? She says, "What if, when Scheherazade disappeared, voiceless, she in her turn took her place under that same bed of love and death, which was transformed into a story-teller's throne, and what if a second sleepless sister forgot her task again? What if this one neglected to keep watch, neglected her duty to wake her sister, prepare the strategy and ensure the sole road to salvation?" (p. 143).

Analysis: This introduction implies that Scheherazade will die if her sisters do not wake her and help her. Without the solidarity of all women, Scheherazade will be murdered by the sultan; she will then take her place under the bed. If she in her turn neglects her duty to wake her sisters in the marital bed above her, she will continue to be reborn in the form of another oppressed woman. She will die again. The murdered Scheherazade who dies only to be reborn into oppression and die again indicates the hopeless cycle of women who are oppressed by men. The solidarity of women is the only hope.

Chapter 1: The Mother
Summary: Isma describes the harems of old where women were guarded by athletic, mute, eunuchs dependent upon whichever master prevailed. No guards are needed these days in Algeria because the older women in the society confine their own daughters to the harem. Isma says, "The matriarchs swaddle their little girls in their own insidious anguish, before they even reach puberty. Mother and daughter, O, harem restored!" (p. 145). Isma visits Touma's home, and Nazim is present. Touma claims she never would have agreed to Hajila's marriage if she had known "the man" was divorced from Isma. She calls Hajila Isma's co-wife, and because this word also means "wound" in Arabic, Isma thinks Touma says, "You were choosing a wound!" (p. 145). Isma claims she does not want anything; she came because she and Meriem will be leaving soon, and she had heard of Hajila's illness. Touma claims that Hajila believes her husband remains the "pillar" of her home (p. 146). Isma claims she is happy to be homeless if having a husband is the cost of having a home. Isma actually meets Hajila face to face and tells her to go to the bath. Isma will be there on Friday.

Analysis: In this chapter Isma speaks directly to Touma. She then addresses Hajila as if she were telling Hajila's story again, and finally she addresses Hajila face to face. Isma thinks Hajila must have wanted to take her daughter's place because she has been resting in the children's room. Perhaps she is implying that Hajila must also return to her childhood to understand herself. As Isma meets Hajila, she says, "You, my daughter and my mother, my half-sister; my reopened wound (so words never lie)" (p. 147). For Isma, Hajila encompasses all aspects of womanhood. She relates her meeting with Hajila to the story of Scheherazade and Dinarzade saying: "With laughter, with tears. The women of the seraglio, sultan's bride or serving-maid, face each other, meet each other's eyes . . . With laughter, with tears! The sun shines through the glass pane of the skylight, high up in the prison" (p. 147). Isma seems relieved to meet Hajila; she extends an offer of friendship when she invites her to the bath. Isma seems to criticize Touma for seeking to marry Hajila to a man who could provide economic stability, but Isma herself actually condemned Hajila to a loveless marriage.

Chapter 2: The Turkish Bath
Summary: Isma lets herself relax in the bath. She feels near to Hajila and the moment when the current will flow between them. Isma explains that the *hammam*, or the Turkish bath is a "place of respite or amaranthine garden. The sound of water obliterates the walls, bodies are liberated under the wet marble. Every night the Turkish bath serves as a dormitory for country-folk in transit and so becomes a harem in reverse, accessible to all—as if, in the melting-pot of

sweat, odours and dead skin, this liquid prison becomes a place of nocturnal rebirth" (p. 148). Here women who share the same man come face to face naked. Isma is hoping to meet Hajila; she says she is in search of her misgivings and her aphasia. She imagines herself at "the same time a child and an old woman" (p. 149). Hajila appears at the bath. Isma pours hot water over her back, and Hajila explains that while she is pregnant, she can only remain in the baths for half an hour. As Hajila and Isma wash together, Isma offers Hajila the key to her apartment. Hajila accepts it without understanding. Isma tells Hajila to get out of her mother's house and consult someone about her pregnancy. Isma tells Hajila that it is her decision whether or not she keeps her child. Finally, Isma says she will not come again, but Nazim will know where she and Meriem will be.

Analysis: Isma says she attends the *hammam* both to recapture her childhood and to act as an observer. She indicates that the *hammam* is a symbol of childhood and a safe place or haven in which women can bond. It is a place of renewal and rebirth—the antithesis of the harem. The *hammam* is defined as "the only temporary reprieve from the harem . . .The Turkish bath offers a secret consolation to sequestered woman . . . This surrogate maternal cocoon providing an escape from the hot-house of cloistration . . ." (p. 152). The waters of the *hammam* symbolize the waters of the womb. Women leave the confines of the harem and pass through the great outdoors in order to arrive at the *hammam*. Within the *hammam*, women meet other women who are not cloistered in the same harem. As they bathe and face one another naked, they can share the truth. The *hammam* seems to symbolize childhood for Isma and public place for Hajila—keys of understanding for both women. As Isma waits for Hajila, she searches for the cause of her misgivings and her loss of the power to understand and use words. She continues to search for the truth of her life. The physical key that she offers Hajila will open a new place for her that is neither her mother's home nor her husband's home. Presumably this is the key to Isma's own apartment—the apartment she is leaving for her motherland. The key may symbolize freedom for Hajila to move into Isma's place and to make her own choice concerning the child in her womb.

Chapter 3: On the Threshold

Summary: Isma walks around the town and escorts her daughter home after school. She is in transit in the capitol, and she begins to envision the place where she hopes to find love. She says, "I will never fall in love again, except in the place of my birth, in my own kingdom" (p. 155). Although Isma dreams of helping Hajila get an abortion, she says, "But I'm afraid of any more traveling. I too want to put down roots. To wear the veil again, in my own fashion . . . To retreat into the shadows; bury myself" (p. 156). Hajila, on the other hand, is trying to escape from her prison. Isma waits for Hajila and follows her on her walk. She watches as Hajila hurtles herself down a flight of marble steps. As Hajila leaps forward, a black car hits her. Hajila is lying on the ground unconscious. Her face is ashen, but she will survive. Isma sees her own face in Hajila's face; she knows that Hajila will lose the fetus. Isma believes the fetus is already dead in Hajila's heart. As Isma leaves the capitol for her mother's home, "The second wife will repeat what the first one only half succeeded in doing: cutting her way through the same undergrowth, starting the same impromptu madness, but in the diamond-sharp light of reason" (p. 159). The first wife, Isma, will fade away to be reborn somewhere else. The second wife, Hajila, "stands on the threshold, devouring the space: and now the first one can put on the veil, or go into hiding. The man, searching for the same wounds, gesticulates in the darkness as the day ends" (p. 159).

Analysis: As the novel ends, Isma addresses Hajila saying: "Turn and turn about on the world stage that is denied us, in the space we are forbidden to infringe, in the flooding light that is withdrawn from us, you and I, turn and turn about, ghost and mirror-image of each other, we play both parts, sultan's bride and her attendant, attendant and her mistress! Men no longer exist, or rather, they do exist, they stamp their feet, they are everywhere, obstructing our path. They spy on us endlessly with unseeing eyes" (p. 158). Now the reader understands that throughout the novel, Isma and Hajila have each played the part of Scheherazade and Dinarzade, sultan's bride and attendant. Men only exist as obstacles for these sisters. Isma concludes saying, "At the end of the long night, the odalisque is in flight" (p.159). The odalisque is the female slaves or concubines of the Oriental harems of the past; their modern-day representatives are both Isma and Hajila. Symbolically the odalisque is the tradition of oppressing women in Algerian society. After a long night of struggle, the tradition of oppression is in flight.

The Lute

<u>Summary</u>: Isma questions women who are freed from the past. She says, " . . . the queen of every dawn, on her dais, can only hope to survive for one day at a time, her salvation is only assured by every night spent in the harem, by every flight into the world of the imagination" (p. 160). Isma closes saying, "O, my sister, I who thought to wake you, I'm afraid. I'm afraid for all women, not just we two or three, Isma, Hajila, Meriem, but all women—barring midwives, barring mothers standing guard and those carrion-beetle-matriarchs, I fear lest we all find ourselves in chains again, in 'this West in the Orient', this corner of the earth where day dawned so slowly for us that twilight is already closing in around us everywhere" (p. 160).

<u>Analysis</u>: Isma seems to indicate that women can only hope to survive one day at a time. Now the harem is a source of strength as is the imagination. However, Isma expresses her fear that women in her society will find themselves in chains again. Her final note seems to put in question her conclusion at the end of the previous chapter "On the Threshold" where she stated, "At the end of the long night, the odalisque is in flight" (p.159). Perhaps Isma wishes the reader to understand that women are on the threshold of dispelling the traditions of oppression. If they do not stand together in solidarity, they may allow the darkness of oppression to envelope them again.

List of Works Consulted

Ali, Abdullah Yusuf. *The Meaning of the Holy Qur'an*. Brentwood, MD: Amana Corporation, 1991.

Amrane-Minne, Danièle Djamila. "Women and Politics in Algeria from the War of Independence to Our Day." *Research in African Literatures* 30.3 (Fall 1999): 62-77.

Bravmann, Rene. *African Islam*. Washington, DC: Smithsonian Institution Press, 1983.

Bruner, Charlotte H., ed. *The Heinemann Book of African Women's Writing*. Portsmouth, NH: Heinemann, 1993.

Cooke, Miriam. "Arab Women Writers." *The Cambridge History of Arabic Literature: Modern Arabic Literature*. Ed. M. M. Badawi. Cambridge, MA: Cambridge University Press, 1992.

Erickson, John. "Translating the Untranslated: Djebar's *Le blanc de l'Algerie*." *Research in African Literatures* 30.3 (Fall 1999): 95-107.

Haddawy, Husain. *The Arabian Nights*. New York: W. W. Norton & Co., 1990.

Jomier, Jacques. *How to Understand Islam*. New York: Crossroads, 1989.

Killam, Douglas, ed. *The Companion to African Literatures*. Bloomington & Indianapolis: Indiana University Press, 2000.

Lane, Edward William, trans. *Best Selections from the Arabian Nights Entertainments*. New York: Hart Publishing Co., 1976.

Mortimer, Mildred. "Assia Djebar's *Algerian Quartet*: A Study in Fragmented Autobiography." *Research in African Literatures* 28.2 (Summer 1997): 102-117.

---. *Journeys Through the French African Novel*. Portsmouth, NH: Heinemann, 1990.

---. "The Evolution of Assia Djebar's Feminist Conscience." *Contemporary African Literature*. Ed. H. Wylie. Washington, D.C.: Three Continents Press, 1983. 7-14.

Rahman, Fazlur. *Islam*. Chicago: University of Chicago Press, 1979.

Tahon, Marie-Blanche "Women Novelists and Women in the Struggle for Algeria's National Liberation (1957-1980)." *Research in African Literatures* 23.2 (Summer 1992): 39-50.

Trimmingham, J. Spencer. "Features of East African Islam." *Islam in East Africa*. Oxford, U.K.: Clarendon Press, 1964. 31-75.

Vogl, Mary. "Assia Djebar." *Postcolonial African Writers: A Bio-Biographical Critical Sourcebook*. Ed. P. N. Parekh. Westport, CT: Greenwood Press, 1998. 135-143.

Zimra, Clarisse. "Afterword." *Women of Algiers in Their Apartment*. Trans. Marjolijn de Jager. Charlottesville: University Press of Virginia, 1992. 159-211.

CHAPTER FOUR

———

Fountain and Tomb
A Novel about Childhood in Cairo
by Naguib Mahfouz

Fountain and Tomb is a semi-autobiographical, episodic novel that offers a small boy's reflections on the life and people of his neighborhood in an alley of old Cairo during the first half of the twentieth century. The first person narrator presents seventy-eight different episodes, some which describe his own initiation into religion, love, and politics and some which describe the affairs of people from his street as they fall in love, search for wealth, enact vengeance on one another, and work their ways towards their eventual deaths. The tone of this short work is mixed. On the one hand, it celebrates the lives of Egyptians under British occupation with a great deal of humor. On the other hand, it is tinged with sadness and foreboding about the difficulties of life, the inevitable loss of community, and the impossible search for meaning and spiritual fulfillment. It conveys a palpable sense of fatalism, as evidenced by the countless occupants of the alley who, metaphorically speaking, travel along seemingly pre-determined paths often leading to unfortunate ends. The laughter and irony of the tales serve as a counter to what would otherwise be an utterly depressing existence. Mahfouz's ability to portray a society where fatalism and lightheartedness are intertwined captures one of the key elements of character in Egyptian literature, if such a thing can be said to exist. But while *Fountain and Tomb* is dependent on the unique qualities of its Egyptian setting, the work also has strong universal appeal. It raises difficult philosophical questions that weigh upon people of every society: What makes people happy? Do humans create evil, or does it exist independently? What is a person's responsibility for his own fate? What do the individual and society owe each other? And why do cultures inevitably change?

The original title of *Fountain and Tomb* is *Hikayat Haritna* or *Tales of Our Quarter*. The work *hikaya* refers to a particular literary genre within the Arabic canon. *Hikayat* are simple oral tales. They stand in contrast to *siyar*, or epic heroic tales (which are often lengthy memorized pieces), or the more complex *quasidas*, or didactic rhymed prose texts. Arab readers would likely read a work entitled *hiyakat* with a different set of expectations than what they would look for in a more sophisticated work such as Mahfouz's famous *Midaq Alley*. *Fountain and Tomb* is a humble set of "tales." It cannot be regarded as one of Mahfouz's definite works; on the other hand, it does contain many of the elements found in his more often read and more widely respected works.

Lessons

Lesson One   The History of Contemporary Egypt
Sufism
Reading Assignment: Episodes 1-40

Lesson Two   *Fountain and Tomb*: A Semi-Autobiographical, Episodic Novel
Reading Assignment: Episodes 41-78

Lesson Three   The Author and His Work
Writing Project for *Fountain and Tomb*

Lesson One
The History of Contemporary Egypt
Sufism

Objectives:
1. Students will identify North Africa by locating Egypt and its neighbors.
2. Students will locate the countries in Africa that are predominantly Muslim.
3. Students will become familiar with the history of Egypt's independence movement.
4. Students will become familiar with the history and the distinguishing characteristics of Islamic Sufism.
5. Students will read the first three episodes of *Fountain and Tomb* and note significant ideas the author conveys about the narrator and the community.

Materials:
1. Classroom World Map
2. Student Handout: Map of Africa, Chapter Two: Africa Overview of the Continent
3. Student Handout: Map of Islam in Africa, Chapter Two: Africa Overview of Continent
4. Student Handout: Independence from British Imperialism
5. Student Handout: Sufism
6. Student Handout: Review of Episodes 1-40
7. Teacher Resource: Historical Highlights of Contemporary Egypt
8. Teacher Resource: Summary and Analysis: Episodes 1-40

Procedures:
1. Distribute Student Handout: Map of Africa. Ask students to locate Egypt on a map of Africa. Have students identify Morocco, Algeria, Tunisia, Libya, and Egypt as the countries of North Africa.
2. Ask students to identify the various countries that are predominantly Muslim in Africa by referring to Student Handout: Map of Islam in Africa.
3. Distribute Student Handout: Independence from British Imperialism. Review handout in anticipation of the novel's references to important political events in the country's history.
4. Inform students of other highlights in the history of Egypt during the twentieth century. Refer to Teacher Resource: Historical Highlights of Contemporary Egypt.
5. Ask students to brainstorm definitions for the term mystic and put suggestions on the board. Distribute and review Student Handout: Sufism so students will be better prepared to understand the crucial importance of the Sufi monastery in *Fountain and Tomb*. Afterwards, have students add to the definition on the board and discuss any connections that can be made to the mystical tradition in western culture.
6. Read the first three episodes of *Fountain and Tomb* aloud in class. Assist students in completing Student Handout: Review of Episodes 1-40 for these three episodes. Answer any questions that might arise over the beginning of the novel. Refer to Summary and Analysis: Episodes 1-40.

Assessment:
Evaluate students' answers for review of Episodes 1-3 to see if they have applied the information provided in Student Handout: Sufism in their understanding of the reading.

Reading Assignment:
Fountain and Tomb, Episodes 1-40
Complete Student Handout: Review of Episodes 1-40

Lesson Two
Fountain and Tomb: **A Semi-Autobiographical, Episodic Novel**

Objectives:
1. Students will gain a heightened understanding of Mahfouz's ideas on politics, history, and love by comparing their observations with others in a small group.
2. Students will develop collaborative skills needed to produce a summary of their group's discussion of one of Mahfouz's three main topics.
3. Students will explore and analyze any unifying elements in *Fountain and Tomb*, especially those concerned with symbolism and point of view.
4. Students will examine how Mahfouz's life and his attention to Arab literary traditions have influenced his writing of *Fountain and Tomb*.

Materials:
1. Student Handout: Review of Episodes 1-40
2. Student Handout: Review of Episodes 41-78
3. Student Handout: *Fountain and Tomb*: A Semi-Autobiographical, Episodic Novel
4. Teacher Resource: Unifying Elements in *Fountain and Tomb*
5. Reading Resource: Summary and Analysis: Episodes 1-40

Procedures:
1. Assign students to groups where they can compare their responses on Student Handout: Review of Episodes 1-40. Allow ample time for students to discuss their assessment of Mahfouz's perspectives on politics, religion, and love. Then allow the groups to choose the topic that generated the most interest for the group and write a one-paragraph group summary that contains the tentative conclusions they reached in their discussions. They should make reference to at least one quote in their summaries and should mention any disagreement or debate that may have occurred in the discussion. Have groups read summaries aloud and then open the discussion up to a larger consideration of the first half of the novel. Answer any questions that arise. Refer to Summary and Analysis: Episodes 1-40.
2. Using Teacher Resource: Unifying Elements in *Fountain and Tomb*, ask students the following questions:
   - Is *Fountain and Tomb* a collection of unrelated stories, or does Mahfouz use any elements to bring his stories together?
   - What thematic motifs are developed in the first half?
   - Do any elements in the first half of the novel seem to have meaning beyond themselves?
   - Can you assign any symbolic meaning to the alley as a whole?
   - Can you assign any symbolic meaning to the *takiya*? To the High Sheikh? To the Sufis' garden?
   - Can you assign any symbolic meaning to the large square located further away from the boys' house? To the smaller square that contains the *takiya*?
   - Can you assign any symbolic meaning to the cemetery?
   - Why did Naguib Mahfouz decide to use a child narrator to tell this story about life in the Cairo alley?
   - What do we learn about the neighborhood from the child narrator that we might not have learned if the narrator were an adult?

- What might the novel have included if it were told from the perspective of an adult instead? In other words, in what ways is the child's perspective limited or incomplete?
- What does the narration reveal about childhood in general?

3. Distribute and review <u>Student Handout: *Fountain and Tomb*: A Semi-Autobiographical, Episodic Novel</u> for a better understanding of the author's narrative choices. Ask students to review again the unifying elements in the novel.

Assessment:

1. Evaluate group summaries to determine their level of sophistication and attention to textual detail.

2. Assess students' contribution to the discussion about the unifying elements in the novel to ascertain their reading comprehension.

Reading Assignment:

Fountain and Tomb, Episodes 41-78

Complete <u>Student Handout: Review of Episodes 41-78</u>

Lesson Three
The Author and His Work
Writing Project for *Fountain and Tomb*

Objectives:
1. Students will continue to develop skills of analysis and collaboration in groups for discussion of the second half of the novel.
2. Students will draw tentative conclusions about Mahfouz's unifying elements, especially symbolism and point of view, during class discussion.
3. Students will become familiar with Mahfouz's biography and his other literary works.
4. Students will begin to draw connections between Mahfouz's childhood and their own in the preparation for the upcoming writing project assignment.

Materials:
1. Student Handout: Review of Episodes 41-78
2. Student Handout: The Author and His Work
3. Student Handout: A Selected Bibliography of Naguib Mahfouz's Works
4. Student Handout: Writing Project for *Fountain and Tomb*
5. Reading Resource: Summary and Analysis: Episodes 41-78

Procedures:
1. Have students go back into their groups to discuss their answers for the Student Handout: Review of Episodes 41-78. Again, let groups decide on one of the three topics after a more general discussion of all three. Ask them to write another summary of their consideration of this topic. Have groups read summaries and move into a larger discussion of the second half of the novel. Answer questions that might arise from the reading. Refer to Summary and Analysis: Episodes 41-78.
2. Ask the class to reconsider the previous day's discussion of symbolism and point of view. See if their ideas on these issues have changed or been extended now that they have completed the second half of the novel.
3. Distribute Student Handout: The Author and His Work and Student Handout: A Selected Bibliography of Naguib Mahfouz's Works. Have students read these handouts for a better understanding of the author's literary career and the influences on it.
4. Ask students to brainstorm the various types of stories that they could tell from their own childhood. List on the board the multiple societal elements that contribute to a child's development. Examples might include relationships with parents, siblings and relatives; interactions with friends; national occurrences; sporting events; neighborhood squabbles; religious observances; holiday celebrations; town happenings; etc. Inform students that they will be asked to provide three episodes from their childhood in the upcoming writing project. Suggest that they refer to the list on the board to brainstorm possible stories.
5. Distribute Student Handout: Writing Project for *Fountain and Tomb*.

Assessment:
1. Evaluate student work on Student Handout: Review of Episodes 1-40 and Student Handout: Review of Episodes 41-78 to judge their thoroughness in reading and their level of analysis.
2. Assess student performance on the Student Handout: Writing Project for *Fountain and Tomb*. An additional assessment, perhaps for extra credit, could be added at the end of the unit by asking students to extend and revise one of their childhood episodes so that it resembles the more fully-formed episodes from *Fountain and Tomb* that could stand on their own as independent short stories, such as Episodes 1, 32, 41, 44, 60, 61 and 62.

Teacher Resource
Historical Highlights of Contemporary Egypt

Phase I   **British Control**

1. 1882 - British troops land along the Suez Canal; British occupy Egypt
2. 1891 - Emergence of a nationalist opposition parties
3. 1902 - Aswan Dam built to irrigate the Nile Valley throughout the year
4. 1903 - French recognize Britain's claim to Egypt
5. 1914 - Egypt declared a British protectorate and Hussein Kamil, a member of the royal family, is declared Sultan of Egypt

Phase II   **Egypt as Monarchy**

1. 1914-1918 - Egyptians suffer many hardships during World War I
2. 1919 - (*Wafd*) moderate nationalists, lead by Saad Zaghloul, petitions British to attend Paris Peace Conference and plead for Egyptian independence
3. 1919 - Zaghloul exiled and returned due to widespread protest
4. 1922 - *Wafd* political party has enormous popular support until 1950
5. 1922 - Token independence; British control of foreign policy and defense
6. 1923 - British constitution imposed; King Fuad becomes the Sultan
7. 1924 - Saad Zaghloul is appointed prime minister but resigns within few months
8. 1936 - Anglo-Egyptian Treaty confines British power to the Suez Canal zone
9. 1942 - Germans and Italians invade Egypt; British drive them out at El Alamein
10. 1948-49 - Coalition of Arab states fight against Jewish state in Palestine

Phase III   **Independent Egypt**

1. 1952 - Abdul Nasser's military coup forces King Faruk into exile
2. 1952 - Land reform decree places limits on land ownership
3. 1953 - Egypt declared a republic under President Muhammed Naguib
4. 1954 - Naguib resigns; Nasser becomes president
5. 1956 - Nasser nationalizes Suez Canal Company; begins Aswan High Dam
6. 1956 - British, French, and Israel invade Egypt for control of Suez Canal but United States and Soviet Union pressure them to withdraw
7. 1967 - Defeat in six day war with Israel; significant loss of Arab land
8. 1970 - Nasser succeeded by vice president, Anwar el-Sadat
9. 1973 - Sadat attacks Israel; negotiations for Israeli withdrawal from Sinai
10. 1977 - Sadat speaks to Israeli Parliament
11. 1978 - President Carter meets Sadat and Menachem Begin at Camp David
12. 1979 - Sadat signs Camp David treaty; some Arab nations break ties with Egypt
13. 1981 - Sadat is assassinated and succeeded by Hosni Mubarak
14. 1987 - Arab leaders agree to allow individual states to determine ties with Egypt
15. 1980-88 - Egypt offers military and technical aid to Iraq in Iran-Iraq war
16. 1989 - Egypt is reinstated in Arab league, after ten-year suspension
17. 1990 - Mubarak supports US-led invasion of Iraq

Student Handout
Independence from British Imperialism

When the Britain conquered Egypt in 1882, opposition quickly emerged over a number of issues. Egyptians were angry that their rights to the Suez Canal had been sold for only four million pounds and that they were being denied any of the canal's sizeable profits. There was also contention over the Sudan. Egypt and Britain were to administer that region jointly, but the Egyptians gradually lost their control. The outbreak of World War I further poisoned Anglo-Egyptian relations. Britain declared Egypt a protectorate in 1914, and the war was a great burden on the population: peasants were called for military service; livestock was requisitioned; and inflation increased food prices.

In the decade before World War I, Mustafa Kamil led a nationalist movement that attempted to oust the British. This endeavor was promoted by intellectuals and did not have popular support. After the war, this changed dramatically. Saad Zaghloul, a charismatic leader, began calling for constitutional reform and improvements in education and agriculture. In 1919, he led a committee (or Wafd) to the British High Commissioner to secure the right to go to the Paris Peace Conference to plead for Egypt's independence. He argued that the conference's emphasis on national self-determination for Europe should be applied to the colonies. The request was denied, and Zaghloul was deported to Malta. This so outraged the people that the British had to return Zaghloul to Egypt and then send him to London for negotiations. A plan for peace failed because of British demands—to maintain control of defense, the Suez Canal, and the Sudan.

Disturbances broke out again in 1921, and the *Wafd* party was formed the following year and gained overwhelming popular support. The British were aware of growing opposition and granted Egypt a token independence that still allowed extensive British control. They imposed a new constitution in 1923 with a monarchy and parliamentary government. King Fuad ruled from 1923-1936, and King Faruk from 1936 to 1952. Both kings hated the *Wafd*, ignored the appeals of the electorate, and represented conservative and landed interests. Britain basically still controlled Egypt through the monarchy. Zaghloul was appointed prime minister to the king in 1924 but was forced from office a few months later.

In 1936, Italy invaded Ethiopia. Fearing that Italy would next attack Egypt, Britain became more willing to make concessions. The Anglo-Egypt Agreement of 1936 reduced the British presence in Egypt, but still allowed Britain to protect the Suez Canal and station troops on Egyptian territory. During World War II, the British forced King Faruk to appoint a prime minister closely aligned to their interests. This seriously undermined the King's authority and re-ignited anti-British sentiment. Britain's support of a Jewish state only exacerbated the rising frustration of the people. One resistance group, the Muslim Brotherhood, fostered anger against the British. Another group led by Abdul Nasser executed a military coup on July 23, 1952. The monarchy was destroyed, the 1923 constitution was abrogated, and an interim military government was established. Egypt was declared a republic in 1953, and the moderate, well-respected Muhamed Neguib became its first president. Soon after, a member of the Muslim brotherhood tried to assassinate Nasser, and Neguib resigned from office because of his complicity in the plot. Nasser was elected president and served until his death in 1970. Known for his anti-imperialist ideas, his socialist leanings, and his determination to maintain a non-aligned position in global politics, Nasser was able at last to usher Egypt into an age of full independence from Britain.

Source: Ayandele, E. A. *The Making of Modern Africa: The Twentieth Century.* London: Longman Group Ltd., 1986.

Student Handout
Sufism

Sufism is the mystical form of Islam. The name means *wool* in Arabic since that is what the first Sufis wore. The early history of Sufism is not clear, but it seems to have emerged around the ninth century as a reaction against the formalism of Islam and the corrupting influence of personal wealth brought on by Islamic conquests. Sufis strive for the perfection of the individual and an intimate union with God. They believe that these goals are best achieved through emotional experiences and the guidance of inner light rather than tradition or reason. They also contend that the coveted state of perfection or *fana* can only be attained through the annihilation of the self in God. For this reason, Sufis withdraw from the world of everyday life and political affairs and seek the divine in the depths of their being instead. Preferring the riches of God to those of society, Sufis view poverty and abstinence as the means to their spiritual ends.

Sufism began on an individual basis, but eventually devotees began organizing into fraternities or orders. The *shaykh* or spiritual master of an order determined the rules of initiation and the path or *tariqa* that the mystics would follow. This master was the focal point of the order and could assert absolute control over the members. In some cases, the leader was even considered a saint by his followers because he displayed signs of nearness to God.

Members of an order occupied a building called the *takiya*. Though they lived in isolation, Sufis were not required to be celibate, and they were allowed to interact with laymen from the neighborhood who wanted to be affiliated with their religious activities. The religious practices of the Sufis emphasized a progression of ascending stations, starting with repentance and abstinence and ending with complete trust in God and acquiescence to God's will. The various orders used different forms of worship to advance in their path. Some practiced the *dhikr* that consisted of chanting the name of Allah over and over with particular breathing and body movements. Others made use of spiritual hymns, dancing, whirling, and drumming. Certain orders took part in public performances of poetry and dancing. When the ecstatic worship activities caused Sufis to go into a hypnotic state, they were considered to be drunk on the spirit of God. Sufis who were members of these more ecstatic sects were also called dervishes.

Ever since its initial founding, Sufism has been in conflict with the more traditional and legalistic forms of Islamic law and practice. Before the twelfth century, some were accused of heresy and even martyred over their interpretations of the *Koran*. Orthodox Muslims have also objected to the performance aspect of Sufi ritual because the *Koran* prescribes a more limited use of music, dancing, and poetry. Sufi beliefs include the adoration of saints, and this is too offends Muslims who disdain anything that detracts from the oneness of God. Finally, Sufis do not believe that God's full revelation was completed with the *Koran*, and they are open to the possibility that new truths can be found anywhere, even in other religious traditions. Their use of hymns, for example, can be traced back to Christian traditions while their praying the rosary was adopted from Buddhist practices.

Nevertheless, Sufism is tolerated in Islam because of its basic tenets—the centrality of God and the importance of surrendering the self to God's will. It is also credited for producing respected religious scholars and some of the most exquisite poetry from the Arab world. In addition, it enjoys tremendous popular appeal, largely because it offers the possibility of spiritual liberation and a personal connection to God within the overarching context of a deeply structured faith.

Source: Martin, Richard C. *Islam: A Cultural Perspective*. Englewood Cliffs, NJ: Prentice Hall, Inc., 1982.

Student Handout
Review of Episodes 1-40

Part I: Naguib is often seen as a great chronicler of contemporary life in Cairo. In the space below each episode make a note of what you learn about narrator or the community he lives in. For example, in response to Episode 1, you might note that *the narrator is fascinated by the High Sheikh*, or *the narrator may have imagined this mystical encounter.* Or, you might observe that *the community believes that there is great mystery surrounding the figure of the High Sheikh.*

Episode 1. (narrator, father, and the High Sheikh)

Episode 2. (narrator, Zaki, Um Zaki, mother)

Episode 3. (narrator, father and mother, Um Barhum, Am Hassan)

Episode 4. (narrator, the flour merchant, his three daughters)

Episode 5. (narrator, mother, the wife of the local police prefect)

Episode 6. (narrator and Darwisha)

Episode 7. (narrator, mother, Hag Bisheer's wife, and three daughters)

Episode 8. (narrator, parents, Hemam and the narrator's sister)

Episode 9. (narrator, mother, and Tawheeda)

Episode 10. (narrator, Um Abdu, Dawlet, Ahsan, and Sheikh Labeeb)

Episode 11. (narrator and father)

Episode 12. (narrator, Saad Zaghloul, Um Abdu)

Episode 13. (narrator and Sabry)

Episode 14. (narrator and Sultan Fo'ad)

Episode 15. (narrator and father)

Episode 16. (Salooma and Am Tulba)

Episode 17. (narrator and So'ad)

Episode 18. (narrator, father and Saad)

Episode 19. (narrator and father)

Episode 20. (narrator and Yehya Mudkoor)

Episode 21. (narrator and Ibrahim Tawfeek)

Episode 22. (narrator and Hasham Zayid)

Episode 23. (narrator and Saad Zaghloul)

Episodes 24. (narrator and Senaya)

Episode 25. (narrator and Fathaya)

Episode 26. (Sitt Nagayah)

Episode 27. (narrator, mother and Nazzlah)

Episode 28. (Moshen, Sowsen and Tawheeda)

Episode 29. (narrator, Ali Al-Benan, and Onsaya)

Episode 30. (Patrick Al-Hamawy)

Episode 31. (Sayeeda Kareem, Sheikh Kareem and Idress Al-Qadi)

Episode 32. (Senan Shalaby, Um Saad, Muallim Halambuhah, Hareedy Hamilowi, and Um Elish)

Episode 33. (Zenab, Zedan, Farag Idduri and Ali, the water pot peddler)

Episode 34. (Henaya, Alwana, Hamam and Hamid

Episode 35. (Radwan Effendi, Auntie Waleeda and narrator)

Episode 36. (narrator and two drunks)

Episode 37. (Am Yansoon Issuramati, Ramadan and Daleela)

Episode 38. (Naain Issaqaf, Sheikhum Iddehl and Fathaya Qaysoon)

Episode 39. (Sabri Gawani)

Episode 40. (deranged man)

Part II: All of Mahfouz's many literary works are concerned with three general themes: politics, religion, and love. Select three episodes from the first half of the novel that illustrate each of these areas. Provide the numbers of the episodes in each category and choose a quotation from one of the selected episodes that best captures the essence of Mahfouz's perspective.

Politics
Episode #___

Episode #___

Episode #___

Quote with page #:

Religion
Episode #___

Episode #___

Episode #___

Quote with page #:

Love
Episode #___

Episode #___

Episode #___

Quote with page #:

Student Handout
Fountain and Tomb: **A Semi-Autobiographical, Episodic Novel**

Mahfouz's *Fountain and Tomb* (1988) is a collection of seventy-eight separate tales about characters and incidents in the old quarters of Cairo. As such, it presents a slice of life of early twentieth-century Egypt. The tales develop a multitude of themes, including the search for spirituality, the emergence of sexuality, the complexities of love, the loss of love and of loved ones, the politics of revolution, the pointlessness of violence, the curse of mental illness, and the challenges of family life. Though *Fountain and Tomb* is one of Mahfouz's later works, it is much in keeping with his realistic writing of the 1940s and 1950s. It highlights the social parameters of Egyptian society and its underlying class issues, much like a Dickens' novel about Victorian London.

The episodic nature of *Fountain and Tomb* is indicative of Mahfouz's later literary career. In the late 1960s, after publishing some twenty-five novels and numerous story collections in which he adopted western literary conventions, Mahfouz began to experiment with popular narrative genres from Arabic literature. Many traditional Arabic prose forms are episodic in structure, including eighth-century animal fables, classical works, picaresque adventures, and popular stories like the tales of the *Arabian Nights*. In utilizing the episodic narrative, Mahfouz rebels against the western literary expectations of plot and structure that he had so successfully mastered in previous novels. In this work, he applies the episodic formula to a child's reflections on his colorful Cairene surroundings.

Many of the stories told in *Fountain and Tomb* come directly from Mahfouz's own childhood. He lived in the Gamaliyya district of old Cairo until he was twelve, much like the narrator who resides on the unnamed alley in the same area. And like this character, he too was the youngest child in a nurturing and supportive lower-middle class family. Mahfouz's neighborhood also had a Sufi monastery that housed Persian mystics who appeared mysterious and enigmatic to the young Mahfouz. They made a deep impression on his developing consciousness and later appeared in many of his writings. Additionally, when Mahfouz was only seven, his quarter was engulfed in a popular uprising against the British. The violence he witnessed shook the security of his childhood and gave him an understanding of both imperialism and nationalism. He began to follow politics closely and became a loyal supporter of the *Wafd* Party because of its liberal, democratic principles and revolutionary agenda.

Mahfouz acknowledges the role that his own life has played in his work. In an interview with Naji H'ir, he explains his purpose in drawing upon autobiography. He says, "My own personality appears, in bits and pieces, in everything I've written. But is always serves as a means to my end: to give expression to a generation, not an individual. I use myself to show the problems of the life of an entire Egyptian generation" (p. 243).

Still, it cannot be assumed that *Fountain and Tomb* is a personal memoir and that the narrator is the voice of Mahfouz. There are many constructed aspects of this novel that give the work a sense of unity. For example, it is doubtful that a young Mahfouz had a mystical encounter with the High Sheikh; rather, this episode appears to have been inserted along with the closing story to provide a frame that emphasizes the narrator's search for spiritual assurance within an uncertain world.

Sources:
El-Enany, Rasheed. *Naguib Mahfouz: The Pursuit of Meaning*. New York: Routledge, 1993.

H'ir. Naji. "An Interview with Naguib Mahfouz." *Tel Aviv Review* 2 (Fall-Winter 1989-1990): 240-243.

Teacher Resource
Unifying Elements in *Fountain and Tomb*

The seventy-eight episodes of *Fountain and Tomb* may at first glance appear to be unrelated and randomly selected. But Mahfouz draws the episodes together through three important unifying elements: theme, symbolism, and point of view. Clusters of tales focus on particular themes such as emerging sexuality, the challenges of love, and the domination of gangsters in the neighborhood. (These themes are discussed more fully in the analyses found at the end of the chapter.)

Mahfouz also creates unifying motifs by assigning symbolic value to the physical structures of the boy's surroundings. For example, the alley the boy lives in represents Egyptian society as a whole. In contemporary Cairo, the old quarters consist almost exclusively of lower-class residents, but this was not the case in the days of Mahfouz's childhood. At that time, the alley housed all classes of people, from the very rich to the very poor. All the residents did share in common the hardships imposed upon them by British occupation, but there was still great diversity in background, occupation, and status. In capturing a cross-section of Egyptian society, Mahfouz fashions a comprehensive model of community and indeed of humanity at large.

It is also of symbolic significance that the alley has two openings. The wider opening looks out toward a large square that represents the city of Cairo and the world at large. This is also the place where residents from his street encounter people from the other neighborhoods. The other opening is to the cemetery with its tombs of the ancestors. This end of the path clearly indicates death and anticipates the fate that all individuals will ultimately face. In between these two locations are the archway, the Sufi monastery, or *takiya*, and the fountain.

The archway lies between the big square and the smaller, more restful square of the narrator's street. In many of the episodes, this archway is shrouded in darkness and

mystery. It represents the entrance into life, but in this alley it is a life that is inherently filled with danger and insecurity.

The significant structure within the square itself is the *takiya*, with its beautiful and tempting garden. The *takiya* resonates on a number of symbolic levels. Firstly, it represents a withdrawal from the world, for the sheikhs intentionally shut their doors on the neighborhood to protect their worship. In addition, the coveted mulberries of the Sufi garden harkens back to other forbidden fruit, especially the apple of Adam and Eve and the pears that so tantalized Saint Augustine when he too was growing up in North Africa. The mulberries in this novel suggest the knowledge of God that the narrator is not meant to access. This meaning is further supported in the boy's encounter with the High Sheikh, an incident that symbolizes the human longing for proof of God's existence. Finally, the luminance of the High Sheikh gives the monastery a sense of lightness and purity, qualities that make it oppositional to the symbolism of the archway.

The fountain does not feature prominently in the tales, but its significance is suggested by the novel's title. Located somewhere between the monastery and the square, the fountain's sustaining water represents the daily lives of the alley's inhabitants. It stands in opposition to the cemetery. The novel's title draws attention to the contrast between these symbols by eliminating the expected articles before *fountain* and *tomb*. The novel's characters move between these two poles, suggestive of the journey they take from birth to death. Along the way, they struggle to carry out daily tasks as they cope with the difficulties life brings.

Mahfouz also pulls the strands of this work together by using a first person narrator who acts as both observer and participant. The fact that this narrator is a child adds a particular flavor to the writing. Firstly, his age allows him a unique opportunity to observe certain aspects of the society. He is invited to massage a naked woman; he spies on a ritual of exorcism from his rooftop vantage point; he overhears women's conversations about birth and adultery; and he witnesses fights and romantic entanglements unobserved.

In many ways, however, the child's perspective is also more limited than an adult's. His understanding is frequently incomplete, and the reader often grasps the implications of the stories more fully than the boy does himself. For example, he delights in failing the primary school exam, thinking that he will be free of the weariness of having to attend school. Later, he attends a political demonstration but cannot answer his father when asked about the purpose of the protest. Similarly, his cousin easily persuades him to distribute pamphlets to the neighborhood without telling him that they are political in nature and therefore subversive. Most tellingly, however, the narrator imagines that an important political figure visiting the alley is actually the Night Rider, a fantastical figure that children believe in. These limitations provide humor and remind the reader that the narrator's young consciousness is only half-formed and that he will need to fill in his lack of understanding as he matures.

Student Handout
Review of Episodes 41-78

Part I: Note what you learn in each episode about the narrator or the community he lives in.

Episode 41. (Ibrahim the Ape and Zalooma)

Episode 42. (Bergowi and Kefrowi)

Episode 43. (Hawash Adad)

Episode 44. (Sitt Sikeena, Sheikh Aml Al-Mahdi, and Muallim Mohamed Al-Zumr)

Episode 45. (Ashur Iddenf and Sitt Fadeela)

Episode 46. (Saad Al-Gebaly and narrator)

Episode 47. (Shalaby Ilaly)

Episode 48. (Saqr Mowazeeni)

Episode 49. (narrator, father and The Night Visitor)

Episode 50. (Gaalus Dananeeri)

Episode 51. (Abdu and Gaalus Dananeeri)

Episode 52. (Zeyan, Sanawi, the *futuwa*, Um Ali, and the midwife)

Episode 53. (Hamooda Halwani, the *imam*, and Qerqoosh the slave)

Episode 54. (Abbas Gehesh, Anabeya Metwali, and Boss Atoof)

Episode 55. (the geography teacher)

Episode 56. (Abdun and Al-Duqma)

Episode 57. (Zaghreb Balaqeeti and Hagar the Hairless)

Episode 58. (people from all the districts)

Episode 59. (Ghanam Abu-Rabyah)

Episode 60. (Khaleem Rumana, the mother of Khaleem Rumana, Bayumi, and Zenab the glass-bead peddler)

Episode 61. (Ibn Ayesha and Sitt Mashallah)

Episode 62. (Hag Ali Khalafawy, the Maharan family, Hag Ali's son, and senior Maharan)

Episode 63. (Shuldoom, Qormah and Qormah's widow)

Episode 64. (Salama and Barhooma)

Episode 65. (Sheikh Labeeb)

Episode 66. (a child behind window bars)

Episode 67. (Am Sukey and Adbu)

Episode 68. (Abdun Lelah)

Episode 69. (Abu Al-Makaram and the *imam*)

Episode 70. (Abdullah, Slave of Allah)

Episode 71. (Yusef Murr and Abd Al-Aker, Contractor)

Episode 72. (Okla Issuramaty)

Episode 73. (Mustafa Al-Dashoory)

Episode 74. (One-Eye and Nono)

Episode 75. (Omar Morgani)

Episode 76. (Abdu Sukry)

Episode 77. (Anwar Gilel and the narrator)

Episode 78. (narrator, father, and Sheikh Omar Fikri)

Part II: Choose three episodes within this half of the novel that illustrate Mahfouz's ideas on politics, religion, and love. Provide the numbers of the episodes in each category and choose a quotation from one of the selected episodes that best captures the essence of Mahfouz's perspective.

Politics
Episode #___

Episode #___

Episode #___

Quote with page #:

Religion
Episode #___

Episode #___

Episode #___

Quote with page #:

Love
Episode #___

Episode #___

Episode #___

Quote with page #:

Student Handout
The Author and His Work

Naguib Mahfouz was born in 1911 to a lower-middle class Muslim family living in Cairo's ancient quarter of al-Gamaliyya. His parents were devout Muslims who nurtured his intellectual interests, particularly in ancient history. Mahfouz's four sisters and two brothers were much older than he, so he turned to schoolmates and people in the neighborhood for companionship. His father was a civil servant whose devotion to the heroes of independence fired the imagination of his young son. When Mahfouz was twelve, the family moved to the modern suburb of al-Abbasiyya, but he never forgot the place of his childhood. The vibrancy of the old Cairene quarters made a lasting impression on him, as did the bloody confrontations between British and the Egyptian people that swept through the streets during the 1919 uprising. Mahfouz named al-Gamaliyya specifically as the setting for many works, including *Midaq Alley* (1947) and *The Cairo Trilogy* (1956-57), and he incorporated typical characters and physical assets from the alley in other works such as *Fountain and Tomb* (1988).

Mahfouz was sent to a mosque school at an early age, initiating his interest in Sufism. Later, he studied in state schools and did well enough to be given entry to university. He did a degree in philosophy at Cairo University and graduated in 1934 near the top of his class. He started a masters program but eventually dropped out and, like his father, began to work for the Egyptian government. This career, spanning from 1934-1971, afforded him a variety of titles: parliamentary secretary to the Minister of Religious Endowments, administrator in charge of an interest-free loan project, office manager to the Minister of National Guidance, head of the Cinema and Theater Censorship office, director of the film production organization, and advisor to the Minister of Culture. Even after he became an established writer, Mahfouz continued government work. Rather than distracting him from his writing,

it offered him the chance to interact with people from different classes and gave him an infinite variety of themes, characters, and plots.

Mahfouz was interested in writing at a young age. He first attempted poetry and detective stories and later wrote articles on philosophy. His first major publications were three historical novels set in ancient Egypt: *Abath al-Aqdar* (*Fate's Mockery*, 1939), *Radobis* (1943), and *Kifah Tibah* (*The Struggle for Thebes*, 1944). These works point out parallels between Egypt's past and its contemporary history, for example depicting the heroic efforts of the pharaohs and the Egyptian people to drive the Hyksos, foreign invaders, out of their country. Mahfouz was credited for giving the historical novel a new nationalistic emphasis, but he also criticized for an inadequate knowledge of ancient Egypt and an incomplete grasp of the genre.

Mahfouz abandoned his focus on the past and next wrote five novels set in the ancient quarters of modern Cairo. *Al-Qahira al-Jadida* (*The New Cairo*, 1945), *Khan al-Khalili* (1946), and *Zuqaq al-Midaq* (*Midaq Alley*, 1947), *Al-Sarab* (*The Mirage*, 1948), and *Bidaya wa Nihaya* (*The Beginning and the End*, 1949) are realist novels concerned with the social problems of ordinary people and tinged with an undercurrent of sadness and tragedy. He followed these novels with Al-Thulatiyya (*The Cairo Trilogy*), the works that earned him considerable recognition in the Arab world. *Bayn al-Qasrayn* (*Palace Walk*, 1956), *Qasr al-Shauq* (1957), and *al-Sukkariyya* (1957) follow multiple generations of a middle-class urban Egyptian family through the years between the world wars and show how material culture from the west brought confusion and discontentment into their lives. To this day, *The Cairo Trilogy* is considered one of the most well-respected pieces of Arabic fiction.

Mahfouz did not write for seven years after the overthrow of the monarchy in

1952; the trilogy had been written but not published before this date. He claimed to be waiting to see the results of the revolution, but critics propose that he was disillusioned by the lack of radical transformation under the military rule of Abdul Nasser. This supposition is affirmed by his next work—*Awlad Haritna* (*Children of Gebalawi*)—that was published as a serialized novel in a Cairo daily press in 1959. It depicts three religious personages who lead a succession of revolutions aimed at creating a more equitable social system but who are easily forgotten after their deaths. Though it is set in Egypt, *Children of Gebalawi* has been interpreted as a universal allegory of the inadequacy of world's religions in meeting the psychological and social needs of mankind. While Muslim leaders attacked it as atheistic, Mahfouz argued it illustrates the transcendence of true religion. It was never published as a novel in Egypt.

From 1960-67, Mahfouz wrote a number of novels—*al-Liss wa al-Kilab* (*The Thief and the Dogs*, 1962), *al-Summan wa al-Kharif* (*Autumn Quail*, 1962), *al-Tariq* (*The Search*, 1964), *al-Shahhadh* (*The Beggar*, 1965), *Tharthara fawqa al-Nil* (*Small-talk on the Nile*, 1966) and *Miramar* (1967)—about the increasing dismay of intellectuals in the poverty-ridden socialist state. These novels focus on individuals rather than groups or places and highlight feelings of alienation and disillusionment. Mahfouz also began to experiment with symbolism, stream of consciousness, and highly poetic and suggestive language at this time, though he never completely abandoned realism.

After the Arab defeat in the six-day war with Israel in 1967, Mahfouz went through another silence and then entered into a period of remarkable variety in theme and style. *Al Maraya* (*Mirrors*, 1972) is a quasi novel made up of a series of vignettes, *al-Karnak* (1974) focuses on people's apathy during the police state of the 1960s, *al-Hubb tahta al-Matar* (*Love in the Rain*, 1973) argues the need for self-sacrifice and anticipates the 1973 "Yom Kipper" war, *Hadratu al-Muhtaram* (*Respected Sir*, 1975)

satirizes governmental bureaucracy, *Malhamat al-Harafish* (*The Everyman Epic*, 1977) allegorizes the struggle between good and evil, *'Asr al-Hubb* (*Era of Love*, 1980) hints at public disenchantment with Sadat, *Al-Baqi min al-Zaman Sa'a* (*Only an Hour Remains*, 1982) demonstrates the failure of leaders to solve the needs of the people, *Rihlat Ibn Fatuma* (*The Voyage of Ibn Fatuma*, 1983) imagines a journey into foreign lands with a variety of societal systems, *Amama al 'Arsh* (*Before the Throne*, 1983) assesses leaders through the ages, *Qushtamar* (1988) presents the life stories of a group of men, and *Fountain and Tomb* (1988) records a child's impressions of neighborhood life in old Cairo.

In addition to being seen as the pioneer of the Arab novel, Mahfouz is recognized for his short stories and film scripts. He has produced over one hundred short stories and has written or co-written eleven adaptations of his own fiction. For all of his literary accomplishments, Mahfouz was awarded the Nobel Prize for Literature in 1988. Many considered this recognition long overdue since Mahfouz's work has such universal relevance and appeal, despite being situated within the framework of the Muslim belief system. Mahfouz did not go to the award ceremony but sent his two daughters in his stead, along with the message that in honoring him, the Academy was honoring all Arab writers. Unfortunately, the attention Mahfouz received for the Nobel Prize also prompted the blind Shaykh Umar Abd al-Rahman to issue a *fatwa* or death threat against him for writing literature that was considered offensive to Islam. This threat was nearly carried out in 1994 when members of a fundamentalist group stabbed Mahfouz in the neck on a street of Cairo. But the viewpoint that encouraged this attack is not shared by the overwhelming majority of Egyptians. Mahfouz is read by the barely literate and the highly educated, and he is greatly respected for his breadth of knowledge, his demand for tolerance, his sensitivity to the plight of the poor, and his remarkable courage.

Student Handout
A Selected Bibliography of Naguib Mahfouz's Works
Translated into English

Al-Karnak. 1974. Trans. Saad El-Gabalawy. *Three Contemporary Egyptian Novels*. Frederickton, NB: York Press, 1979. 67-132.

Al-Liss wa al-Kilab. 1962. *The Thief and the Dogs*. Trans. Trevor Le Gassick and M.M. Badawi, 1984. New York: Quality Paperback Book Club, 1989.

Al Maraya. 1972. *Mirrors*. Trans. Roger Allen. Minneapolis: Bibliotheca Islamica, 1977.

Al-Sukkariyya. 1957. *Sugar Street* (third novel of the *Cairo Trilogy*). Trans. William Maynard Hutchins and Angele Botros Samaan. New York: Doubleday, 1992.

Al-Summan wa al-Kharif. 1962. *Autumn Quail*. Trans. Roger Allen, 1986. New York: Doubleday, 1990.

Awlad Haritna. 1959. *Children of Gebelawi*. Trans. Philip Stewart. London: Heinemann, and Washington, D.C.: Three Continents Press, 1981.

Bayn al-Qasrayn. 1956. *Palace Walk* (first novel of the *Cairo Trilogy*). Trans. William M. Hutchins and Olive E. Kenny. New York: Doubleday, 1990.

Bidaya wa Nihaya. 1949. *The Beginning and the End*. Trans. Rames Hanna Awad. Cairo: American University in Cairo Press, 1985.

Fountain and Tomb. Trans. Soad Sobhy, Essam Fattouh and James Kenneson. Washington, D.C.: Three Continents Press, 1988.

Hadratu al-Muhtaram. 1975. *Respected Sir*. Trans. Rasheed El-Enany, 1986. New York: Doubleday, 1990.

Miramar. 1967. Trans. Fatma Moussa-Mahmoud. 1978. Washington, D.C.: Three Continents Press, 1990.

Qasr al-Shauq. 1957. *Palace of Desire* (second novel of the *Cairo Trilogy*). Trans. William Maynard Hutchins, Lorne M. Kenny, Olive E. Kenny. New York: Doubleday, 1991.

Rihlat Ibn Fatuma. 1983. *The Journey of Ibn Fattouma*. New York: Doubleday, 1992.

Zuqaq al-Midaq. 1947. *Midaq Alley*. Trans. Trevor LeGassick. 1966. Washington, D.C.: Three Continents Press, 1990.

Student Handout
Writing Project for *Fountain and Tomb*

Part I: Creative Writing

In *Fountain and Tomb*, Mahfouz demonstrates that many individuals and events contribute to the narrator's development. Some of the events he describes happen to the narrator personally and indicate his own development. Many others are about various people in the neighborhood, but the narrator is also affected by their stories.

For this assignment, you will be asked to write three episodes about people and events that contributed to your development in childhood. These can be about things that happened to you personally or about people whose stories had an effect on you at the time. To decide upon your episodes, you should consider the many factors that shaped your early years: parents, interactions with siblings, relatives, friends; national occurrences; sporting events; neighborhood squabbles; religious observances; holiday celebrations; town happenings; etc. Try to create episodes that reflect different influences so that your writing can imitate some of the variation that is found in *Fountain and Tomb*. Mahfouz created episodes that ranged in length from one paragraph to a couple of pages. Try to vary your length as well, or at least avoid writing three very short episodes. Brainstorm possible stories for your episodes below:

Episode #1:

Episodes #2:

Episode #3:

Part II: Analytical Writing

Write a short essay in which you compare the impact that the episodes you wrote about in Part I had upon your own development to the impact that the narrator's stories had upon his maturation process. What did he learn about politics, religion, and love from his environment? What did you learn from the events and individuals you describe in your episodes?

Reading Resource
Summary and Analysis
Fountain and Tomb

Episodes 1-40
<u>Summary</u>:

1. The young narrator enjoys playing in the square between the archway and the *tayika*, or monastery, where the Sufis live. These Sufis, also known as dervishes, are Islamic mystics who seek God through prayer, chanting and dancing. The children of the alley are drawn to the mulberry trees in the monastery garden because they are so green and have dark berries, but the monastery surrounds the garden, like a fortress. The gate and windows to the garden are shut, isolating it from the community. Whenever the children spot one the Sufi priests in the garden, they yell, "If God wills, you dervish, you might get your wish" (p. 11). The priests never respond but just vanish behind the inner gate. The narrator is curious about the Sufis, but his father instructs him not to disturb their peace. Even so, he is still tempted by the mulberries.

One day, the narrator sees an impressive old priest who seems to be the overseer of the monastery. He says, "Everything about him is munificent beyond imagining. I look at him so intently that I become intoxicated, the sight of him filling the whole universe" (p. 12). The boy tells the Sufi that he loves mulberries, and the priest chants, "My nightingale, *khoon deli khord wakuli hasel kared*" (p. 12) which in translation means from Persian means "a nightingale wore himself out and harvested a rose." He also appears to toss the boy a berry, but when the narrator bends down to get it, it is not there. When he looks up, the garden is empty. He tells his father about the incident, and his father wonders if his son has seen the High Sheikh, though this is unlikely since this priest never leaves his retreat. The father tells him not to repeat this story to anyone. The narrator goes back to the square, hoping to see the dervish again but is disappointed. Later, he wonders if this encounter really took place or if he just imagined it. Even if it was just a fantasy, the narrator says, "this supposed vision of the sheikh burrowed deep down into my very marrow, a memory of great purity" (p. 12).

2. The narrator is looking down at his neighbors from his rooftop. He decides to go to the house of Um Zaki, a fun-loving widow, to see if she has any sweets to give him, but when he looks through the skylight, he sees her sunbathing on her sofa, completely naked. He shouts at her, and she tells him to come down so that he can rub her back. He is happy to do so and massages her enthusiastically. She suggests that he not tell his mother and he agrees. She commends him on understanding so much at such a young age. Whenever Um Zaki visits the narrator's house, he stays close by to hear her bawdy stories, despite the mother's efforts to send him away. Um Zaki's son is a carpenter. He is proud of his mother, though she makes off-color jokes, since she never does anything to shame him. Also, she is well liked by every household, even in a neighborhood that is marked by strife. Um Zaki suffers from deteriorating health. People suggest that the *jinn* or invisible demons cause her illness, and she decides she must have an exorcism. On the day of the ritual, a number of Sudanese women descend on the house. The narrator watches through the skylight as they dance around Um Zaki, as if dancing with the demons that possess her. Um Zaki writhes wildly until she falls unconscious. Days pass, but her health continues to decline. Her laughter disappears, and she despairs over her fate. Her son must send her to a government hospital. The narrator cries as she is taken away.

3. One morning, the narrator's parents are especially kind to their young son. Um Barhum, the Syrian neighbor, keeps him company while his parents are away. Then, Am Hassan, the barber, and his apprentice arrive and use special instruments to circumcise him. The boy is in pain for some time. His mother feeds him sweets for days as an apology for allowing the operation. Many friends come to greet him. He walks with his legs apart and holds his *gallabiya*, or robe, away from his body.

4. The narrator is on his way to the arch when he notices the flour merchant with his three daughters getting into a cart. He is transfixed to the spot by the daughters' beauty. When one of them asks why he is blocking their way, he says the words supposedly spoken to him by the High Sheikh. The girls laugh, calling him a crazy dervish. His head whirls with his new awareness of beauty and of desire. He says, "Their ravishing portraits hang deep in my deepest gallery. Seed of love planted too early to grow" (pp. 16-17).

5. The narrator is happy because he is going with his mother to visit the wife of the local police prefect. She is an enormous woman who gives him a huge hug every time she sees him. He says, "I sink into deep softness and feel her great paunch, a lush mattress which floods my being with warmth" (p. 17). The narrator listens as the two women discuss the possibility of "demons living in the vaulted archway"(p. 17), all the while anticipating their departure when he will again experience the warmth of the woman's hug.

6. At the mosque school, the narrator steals glances at Darwisha. Later, during his family's trip to the cemetery, he bumps into her by accident and asks where she plays. He goes to her lane that afternoon and finds her standing on her doorstep. They sit down together, side by side, and kiss. He is overwhelmed with feeling and says: "I know drunkenness before touching liquor. We forget time and fear. We forget our families and the alley. Even the phantoms cannot part us" (p. 18).

7. On hot summer nights, the narrator and his family go up to the rooftop and stay up late. Sometimes, the wife of the Syrian neighbor, Hag Bisheer, and their three daughters accompany them. The girls sing songs, and the boy is so enchanted by them that he joins the singing. The neighbor's wife compliments him on his voice and says he should become a singer, but the mother hopes he will become a government official like his father and brothers instead. One day, the narrator hears that the Syrian neighbors are moving back home. He is heart-broken. He watches them leave and cries for a long time, having tasted "the bitterness of separation, gloom, and an empty world" (p. 21).

8. The narrator enjoys festivals at the cemetery. When they visit the family vault "with its austere dignity, towering tombstones, and hidden secrets" (p. 21), he breaks into "leaps of joy and bursts of exploration" (p. 21). His delight in cemeteries changes when Hemam, the narrator's cousin, comes to stay with them. He is fourteen and an affable companion, but one day he falls ill. The whole family grows deeply concerned and anticipates the boy's death. The narrator grieves saying, "I see that it's a parting without end so I cry with the mourners, and my heart suffers more than its age can bear" (p. 21). He no longer enjoys the cemetery and now wonders about what lies beneath. The grief fades with time, but the experience leaves a mark. He laments, "There is nothing but sorrow and lost love and fear and cruel memory and the heavy weight of the mysterious unknown" (p. 22).

9. A neighbor tells the narrator's mother the gossip about Tawheeda, the daughter of Um Ali and Am Ragab. She has gone to work for a government ministry. Both women are shocked that a girl from such a nice family would take a job where she has to mix with men. She is the first woman from that part of town to take such a job, and the people in the alley blame her father for not having greater control over his daughter. The narrator watches her as she comes home from work with her face unveiled and an exhausted look in her eyes. The narrator mimics the community in wondering, "What are men coming to?" (p. 22).

10. The narrator describes Um Abdu, the best-known woman in the alley. She is very tough and has a hot temper but remains on friendly relations with everyone. She usually wins arguments because of her "whiplash tongue" (p. 23) and her "knowledge of everyone's secrets" (23). She also has two daughters, Dawlet and Ahsan. Dawlet is married to an educated young man who was willing to overlook the social gap between them. The beautiful Ahsan has the fiery disposition of her mother and rejects many suitors because she is hoping for a match as impressive as her sister's. The narrator is on friendly terms with Ahsan, though he is much younger. She lets him help her with the laundry and sends him as a messenger to Sheikh Labeeb. He is a wealthy business owner with a wife and children. Ahsan marries him but then leaves him, bringing disgrace upon her mother. Many years later, the narrator meets up with Ahsan at a nightclub. He asks how she got there, and she responds, "The same way you did!" (p. 24).

11. The narrator has finished mosque school and has taken the primary school entrance exam. When the results are announced, his name is not included among those that secured a place. He is delighted to be freed from the wrath of his teachers, thinking, "life will be soft and carefree from now on" (p. 25). But his father informs him that he will not stay home and be idle in the alley; rather, he will return to the mosque school for another year "so the whip can treat your idiocy" (p. 25). He objects, but the father announces, "Prepare for a long life of learning. You shall learn step by step until you become a civilized human being" (p. 25).

12. Thousands of people are protesting against the British government and in support of Saad Zaghoul who has been sent in exile to Malta. Their screams "rattle the walls of our alley and deafen our ears" (p. 25), and even the women take part. The narrator thinks the turmoil is "exciting and entertaining, truly magnificent" (p. 25), except for the chase that he witnesses where British horsemen crash down the alley and beat people in their way. Um Abdu comes to tell them about the heroes and martyrs of the fight. She also claims that the British horses became unsettled in front of the monastery and knocked their riders to the ground.

13. The narrator's cousin Sabry is sent to live with them in Cairo for a while because he has been suspected of being involved in political activities at his hometown in the countryside. After staying there for some time, he asks the narrator to distribute papers for him to shopkeepers and passers-by. The narrator later discovers that he was distributing political pamphlets.

14. There is another demonstration, this time against Sultan Fo'ad, for it is believed that the Sultan has betrayed the nation. The narrator's father worries about Saad Zaghloul being "sick and in exile" (p. 28), but the boy refuses to believe that Saad could die as Hemam did.

15. The narrator's friends come to hear his father talk about the revolution. Everyone is discussing it; even the children are using the language of demonstrations in their games. There is an increased presence of British patrols. The father is moved to tears by someone's recounting the legend of Saad, and seeing this, the narrator also experiences "a flood of tears streaming down my cheeks" (p. 28).

16. Salooma is the first martyr of the neighborhood. He assisted his father, Am Tulba, in selling cotton candy from a cart. When a demonstration passed through, Salooma joined in. Later, the British opened fire on the demonstrators, shooting Salooma in the head. People come to console Am Tulba, and he is overwhelmed by the attention that his son's death has generated. Salooma is given the finest funeral in the neighborhood, and he has become a symbol for the

revolution. His father is given a prominent position, and "alley commentators speak of the wonder of life which changes values in an instant among instants of wonder" (p. 29).

17. One morning, the narrator's aunt and her daughter So'ad come to visit and shop for So'ad's apartment. Smitten with her beauty, he quickly falls in love with the girl and offers to take her on a tour of the alley. She ignores the offer and scolds him for looking at her with desire. Her mother has agreed to supply So'ad's fiancé with a photograph of his bride. The narrator's parents think this request represents improper behavior. The narrator dreads So'ad's imminent departure. He grieves, and his mother teases him without realizing the depth of his suffering.

18. There is great celebration on the day that Saad Zaghloul returns from exile. The narrator's father returns from the celebration with his clothes disheveled and his voice hoarse from shouting. All believe that freedom is coming soon and that the British will leave "never to return!" (p. 31). That night, there is a big festival. Everyone attends, including Sheikh Labeeb and Am Tulba, the father of the martyr. The narrator is awake for a long time at his window, and a mysterious power charges him with "magic vitality" (p. 32).

19. The father questions the narrator and discovers that he has been attending the demonstrations. He grills his son on its purpose and discovers the boy doesn't fully understand. All the same, the narrator says these demonstrations are the "most enjoyable thing in the world" (p. 33), and his father responds, "As long as the British don't participate" (p. 33).

20. The narrator borrows a book from his friend, Yehya Mudkoor, and is soon addicted to books. Yehya, on the other hand, eventually gives up on reading in pursuit of his soccer career.

21. The school boys frequently play pebble soccer led by Ibrahim Tawfeek, a half-crazy boy who is always "clowning and taking dares" (p. 33). One day, one of the boys dares him to eat a hot horn pepper, and he boasts that he can eat ten. The boys take bets and Ibrahim makes his way through all the peppers. He returns to class in great discomfort and eventually the teacher sends him to the dispensary, "but he never gives up clowning and taking dares" (p. 34).

22. The narrator shares a bench with Hasham Zayid at school. His mother owns several houses and businesses, and therefore he is much admired. He fails out of school, but after his mother dies, he becomes a very influential man. The narrator avoids him because he has put on airs and imposes his will on people. He is always looking for a fight, and everyone in the neighborhood shuns him. Though surrounded by many who seek his money, he doesn't have even one friend, and he has never married. He recalls his mother with great sorrow at some moments, but at other times, he criticizes her with bitter sarcasm. One day when he is attacking her memory, he bursts into tears. Knowing that others will think him weak, he laughs it off, but later vents his anger on anyone who saw him cry. Then, suddenly, he disappears from the alley, and it is suspected that he has either emigrated or been murdered.

23. The narrator wakes one morning to the sound of wailing. His mother, father, and the servants are all crying. Saad Zaghloul has died. He says, "I cry from my soul, 'Saad!' I go back to my room. Gloom hangs everywhere" (p. 36).

24. The narrator is watching a cat nurse its kittens. Suddenly, he hears Senaya, the postman's eldest daughter, behind him. She is delighted to see the scene and presses close to the narrator. He turns around and crushes her to his chest. They begin a relationship that is full of joy and regret. They are passionate, but there are still barriers between them that they do not cross. They experience the sweetness of love but also the pain of their unfulfilled desires. Two years later, Senaya marries and when he meets her many years later, she is a respectable woman and mother. She is now looks fat and sleepy, but the narrator remembers when "she was a butterfly of many hues, a fresh apple, a sweet flower, a flowing stream. Those were happy days" (p. 37)

25. Later, the narrator loves Fathaya, Senaya's younger sister. They share glances, but Fathaya doesn't believe the narrator loves her as she loves him. He tries to give her up, but something always draws him back. However, his life path cannot accommodate an early marriage, and many other suitors woo her. Her father insists that she accept one man, rather than wait. She meets the narrator again when she is sixty and a widow. He is drawn to her again but decides not to pursue her. He "meekly submits to the sorrow of farewell" (p. 38).

26. Sitt Nagayah is a wealthy but lonely woman in the neighborhood. She is considered ugly, but she has a light spirit, and she is able to mock herself and others. She takes care of multiple cats and dogs, and she believes she can talk to her pets in their languages. She also speaks to an invisible demon that she considers to be her brother. People stay away from her because she is odd, but she knows her dogs, cats, and brother will mourn for her when she dies.

27. A guest comes to tell the narrator's mother about Nazzlah, the wife of Hassan, who chased her husband until he married her and then left him when he became ill. After he dies, Nazzlah then seduces his brother, Khalil. They marry and have a son, and then Khalil dies. Nazzlah has a reputation as a whorish woman, so the narrator is surprised that his mother treats her kindly when she moves into a nearby apartment near them. His mother explains, "I've heard a lot, but what I see is a weak woman with a son, no husband, and no money.... Allah alone knows what's inside the heart" (p. 41). The narrator watches Nazzlah from his window and develops an attraction to her. Then, a neighbor throws lye in Nazzlah's face because she suspects her of seducing her husband. Nazzlah loses her beauty and takes a job in the local bathhouse. The narrator is saddened by this turn of events.

28. Mashen visits the narrator's father often. He complains endlessly that money owed to him is tied up in an endowment to a religious institution. Because he has no money, he has to work in a lumberyard and marry Sowsen, a women lacking in beauty and status. Over the years they have no children, and Sowsen prays that the inheritance Mashen is due never comes for fear that he will throw her out for a new wife. Mashen feels great self-pity throughout his life and regrets having no heir. Suddenly, when Mashen is almost seventy, four thousand pounds is released to him. He changes his life completely, marrying a girl under twenty, buying a fancy house, and overindulging in food. He prays that the heir apparent is on its way, but within six months he becomes ill. He has no regrets and buys an expensive tomb for his burial.

29. Ali Al-Benan, the narrator's friend, owns the coffee-bean shop. He inherited the business when his father died, though he was only an adolescent. He asks the narrator about Onsaya, a girl with a dubious reputation. He is aware of the rumors about her. The narrator cannot understand Ali Al-Benan's interest in her, until he confesses that he loves her and plans to marry her. He is determined to do so despite people's objections.

30. Patrick Al Hamawy's father arranges for his son to be married at fourteen for he wants to enjoy his last child's life before he dies. Patrick torments his fellow students by telling tales of the sexual pleasures of married life. He is successful in school and is sent to England for two years. When he returns, he can't fit in and he is appalled by the superstitions and ignorance of his wife. He divorces her, despite the shock it causes in the alley, and he brings home a white foreigner as a second wife. The neighborhood rejects her, finding her behavior too immodest and her understanding of Islam too shallow. This causes problems in the marriage, for the wife begins attacking her husband's traditions and making great demands of him. He refuses to divorce her, but she eventually leaves him and returns to her own country. The neighborhood pushes him to take back his first wife, but Patrick is convinced that what he wants most is to be alone.

31. Sayeeda Kareem is the daughter of a sheikh, and she falls in love with Idress Al-Qadi, whose father is a vendor of sweets. The two are discouraged in their love, but after Idress finishes high school, he convinces his father to make a formal request for Sayeeda's hand. The sheikh refuses, thinking this peddler's son to be far beneath him. A marriage proposal comes from an acceptable suitor, but Sayeeda staunchly rejects it, despite the anger of the neighbors. Her father dies sometime afterwards, and the community blames her for the grief she put him through. When Idrees finishes college, he again asks for her hand, but Sayeeda's uncle refuses. Years pass, and neither of the lovers marries. Idress becomes a government official who goes off to other Arab countries. When he returns to Cairo in his mid-fifties, he is still a bachelor and he again asks for her hand, even though Sayeeda is no longer young and beautiful. The wedding crowns "two lives melted away by fidelity, perseverance, and pain" (p. 47).

32. Senan Shalbaby works in the flourmill. One day, he catches a glimpse of a beautiful woman in the window of a house nearby. He decides he must have this woman, but she never comes out of the house. He approaches Um Saad, the woman who seems to be in charge of the home. He beseeches Um Saad to let him court the woman in the window and is told that she is a professional lover and extremely expensive. Senan still desires her and pays Um Saad a ten-piaster coin, which is a third of his monthly salary. This only gains him an audience with Halambuhah, her pimp, and he charges Senan a full Egyptian pound. Senan sells a ring inherited from his father for this charge, but he is then told he must pay two more pounds to Hareedy Hamilowi, the woman's fiancé. He is completely distraught because he could never procure this amount of money. In desperation, he murders Um Elish, an egg peddler, and steals her money. He gives Hareedy Hamilowi the two pounds and enters his beloved's room. He falls to her feet and in a fit of passion and honesty tells her he has committed murder for her. She doesn't understand, and the act of love is never consummated. Rather, footsteps on the stairs announce the arrival of the police and signal the future that awaits him.

33. The narrator recounts a time that the community refers to as the Age of Zenab. Zenab is an incredibly beautiful girl. Her parents keep her in seclusion and many men "fawn over her and drool like dogs" (p. 50). Her mother anticipates a great match and causes a rift in the family by rejecting her nephew's proposal. Then, two men who propose at the same time get involved in a fistfight and give each other permanent injuries. When Farag Idduri, the schoolteacher, asks for her hand, he is granted it, but Ali the water pot peddler warns him to stay away from her and then attacks him and pokes his eye out. All decent men give up the idea of proposing, and soon it is only the gangsters and tough guys who are vying for her attention. The parents feel themselves cursed by their daughter's beauty, and her father worries about Zenab's safety. One morning, it is discovered that the family has secretly left town. The narrator feels great frustration. He sadly asks, "Is it impossible for beauty to thrive in our alley?" (p. 50).

34. Henaya, the well-educated daughter of Alwana, is considered a heroine for her persistence in love. She was determined to be with Hamam, an ugly man with a bad reputation and a foul temper who worked as an apprentice to a *gallabiya* maker. She refuses a marriage offer from Hamid, a salesman with considerable wealth. Her mother vows to rid her child of her illogical obsession, but Henaya remains adamant, even after Hamam is sentenced to two years in jail for mugging someone. She grows very despondent during these years but is renewed with life on his release. He can't find a steady job but is able to go into a business when she sells one her gold bracelets. Alwana unsuccessfully attempts to stop the wedding. However, it proves to be a happy and prosperous marriage. Henaya helps her husband, and eventually they open a shop. "And as for the old memories, no one finds it necessary to bring them up anymore" (p. 53).

35. Radwan Effendi and his wife have two children. He loves their daughter, and his wife loves their son. The boy bullies his sister and the father imposes harsh punishment upon him. Soon after finishing high school, he becomes consumptive and dies. The mother collapses, and the father is ashamed of his treatment of the son. One year later, the daughter comes down with the same illness and dies. The father moves to the graveyard to be near the tombs of his children, and one year later he dies too. The wife becomes friendly with the narrator who calls her Auntie Waleeda. His mother says, "Our Lord be with her and all wounded souls" (54).

36. One night, a drunk falls in the street. Some kind people put him on a huge breadboard and carry him home. One their way, they meet another drunk, and the first drunk mocks him for his shameful state. The narrator says, "Later, under very serious circumstances, this scene comes back to me heavy with implications that never occurred to me at the time" (p. 54).

37. Am Yansoon Issurmamati is a decent man of advanced years. His son Ramadan dies suddenly, leaving behind a fiancé named Daleela. Everyone is surprised when the old man marries this girl, forty years his junior, within a month of his son's death. Rumors fly and it is eventually decided that Ramadan must have impregnated Daleela. The father must be marrying her to get her out of a jam. There are many opinions about this "most unusual marriage in alley history" (p. 55): some bless it, others think Am Yansoon a fool, and others enjoy whispering, "There goes the father of his own grandson" (p. 55).

38. The narrator is outside playing when he hears the announcement of Naain Issaqaf and Sheikhun Iddehl's marriage. When Fathaya Qaysoon hears the news, she throws on her headdress and tears out in search of the groom screaming, "I'll rip his face into such a horror even his own mother won't know him!" (p. 56). Everyone is anxious about the outcome and expects the worst.

39. Sabri Gawani is a mystery. He comes from a poor background and works in a notions shop. Then he gets chosen to go around to similar shops in different areas and begins to improve his lifestyle. He dresses better, eats extravagantly, and he spends his free time smoking a *hookah* and drinking ginger tea. He then marries a girl of good social standing, and walks around with a look of "contentment, confidence, and security" (p. 56). One night he gets drunk at a friend's wedding. He never returns home, and no one knows what happened to him.

40. A deranged man sits behind a barred window in the neighborhood. Everyone avoids looking at him so as not to get him excited. Before he was locked up, he would jump out in front of women and tear off their veils, looking for the beautiful girl he fell in love with in a dream. His relatives sought healing, but no cure was found. People try to convince his father to commit him to a hospital for the insane, but he refuses; instead, the son remains behind bars, occasionally saying, "O darling, where are you?" (p. 57).

<u>Analysis:</u>
The symbols associated with the *takiya*, the archway, the cemetery, and the fountain create unifying patterns within the numerous tales. Other patterns are achieved through the clustering of certain episodes along particular themes. The episodes found in the first half fall into motifs that emphasize a young boy's initiation into the world. The opening episode of course highlights the narrator's awakening sense of spiritual longing. (Religion and faith are inherent elements in many of the following tales, but the boy's engagement with this topic is not mentioned explicitly again until the final episode of the novel.) Nine of the tales (Episodes 2, 4-7,

10, 17, 24, & 25) capture the narrator's awakening to physical attraction, desire, and romantic love. He starts off seeking the physical closeness and comfort of his mother's friends and then moves through several attractions to girls of various ages. He learns to kiss and to fondle a girl, but his desires are not purely sexual, as is suggested by the last of these episodes (Episode 25) where he seems to truly fall in love with a girl, though he is not yet ready to commit to marriage. At moments, the boy's propensity for romance appears humorous and slightly obsessive, but Mahfouz seems to elaborate on this theme to show the power of sexual and romantic awakenings and the process by which a child gradually comes to understand these feelings.

The novel's first half also presents many episodes (Episode 9–27-34, 37, & 38) that show the complications, pleasures, and stresses of adult love. The narrator describes men and women who love foolishly, like the man who loves a promiscuous woman (Episode 29), the man who commits murder in order to marry a prostitute (Episode 32), and the woman who wants to rip the face off her lover when he becomes engaged to another (Episode 38). He records the stories of successful marriages as well, such as those achieved by the couple who are finally allowed to marry some thirty years after their original request (Episode 31) and the woman who marries and reforms an ugly criminal (Episode 34). Observing the actions of adults in love proves to be part of the child's formation. He learns to understand the nature of love in part by witnessing how people love--in some cases for better and others for worse.

Another prominent cluster of episodes (Episodes 12-16, 18, 19, & 23) records the main events of the revolution starting with its eruption in 1919 and ending with the death of its leader, Saad Zaghloul, in 1927. While the narrator does not fully understand the circumstances, he feels the emotional ramifications of the demonstrations. For example, in describing the celebration of Saad's return from exile, he says, "a mysterious power charges my small heart with magic vitality" (p. 32). His intense excitement and deep admiration for the leader of the rebellion suggest that emotional knowledge precedes intellectual understanding in the mind of a child.

A final theme in the first half of the novel (Episodes 7, 8, 17, 24, 25, 27, 33, & 35) focuses on the experience of loss. After discovering the ability to make intimate attachments, the narrator quickly learns that intimacy includes loss. He laments the departure of the Syrian neighbors who would sing with him on the roof (Episode 7), the friendly So'ad who leaves the alley to wed (Episode 17), the beautiful Zedan who flees from gangsters that are vying for her attention (Episode 33), and, most tragically, the death of his sister's son Hemam (Episode 8). By the end of the first half of the novel, the narrator has learned the difficult lesson that joy and delight in life are necessarily countered by sadness, emptiness, and gloom.

Episodes 41-78
Summary:
41. The blind man Ibrahim the Ape is the largest man the narrator has ever seen. "A minaret, he picks his way around by poking with a dreadful great staff, his feet shuffling along like immense turtles beneath him" (p. 57). All the other beggars move to another vicinity when Ibrahim is in the area. He sits just outside the vaulted archway, and passers-by are generous with meals, money, and pleasantries. He is well liked because he "never throws his weight around" (p. 57). One day, another blind beggar named Zalooma takes up a spot near him and calls out for succor. Ibrahim attacks him and a crowd gathers to break them up. They chastise Ibrahim for his heartlessness and someone throws a broken basket at him. The Ape revolts and begins clobbering everyone in his path. "Soon the Ape is a blind destructive force that engulfs the whole alley" (p. 59). Everyone flees from him. The police arrive, but Ibrahim flings them off in all directions. The police threaten to shoot him, but they fire hose him instead. The Ape falls to the ground, defeated, and is carried off in handcuffs. He stays away for a while, but then one day "he takes up his old life, parking his enormous frame at the archway like a myth" (p. 60).

42. Bergowi works in a restaurant, and Kefrowi stops in for a drink of water. Bergowi jokingly tells him to take it from the donkey trough, and this starts a fight. They begin with insults and escalate to blows that leave Kefrowi dead. The clans of the two men rush to the scene and start a battle of their own. Many are killed, and the others go to prison. Both families mourn for a long time. The narrator is saddened by these events, but a number of people in the alley speak of the bloody fight "with a pride utterly disdainful of jails and gallows" (p. 60).

43. Hawash Adad is a big spender, and he has an extravagant holiday party that lasts late into the night. In the morning, terrified screams come from the house because everything has been destroyed. The guests claim that all was in place when they went to bed. Some people think the party ended in a "drunken free-for-all" (p. 61) that has been hushed up; some think that Hawash's enemies drugged the party goers and wrecked the house for vengeance; some feel God was giving Hawash what he deserved, and finally others believe "a *jinn* did it because of a vow Hawash made and never fulfilled" (p. 61). The mystery is never solved.

44. The narrator recounts an old story. Sheikh Aml Al-Mahdi is the *imam*, or prayer leader, of a newly built mosque. One night he sees a woman open a window and a man's hand stifle her cry. The man then jerks her inside and batters her to death. The sheikh knows the victim, Sitt Sikeena, and the man, Mohamed Al-Zumr, a respected businessman who donated the money for the construction of the mosque and the *imam's* salary. The sheikh feels Allah is testing him. At the inquest, he is asked what he heard. He lies and says he was too sick to go out that night. The sheikh feels he has damned himself with this falsehood. Later, the police arrest the assistant in the laundry who entered the victim's house because some of her jewelry was found in his house. The sheikh is completely unnerved by this development. He confronts Muallim Mohamed Al-Zumr one night at the fountain and then locks himself in the mosque for two days. On the third day, he is in the minaret's high window, completely naked and seemingly crazy.

45. Ashur Iddenf is a poor man of forty with a family of ten children who works in the saddlery. He envies everyone else and complains that Allah has neglected his children. One night, Am Ashur is summoned inside the house of Sitt Fadeela, a widow who is about to inherit a huge fortune. She wishes to marry him, as long as he agrees to a clause that allows her to divorce him. He eagerly accepts the plan, as do his first wife and children, for they will receive a generous monthly allowance. Am Ashur is very happy; however, in time, he begrudges the control Sitt Fadeela has over him, and he feels trapped. "Silk chains to replace his old iron ones draw tighter on his throat and boredom floods him" (p. 66). Eventually, anger boils up, and he slaps her. She kicks him out. On his own again, he has difficulties supporting himself and gets into trouble. Sitt Fadeela offers to take him back, but he refuses. "And Ashur is thus justly hailed as a rarity of an extraordinary new type in our alley" (p. 67).

46. Saad Al-Gebaly works at a local moneylender's but he has big dreams. He sells a piece of land, quits his job, and does quite well with a perfumery business. However, he lacks real business sense, making a bad investment and spending his money entertaining. He declares bankruptcy and lives such a poor life that his health is damaged. But he has a strong faith, and he doesn't despair over his children's fate. "Fear is blasphemy," he explains, "God protects us from fear" (p. 68). At the end of his illness he admits that he brought on his fate himself.

47. Shalaby Ilaly is a kind man, but he has an excessive admiration for his father. The father was not a particularly impressive man, but he takes on mythic stature in his son's mind. Shalaby therefore is shocked when he discovers that his father left no inheritance. In addition, Shalaby finds that people reject him on the grounds that he is his father's son. He digs around and realizes that his father was jailed for theft when a young man. This "rams a brutal contradiction through the center" (p. 69) of Salady's life. After that, he lives an exemplary life, but he stops caring what others think of him since they will automatically judge him on his father's merits. He continues to speak of his father's marvelous deeds, though deep down he acknowledges the truth.

48. Saqr Mowazeeni is envied by the other children because his father is a minor government official. Saqr gets a similar job after graduating from school. His father soon dies, leaving the son buried with the responsibilities of a big family. Saqr desires a beautiful life but also feels a commitment to duty and honor. Because his father held such an important position, the women in the household are not accustomed to earning money, and Saqr must support four of them on a small salary. They cannot find husbands because only poor men ask for their hands, and they refuse. As a result, Saqr is unable to wed, though his deepest desire is for a simple house, a wife, and children. As the years go by, he resents his family. The neighborhood views Saqr with a mixture of sympathy and disgust wondering, "Maybe he stands for spineless surrender to the decrees of fate, or utter flaccidity" (p. 71).

49. As a child, the narrator is told about The Night Visitor that comes to children in their dreams and grants them their wishes. As he grows up, he makes fervent requests of this supernatural being. One day a procession led by a glorious man goes through the alley. The leader stops at each shop and visits the mosque and the government school. His tour is celebrated, and the narrator is in awe. He is convinced that this man is The Night Visitor, and so he shouts, "Long Live the Night Visitor!" (p. 72). Everyone is silent and the *iman* yells at him for his insolence. He is shoved homeward and is further humiliated by his father who says, "What a simpleton! How could you forget The Night Visitor comes only in dreams?" (p. 72).

50. For a time, the alley is controlled by the thugs and bullies who operate a protection racket. Gaalus Dananeeri is one of the worst gangsters, and he causes the residents much suffering. He is a giant with great strength and agility. His cruelty is legendary, and he growls and shouts abuse at people. He refuses a man a grace period on a loan and the man hides in his house until he is able to get the money. Once, when the school principal punishes the son of a thug, he makes the principal strip naked and walk home nude. He forces men to divorce their wives so that he can marry them. And once he punished the whole town by demanding that they forgo any celebration of the Lesser Feast day. "His reign is a time of terror, cowardice, shame, and hypocrisy, a season of nightmare, hushed moan and misery, an age of devils and scabrous stories, the heyday of hopelessness and blocked roads" (p. 74). But, Gaalus does provide them protection from other quarters, for people know that "messing with us is asking for catastrophe" (p. 74). However, for all Gaalus's towering strength, he is stabbed to death by a child. The killer is the son of one of his victims from another alley. When the news spreads, people are both horrified and relieved. They decide to mourn as though they are seeking vengeance, even though they are delighted. This creates deeper conflicts with the neighboring areas, and Gaalus' death becomes just as much trouble as his life.

51. One day, the narrator is playing with Abdu, the neighbor's son, who convulses and falls to the ground. He is brought into the house and his condition gets worse. He ends up an imbecile. On a day when Gaalus Dananeeri is parading through the alley, Abdu says to him, "You aren't worth a good God damn, Gaalus. Up yours!" (p. 51). Everyone thinks Abdu is done for, but Gaalus, takes him by the arm and walks along with him. All are surprised since Gaalus has never shown kindness or compassion. This teaches the narrator that the alley has two classes of people that are considered sacred—"gangsters and idiots" (p. 51). He begins to wish for the glory of a gangster or the blessings of an idiot.

52. Zeyan the copper-polisher's helper has a burning love for Um Ali, the midwife, even though she is twenty years older than he. He knows that he can never win her favor without wealth, and so he thinks of joining Sanawi's gang. Sanawi is willing to let him join if he proves himself by obeying the command of the *futuwa*, or gangster chief who instructs him to: "Kill Um Ali the midwife" (p. 52). He tries to back out but is told that the *futuwa* will be very unhappy and will destroy his life. When Zeyan tells his mother his troubles, she urges him to run away. And so he leaves before dawn, "with fifty piasters and a vagabond's bundle, abandoning family, friends, and job to face hardship and the unknown" (p. 77).

53. Hamooda Halwani is another extortionist in the neighborhood. Unlike the other *futuwas*, he lives long enough to retire. In retirement, he repents and spends his time at the mosque. He tells the *imam* about a number of murders of immoral people that he committed which could actually be considered good deeds. He then admits that he also committed murders for no good reason, but he is certain that Allah has forgiven him. The *imam* asks about the Qerqoosh, the slave, and Hamooda confesses that he killed this man because Qerqoosh had made plans with a friend for the next day and had infuriated Hamooda with his "puffed-up self-assurance and faith in the future" (p. 79).

54. Abbas Geheshis is a young punk who cannot keep a job. He falls in love with Anabeya Metwali, the policeman's daughter, but he knows he cannot gain her favor on his own merit. So, he asks his friends to surround Anabeya when she is out shopping. He fights them off, allowing her to go on her way. She thanks him and is awed by his prowess. Rumors of this event spread and people begin to hail Abbas as the protector of the alley. This gives him the idea to become a gangster who will offer protection for a fee. He extorts large sums of money this way, so that when he goes to ask for Anabeya's hand, he is immediately granted his wish. The wedding takes place, but it is followed by a procession though all the neighboring quarters. Unwritten law says that he must face the challenges of his enemies, and so he and his followers get very drunk and walk freely through one neighborhood after the next. But they come to the street ruled by Boss Atoof. As Atoof approaches him, Abbas grows frightened and rushes past his foe and down the street. The people on the square break out in uncontrollable laughter. Abbas is never heard from again, and his marriage is eventually annulled.

55. When the fighting between districts grows particularly fierce because *futuwas* are warring with one another, the important men from the alley decide to build a secret gate in the east wall so that residents can have a safer means of entering the town. "Thus, we make a secret opening to the world outside, avoiding the cemetery path and the great square that bound our alley" (p. 81). The geography teacher warns that this pass is potentially more dangerous than the *futuwas* because it would allow for a torrent of rainwater in the whole quarter should there be a storm. The teacher is mocked and called "Professor Falseprophet" (p. 82). For years, the pass serves them well, but during a bad winter, it rains for three days and a flash flood destroys homes and businesses and unearths corpses from the cemetery. The disaster is unforgettable, and memory is "wet with tears" (p. 82).

56. Abdun the Sweet is a menial worker who wants to join the gang of Al-Duqma, the current *futuwa*. One man informs him that the *futuwa* prizes purity and cleanliness. So Abdun buys a new *gallabiya* and goes off for a bath. Another tells him he needs to become knowledgeable in legends since the *futuwa* is a great lover of stories and fables. Abdun decides to take his time with this study, so in the meanwhile he marries and has children. Others warn him that Al-Duqma expects his thugs to be very strong but not stronger than he is himself. Abdun grows confused about how he can satisfy the *futuwa's* expectations. His life falls to pieces in confusion; he loses his job and gets a divorce. He finally goes to the *futuwa* who refuses his service. Abdun is shocked that Al-Duqma knows that he threw his life away to prepare to be a gangster and yet he willingly brushes him aside. The Boss replies, "I brush you aside because of that" (p. 84). "The story of Abdun the Sweet becomes proverbial in our alley" (p. 85).

57. Zaghreb Balaqeeti is one of the most powerful bosses of the alley. He is extremely skilled in fighting, and he beats the *futuwas* of other neighborhoods. Everyone loves him and appreciates the security he provides. He is unprecedented because he expects his followers to work hard, and he sells dope instead of extorting protection money. Even though he is kind, "the Boss is the Boss" (p. 85). The people find that Zaghreb meddles too much in their lives and they feel imprisoned by his rule. More educated residents are moving into the alley, and they think that the protection business is an anachronism that should be abolished. "For the first time, a good *futuwa* is cursed as much as a bad one" (p. 86). When Zaghreb hears of this, he is furious threatens everyone for their lack of gratitude. Some of the people try to get Hagar the Hairless, a giant man who is "a bit touched in the head" (p. 86), to attack Zaghreb by saying to him, "To you were strength and power given to break our chains" (p. 86). He misunderstands and begins attacking innocent people. The alley panics, and the people stone him until he drops dead. Now there is open resistance to Zaghreb's rule, and eventually "the Boss is eliminated and the gates open on a new age" (p. 89). Hagar the Hairless somehow becomes a symbol for this new life.

58. Spring comes to the neighborhood riddled by gang wars and disagreements with other quarters. "Rancor boils, hearts seethe with hate, murder lurks everywhere, and all our tomorrows stink of disaster" (p. 89). Then, at noon on a sunny day, dark clouds gather and form huge masses. People run into the street, looking for security amongst others, and the world goes dark. People reach out to one another, "and no one either knows or cares whose hands he holds" (90).

59. Ghanam Abu-Rabyah grows up in a humble family, but he does well enough in school to secure a job at the Ministry of the Interior. He gradually works his way up to the position of budget chief for secret security. One day he disappears, and people think he has either run away or been murdered. But then, he reappears just as suddenly, saying that he was arrested for slugging an official at the ministry. People consider him a hero because of their automatic distrust of the government. But another story soon surfaces about Ghanam's disappearance after he goes into early retirement. It suggests that Ghanam has embezzled a large amount of money and that he was never prosecuted for this crime because he knew too much about the secret monies being distributed to ministry officials. The administrators tried to get him to return the money for a full pardon, but he refused, arguing that since so many thousands are given to immoral officials, he should get his share, too. They arrested him to scare him, but he would not budge. Finally, they released him, on the understanding that he would remain silent about the finances and retire from the ministry. Because of his wealth, Ghanam Abu-Rabyah becomes "one of the most notable men in the whole neighborhood" (p. 92).

60. Khaleem Rumana works at the copper shop, but one morning he does not go to work and is found wandering aimlessly in front of the *takiya*. His mother goes to him and discovers that he has completely lost his memory. Cures are recommended and attempted, but eventually everyone accepts that he is just "an empty shell without memory or human contact, a living corpse" (p. 92). But one day, he recovers and tells his mother he is late for work. Then, he asks about Bayumi, his best friend and, as a few people know, his lover. He is told that while he was away, Bayumi was arrested, tried, and hung for the murder of Zenab, the glass-bead peddler. Now, Khaleem goes through another personality change, this time becoming silent and uncooperative. When his mother suggests that other people have suffered worse disasters, he walks out of the house and goes to the police station to confess to Zenab's murder.

61. Ibn Ayesha is a thief who sneaks into Sitt Mashallah's house one night when she is at a wedding. He hides under her bed when he hears her return with a lover. During the lovemaking, Ibn Ayesha has a hallucination brought on by the opium he took before coming to the house. He imagines that he looks down on the bed from above, seeing a naked woman in the form of a tree and a monkey man playing in the branches. Then a storm disturbs the scene and there is a confusion of screams and brutal blows. When the police arrive, they pull Ibn Ayesha out from under the bed and put him under suspicion for the murder of the adulterous couple. Soon, the real killer is found, and Ibn Ayesha tells the story over and over. Later in life, he seems to be mentally destabilized by the incident. "It is said the Sufi madness fell upon him while he was under the bed of Sitt Mashallah" (p. 95).

62. Hag Ali Khalafawy is one of the richest men in the alley, but he is also known for his generosity. He bestows considerable charity upon the Maharan family, though no one knows why. On his deathbed, he tells his son about his guilt concerning the Maharans. He was partners with Maharan senior when a young man. They were traveling together when Maharan died, and Hag Ali stole his money and invested it to make a fortune. He explains, "The very same money made us what we are today—just as the loss of it made the Maharans what they are" (p. 96). He demands that his son return the family fortune to the Maharans, but the son wonders why the father didn't concern himself with restitution of this kind while he was alive and healthy. The father dies before he can see his desire carried out, though some suggest the son helped him on his way. "Well, that's how the story goes—embellished with accurate details only an eyewitness could possibly know. But that's how stories are told in our alley" (p. 96).

63. Shuldoom and Qormah begin to hate each other in childhood when one tears the other's *gallabiya* and starts a fight during a festival celebration. This animosity grows over the years, at neighborhood games or in school. When Shuldoom's father is buried, Qormah sings a wedding tune nearby. When Shuldoom is engaged, Qormah tries to steal his bride away. Even as they grow older, "the secret knot that bound them would not unravel" (p. 97). Qormah is successful in business, and Shuldoom accuses him of embezzlement. Then he steals funds from his own boss and is sent to prison. When he is released, he cannot find proper employment, so he joins the racket with the fervent hope of getting vengeance on his enemy. Qormah knows he will be Shuldoom's first extortion target, so he plans to either make peace with him or buy him off. But Shuldoom's demands are too great, so Qormah plans to have him killed. Shuldoom beats him to it, but then a killer hired by Qormah's widow murders Shuldoom the same night. The narrator's father comments, "Hate is of the devil, but men are a source of wonder" (p. 98).

64. Salama is a humble cop known for his honesty, a rare trait in a time of *futuwas* when the law is easily disregarded. Salama's incorruptibility impresses everyone, but then he decides to marry a widow with a grown son named Barhooma who has a bad reputation. He catches Barhooma stealing from a shop and makes him return the goods. In not arresting the young man, Salama worries that "he'd squandered the very thing that set him apart for everyone else and made him what he was" (p. 98). When Barhooma acts up again, Salama tries to discipline him, but the stepson threatens to tell the police about Salama's cover-up. Salama feels he is losing something of himself that is irreplaceable, and he notices that people are regarding him with less respect. He therefore decides to confess to the police. Barhooma is arrested, and Salama resigns from his job, though he is hired as a watchman immediately because he is so trustworthy. "His action was considered a good example by some and a species of idiocy by others" (p. 99).

65. The venerable Sheikh Labeeb is an institution in the alley. Every day, he sits in front of the arch and offers prayers and prophecies. The women listen to his every word and interpret the utterance as they see fit. His prophecies are famous and the broken-hearted cling to his pronouncements. Sheikh Labeeb lives so long that things begin to change and people no longer venerate his sanctity. "He threatens people with hellfire in the world to come, curses the age, and sighs with regret for the good old days full of good folk now long gone" (p. 101). Eventually, he gives in and takes up his role as a beggar, crying, "All things earthly pass away" (p. 101).

66. A child's face appears behind the bars of a basement window. He wants to come out but is locked in by parents who have left him alone. Passers-by continue on their way, seeing what they want to see.

67. Am Sukry is the man in the mosque that wafts smoke over people with a censer for a small fee. He has a large family that lives together in one room. He decides to send his youngest child, Abdu, to the mosque school. Abdu does well, and the sheikh advises that he be sent to primary school. Am Sukry debates whether or not he can afford the schooling, but decides to go ahead with it. After grade school, he is delighted to have a son who can qualify for a government job, but Abdu wants to go to high school. The boy then wins a scholarship to engineering school in England. Am Sukry gains great fame for his son's intelligence. Adbu secures a very high post in the ministry and eventually brings electricity to the alley.

68. Abdun Lelah's story is quite remarkable. He is a baker's boy who takes the dough from everyone's houses and brings it back to them as fresh-baked bread. He falls in love with the street sweeper's daughter and has a happy marriage. He never complains about his work and is a prayerful man. He has no amusements in life, but always has a genuine smile of patience for his boss, his customers, and his friends. "It's as if he never heard an insult doubled and redoubled there, never saw a fight, never dealt with sinners and troublemakers" (p. 103). One day, he comes out of his house nicely dressed and hugs everyone, saying, "The time is at hand" (p. 103). He climbs to the top of the archway and jumps off. No one can understand why. The narrator says, "Far easier to know why I live on than why Abdun jumped" (p. 103).

69. Abu Al-Makaram is called the Father of Generosity because he is the moneylender in the neighborhood, even though the Prophet clearly forbids usury. He stays inside most of the time and scurries quickly through the alley when he needs to go out. When he reaches seventy, he calls in his loans and retires. He is tormented by a dream so he goes to the *imam* to discuss it. In the dream, someone dressed in a bright light tells him to burn his money. The *imam* tells him to give his money to the poor. Instead, he is seen "standing naked before a bonfire of money" (p. 104). Later, he dies outside beneath the arch, penniless. He is given a pauper's grave. Then a rich man has a dream visit from Saint Khudr who reports that Abu Al-Makaram is one of God's favorites and that a shrine should be erected over his place of rest. The shrine is built and people come to remember Abu Al-Makaram as blessed by God. The narrator does not understand why he should win favor with God since he did not give his money to the poor. The father responds that if he had done that, he would have only been generous and not God's favorite.

70. One autumn day, a naked man comes staggering out of the arch and collapses. He cannot answer any questions, but he appears to have been mugged. His mind is gone and he lives in the neighborhood, relying upon the charity of others. They name him Abdullah, Slave of Allah, and he is treated with reverence. One man explains Abdullah's sanctity by saying, "Whoever enjoys the kingdom of life ignorant of his origin and purpose, ignorant of the meaning of life, is worthy of the reverence due to sanctity!" (p. 106).

71. A strange man enters the coffeehouse and asks the *imam* to give him information about Yusef Murr, a respectable man who is married with three sons. The stranger is not at liberty to say who has entrusted him to make these inquiries, but he admits that his name is Abd Al-

Akher, Contractor. Everyone assumes that Yusef has tried to arrange a second marriage and that the intended's family sent Abd Al-Akher, but he denies this vehemently. Curiosity about the stranger fades until he enters the square once again. Yusef learns of his presence and runs after him. He does not return for some time, so his father goes looking for him and finds him dead on the ground. The coroner says it was a heart attack but everyone believes the stranger caused his death. People remember that the name he gave meant, "slave of the hereafter," and "a wave of supernatural mystery rolls through the air" (p. 108).

72. Okla Issuramaty's father owned a circus and, even as a child, he was known for his talent in the ring. Okla quits the circus after his father dies and joins the racket. For some reason, he is able to attract many women. He falls in and out of love and has numerous conquests, but them he settles down into a sudden marriage with a widow much older than he and not particularly attractive. He gives up the protection game, and he opens a candy store. He bores of this and then starts a restaurant that is also very successful. He desires more possessions and starts dealing in drugs and real estate. He buys a fancy house in the alley, but then sells it for a better house downtown; he relocates again to a country estate. Next, he begins traveling around Egypt, to other Arab countries, and eventually to Europe. He does not return to the quarter anymore, and his friends can no longer understand his desire for continual acquisition. Rumor abounds about him, but eventually the community considers him lost. Then, one morning, the naked corpse of an elderly Okla Issuramaty is found in the courtyard in front of the *takiya*. People are stunned. "His death was a legend, his death a slap in the face…" (p. 110).

73. Mastafa, the schoolteacher, is a friend of the narrator's father. Although he believes in God, he feels that God has decided "to leave us to our own devices" (p. 110). He argues that people would be better off if they didn't expect a God who intervenes. They might achieve a greater sense of wholeness if they considered themselves more in control of their own fate, and through that enlightened perspective, they might better understand the divine. Mastafa wants to spread these ideas, but the narrator's father warns him against taking the language of religion from people whose lives are run down by poverty, disease, and strife. Mastafa takes this advice; but even so he is driven from his job and from the alley for having such outlandish ideas.

74. One-Eye decides to have a few drinks in the *booza* to get ready for a rendezvous with a woman in front of the *tayika*, but he keeps drinking until he becomes drunk. He wanders out after midnight, not sure of where he is and bumps into Nono, the madman. He pleads with Nono to guide him to the *tayika*, and Nono marches him about for a long time. One-Eye becomes exhausted after some time and finally collapses into a deep sleep. He awakens the next morning and discovers that he is right in front of the *booza*, the place he started from the night before.

75. Omar Morgani enters the bar with an elegant walking stick. He salutes the patrons and cheerily remarks about the bliss of life. He continues to gush over the life's joys and pleasures, despite the fact that a surly drinker shouts at him. When Omar begins dancing and singing, the drinker raises a club and flings it at his head. At that, "his warbling mouth snaps shut, his features stiffen as the pearls of happiness scatter, and he falls to the ground…" (p. 113).

76. The government announces that it is going to tear down the *takiya* for an urban renewal project. The neighborhood is distraught at the idea of losing their spiritual security. Eventually, it is discovered that the person driving the project is Abdu Sukry, the engineer from the alley. Abdu insists that the *takiya* blocks the natural flow of the main street and needs to be cleared so that they can expand to the north. A compromise is reached after much debate. The *takiya* will not be touched until the cemetery removal project is completed. Everyone thinks that this will never happen, so they go along with the plan.

77. Anwar Gilel sits on the old fountain steps and laughs uproariously. The narrator offers the following explanation: "I've just realized that I'm a student among competing students in a school which throws together students from antagonistic little lanes, in an alley in the middle of warring alleys, that I'm a creature among millions of creatures both seen and unseen on a ball of mud awhirl a solar system over which I have no control, that this system is itself lost in endless space, that all life, myself included, is but a dewdrop on one leaf of a lofty tree, and that I have to accept all this and at the same time lead my life as if sorrow and joy were of any importance! That's why I can't stop laughing..." (p. 115). He comments that the ignorant must lead much happier lives than he.

78. The narrator gets to know Sheikh Omar Fikri through his father, who assists residents in the alley in matters of housing, marriage, divorce, funerals, etc. Sheikh Omar says he can offer service for any sphere of life, so the narrator asks him if he can get him an audience with the High Sheikh of the *takiya*. The father apologizes for his son's impertinence. The sheikh admits that he also once wanted to see the High Sheikh. He couldn't get to him by conventional means, so he tried to mix in the company of those great with age and famous in piety since a few of them said that they had seen him. But they could not agree on a description and Sheikh Omar Fikri concluded that they had never seen him. He even went to the Bureau of *Waqf* but could not get any further information about the High Sheikh. He finally decided to be logical and accept that he would never see this man. The narrator then asks why the dervishes slam the door of the *takiya* in their faces. Sheikh Fikri answers, "The *takiya* was originally built in the open because this order sings of seclusion, isolation from people and the world, but as time passed the city overtook and surrounded them with the living and the dead. As a last resort, they closed their doors to attain solitude" (p. 117). The narrator knows that he can't legally have access to the High Sheikh, and he has no intention of breaking the law, but he can't imagine the *takiya* without him. But, as time goes by, he stops looking at the *takiya*, except at funerals. "I try to remember the figure of the Sheikh—or whoever it was I once upon a time thought was the Sheikh—and then I just go on along the narrow path leading to the cemetery" (p. 118).

Analysis:

The narrator is a character in most of the tales represented in the first half of this episodic novel. In fact, thirty out of the first forty tales speak of his interactions with the different personalities he describes. This is not the case in the second half. Only twelve of the tales involve the narrator directly; the others describe actions of individuals in the community without showing their direct effect on the narrator. This seems to suggest two things: first, the narrator is observing things outside of himself, part of the natural process of maturation, and secondly, the narrator is becoming more a part of the community. In fact, he often records the alley's impressions of the events and people described rather than identifying his own perspective.

Another difference in the tales in the second half is that they are considerably darker than those in the first. Many of them (Episodes 41-44, 53, 58, 60, 61, 66, & 75) are tales of senseless murders and festering hatred. One man admits to murdering his victim for no reason other than the fact that he was confident he would be alive the next day (Episode 53); a deadly feud erupts between two clans because of a casual insult mentioned in a restaurant (Episode 42); and a cheerful man is attacked in a bar because another patron finds his mood too light (Episode 75). These stories point to an atmosphere of distrust, danger, and anger that characterizes the community. These episodes also prepare the reader for a series of tales (Episodes 50-54, 56, & 57) about the gangsters or *futuwas* who dominate the inhabitants of this Cairene back street. These strongmen extort protection money from the people and generally foster fear and instability. They can also be seen to stand for the autocratic rulers who have dominated Egypt's political life. But Mahfouz acknowledges the community's ambiguous feeling about the *futuwas*.

While disdaining the *futuwas'* power, the people simultaneously value the protection they provide against the aggression of neighboring alleys. The awe and admiration that come through in these episodes echo the community's appreciation for the service they provide at a time when protection from lawlessness was not guaranteed by the police or the state. In describing the futuwas in this manner, Mahfouz is indirectly criticizing the government. Mahfouz was given greater liberty to do so than many of his colleagues who spent time in prison for the accusations suggested in their writings. As such, he was one of the few "steam valves" for the intelligentsia and the reading public as a whole.

The family in *Fountain and Tomb* functions in a fashion similar to the *futuwas*. The Egyptian family is a prominent social institution as is demonstrated in many of the episodes by the close ties exhibited between parents and children. But family obligations can also negate the rights of the individual. One man is crushed to find that his only inheritance from his father is a legacy of poverty and shame (Episode 47); another man is denied a life of his own because he is burdened by the responsibilities to his dead father's sisters and daughters (Episode 48); and a third man must contend with a father who asks his son to pay for his sins by returning the family fortune to its rightful owner (Episode 62). In this capacity, the family, like the *futuwas*, is symbolic of the oppressive state.

This section also has many stories that involve mental illness, whether in the form of retardation, Sufi madness, suicidal depression, or complete memory loss. They illustrate the way the community contends with madness and serve as a reminder of the fragility of life, especially in a hostile and challenging environment.

Finally, the novel works its way towards a conclusion with a palpable sense of oncoming change. The influence of an intruding modern world asserts itself in the girl who goes to work in a company where she will mix with men (Episode 9), in the fiancé who demands a picture of his bride before the wedding rather than marrying sight unseen (Episode 17), in the geography teacher who proves to be scientifically correct when predicting that the construction of a new path would lead to the flooding of the alley (Episode 55), in the gangsters who disappear because there is no longer a need for them (Episode 57), in the sheikh who becomes a beggar because no one will buy his prayers and fortunes anymore (Episode 65), and in the engineer from the alley who brings electricity into the quarter (Episode 67). The most telling indication of cultural shifts is the proposal to tear down the *takiya* for the sake of urban expansion (Episode 76). These tales whisper of diminishing values and norms that kept the community together in the past. They also point to alterations in spiritual practices. Under the modern impact of materialism and rationalism, Sufism has lost a certain prominence in the hearts of the majority of alley dwellers, and in many countries such as Egypt, *takiyas* are now under governmental control.

The inevitability of change is reinforced by the metamorphosis of the narrator in the novel. He does not reveal his age at any point, but his conversation with Sheikh Omar about the High Sheikh at the end of the novel is much more sophisticated than his understanding of the *takiya* during the novel's first episode. Some of the novel's episodes (Episodes 10, 13, 22, 25, & 55) also move forward in time and give the narrator's reflections as a much older person. This shifting of perspective between younger and older narrator points to his growth and further emphasizes the themes of transformation and loss.

At the close of the novel, Mahfouz reintroduces the topic of religion and faith in a very explicit way, thus completing the overall unifying frame. In Episode 78, Sheikh Omar Fikri recounts his own search for the High Sheikh and his eventual conclusion that he would never set his eyes on this mysterious figure. In the long run, the narrator also accepts the inevitable. In the final paragraph he indicates that he only thinks of this childhood experience when he passes by the *takiya* on the way to a funeral. "I try to remember the figure of the Sheikh—or whoever it was I once upon a time thought was the Sheikh—and then I just go on along the narrow path leading to the cemetery" (p. 118).

This ending does not answer the question of whether the High Sheikh was real or a creation of the imagination and, by implication, whether or not God really exists. It further suggests that while humans pursue the divine throughout their lives and until they are in their graves, they must gradually come to terms with the elusiveness and inscrutability of God. They cannot isolate themselves from the world as the dervishes do but must interact with life as responsibly as they can. In Episode 73, the schoolteacher Mustafa Al-Dashoory argues that people might be better off if they did not claim God and assume God's interest in their lives. He comments that mankind "might achieve a certain wholeness in themselves and in society" (p. 111) if they took more personal responsibility for themselves and their communities. In saying this, Mustafa becomes a mouthpiece for Mahfouz and articulates the ultimate conclusion of this episodic novel. For the stories from the neighborhood illustrate, if nothing else, that people are a mixed bunch, that some act with the good of the community in mind while others are driven by selfish motivations, and that, as a result, a lot of unnecessary suffering occurs. In this work, Mahfouz laments these aspects of human nature at the same time that he finds humor and irony in the characters who inhabit these stories.

List of Works Consulted

Al-Ghitani. "From 'Naguib Mahfouz Remembers.'" *Naguib Mahfouz: From Regional Fame to Global Recognition*. Eds. Michael Beard and Adnan Haydar. Syracuse, NY: Syracuse University Press, 1993. 37-51.

Altoma, Salih J. "Naguib Mahfouz: A Profile." *International Fiction Review* 17.2 (Summer 1990): 128-132.

Ayandele, E.A. *The Making of Modern Africa: The Twentieth Century*. London: Longman Group Ltd., 1986.

Beard, Michael. "The Mahfouzian Sublime." *Naguib Mahfouz: From Regional Fame to Global Recognition*. Eds. Michael Beard and Adnan Haydar. Syracuse, NY: Syracuse University Press, 1993. 95-105.

El-Enany, Rasheed. "The Dichotomy of Islam and Modernity in the Fiction of Naguib Mahfouz." *The Postcolonial Crescent: Islam's Impact on Contemporary Literature*. Ed. John C. Hawley. New York: Peter Lang Publishing Inc., 1998. 71-83.

El-Enany, Rasheed. *Naguib Mahfouz: The Pursuit of Meaning*. New York: Routledge, 1993.

Fattouh, Essam, James Kenneson and Soad Sabhy. "Introduction." *Fountain and Tomb*. Washington, D.C.: Three Continents Press, 1988. 1-6.

H'ir, Naji. "An Interview with Naguib Mahfouz." *Tel Aviv Review* 2 (1989-1990 Fall-Winter): 240-243.

Le Gassick, Trevor. "Introduction." *Critical Perspectives on Naguib Mahfouz*. Ed. Trevor Le Gassick. Washington, D.C.: Three Continents Press, 1991. 1-8.

Le Va, Britta. *The Cairo of Naguib Mahfouz*. Cairo: American University in Cairo Press, 2000.

Martin, Richard C. *Islam: A Cultural Perspective*. Englewood Cliffs, NJ: Prentice Hall, Inc., 1982.

Moosa, Matti. "Naguib Mahfouz: Life in the Alley of Arab History." *The Georgia Review* 49.1 (1995 Spring): 216-230.

Sasson, Somekh. "The Essence of Naguib Mahfouz." *Tel Aviv Review* 2 (1989-1990 Fall-Winter): 241-250.

CHAPTER FIVE

––––

Woman at Point Zero
A Novel about Violence and Women
by Nawal El Saadawi

     Nawal El Saadawi is a psychiatrist who was drawn to conduct research in prisons because so many Egyptian intellectuals, including her husband and herself, had been incarcerated for political offenses. *Woman at Point Zero* focuses on the experience of a prostitute on death row in order to illustrate the oppression of women in Egypt. The protagonist, Firdaus, emerges as an "every-woman" who seeks to live a meaningful and independent life and symbolizes the violence against women in society. She is oppressed by both men and women and finally takes matters into her own hands, murdering her oppressor and defiantly facing death instead of living a life of misery and fear. *Woman at Point Zero* is a symbolic novel that uses prostitution as a vehicle to illustrate the oppression of women.

Lessons

Lesson One	Introduction Women and Islam Reading Assignment: *Woman at Point Zero*, pages 1-51
Lesson Two	The Author, Character, and Plot Development Women in Ancient Egypt Reading Assignment: *Woman at Point Zero*, pages 51-108
Lesson Three	Patterns in *Woman at Point Zero* Creating a Frame Story

Lesson One
Introduction
Islam and Women

Objectives:
1. Students will become familiar with the role of women in Islamic societies and explore issues such as female circumcision, the veil, forced marriage, polygamy, domestic abuse, lack of education, and poverty.
2. Students will identify Islamic nations in northern Africa by locating Egypt and her neighbors.
3. Students will discuss the significance of a frame story.
4. Students will begin to plan their own research for a frame story about the oldest or most interesting woman they know.

Materials:
1. Classroom World Map
2. Student Handout: "Women and Islam" by Nawal El Saadawi
3. Student Handout: "Some Problems of Contemporary Arab Women" by Nawal El Saadawi
4. Student Handout: Map of Africa, Chapter Two: Africa Overview of the Continent
5. Student Handout: Map of Islam in Africa, Chapter Two: Africa Overview of the Continent
6. Teacher Resource: Historical Highlights of Egypt
7. Reading Resource: Summary and Analysis: Author's Preface

Procedure:
1. Explain that *Woman at Point Zero* is a symbolic novel about oppression and a woman prostitute in Egypt.
2. Distribute Student Handout: "Women and Islam" by Nawal El Saadawi and discuss the ambiguity of the traditional Islamic teachings on the role of women.
3. Discuss the Prophet Muhammad's view of women and how the role of women changed in Islamic societies after the eighth century A.D. More information concerning the "veil" and the "harem" are available in the unit on *A Sister to Scheherazade* by Assia Djebar.
4. Distribute Student Handout: "Some Problems of Contemporary Arab Women" by Nawal El Saadawi and discuss issues such as female circumcision, the veil, forced marriage, polygamy, domestic abuse, lack of education, and poverty.
5. Ask students to locate Egypt on a classroom wall map.
6. Distribute Student Handout: Map of Africa and ask students to identify Egypt and her neighbors.
7. Distribute Student Handout: Map of Islam in Africa and ask students to identify Islamic nations in Africa.
8. Inform students of important events and periods in the history of the Egyptian people. Refer to Teacher Resource: Historical Highlights of Egypt.
9. Read the Author's Preface aloud and ask the students to consider El Saadawi's reason for including this piece in the English translation. Refer to Summary and Analysis: Author's Preface.
10. Ask students to read the first chapter of *Woman at Point Zero* aloud or silently.
11. Discuss the author's use of a frame story. Refer to Summary and Analysis: Chapter 1.
12. Explain that each student will be writing their own frame story about a woman whom they will interview. This woman should be the oldest or most interesting woman they know. Ask students to think about three possible women they might interview for their frame story.

Assessment:
1. What is a frame story?
2. How might the students begin their own frame stories of women they interview?

Reading and Writing Assignment:
1. *Woman at Point Zero*, Chapter 2, pages 11-51.
2. Students will be asked to identify the name of the woman whom they will interview and indicate the time and place of the interview on the third lesson of this unit.

Thought Questions:
1. Why does Nawal El Saadawi tell Firdaus' story in *Woman at Point Zero*? (Author's Preface)
2. Why do you think Firdaus agrees to tell the psychiatrist her story? (Chapter 1)
3. Describe the relationships between Firdaus and her father, mother, and uncle. (Chapter 2)
4. Describe the relationship between Firdaus and Miss Iqbal. (Chapter 2)
5. Why does Firdaus detest her husband? (Chapter 2)

Lesson Two
The Author, Character and Plot Development
Women in Ancient Egypt

Objectives:
1. Students will discuss Firdaus' childhood relationships and the concept of female circumcision.
2. Students will determine whether or not Firdaus is right to be unhappy in her marriage.
3. Students will consider the relationship between Nawal El Saadawi's life and work.
4. Students will re-evaluate the significance of the Author's Preface in the novel.
5. Students will identify major and minor characters in the novel.
5. Students will compare and contrast Firdaus with women of ancient Egypt.

Materials:
1. Reading Resource: Summary and Analysis: Preface, Chapter 1, Chapter 2, pages 1- 51.
2. Student Handout: Some Problems of Contemporary Arab Women by Nawal El Saadawi
3. Student Handout: The Author and Her Work
4. Student Handout: A Selected Bibliography of Nawal El Saadawi's Works
5. Student Handout: Characters
6. Teacher Resource: Characters
7. Student Handout: Women in Ancient Egypt

Procedure:
1. Discuss the thought questions and review Firdaus' childhood relationships. Refer to Summary and Analysis: Chapter 2, pages 11-51.
2. Discuss female circumcision and refer to Student Handout: "Some Problems of Contemporary Arab Women" by Nawal El Saadawi distributed during the last class.
3. Ask students to decide whether Firdaus is right or wrong to be so unhappy in her marriage. Refer to Summary and Analysis: Chapter 2, pages 11-51.
4. Distribute Student Handout: The Author and Her Work and Student Handout: A Selected Bibliography of Nawal El Saadawi's Works. Discuss the relationship between the author's life and work and ask students to re-evaluate the significance of the author's preface.
5. Distribute Student Handout: Characters and ask students to identify the major and minor characters in the novel. Refer to Teacher Resource: Characters.

Assessment:
1. Distribute Student Handout: Women in Ancient Egypt and ask students to compare and contrast Firdaus with the women of ancient Egypt.
2. Ask students to identify two ways in which Firdaus exemplifies the women of ancient Egypt and two ways in which she is an antithesis of the women of ancient Egypt.

Reading and Writing Assignment:
1. *Woman at Point Zero*, Chapter 2, pages 51-108.
2. Students should confirm the time and place of their interview for their frame story.

Thought Questions:
1. Describe Firdaus's life under the control the female pimp Sharifa. (Chapter 2)
2. Explain how Firdaus' life changes when she becomes an independent prostitute. (Chapter 2)
3. How is Firdaus' relationship with Ibrahim different from her other relationships? (Chapter 2)
4. Why is Firdaus arrested and imprisoned? (Chapter 2)

Lesson Three
Patterns in *Woman at Point Zero*
Creating a Frame Story

Objectives:
1. Students will analyze thematic and literary patterns in *Woman at Point Zero*.
2. Students will plan the frame story for their story about the oldest or most interesting woman they know.
3. Students will begin their preliminary research on gender inequality in the United States and make connections between women in the Islamic and western worlds.
4. Students will design interview questions for the internal story about the oldest or most interesting woman they know.

Materials:
1. Reading Resource: Summary and Analysis: Chapter 2, pages 51- 103.
2. Student Handout: Patterns in *Woman at Point Zero*
3. Student Handout: A Frame Story of the Life of an American Woman

Procedure:
1. Discuss the thought questions and review Firdaus' relationships with Sharifa, Ibrahim, and the prince. Refer to Summary and Analysis: Chapter 2, pages 51-103.
2. Ask students to identify why Firdaus killed the pimp and analyze the significance of her action.
3. Continue identifying major and minor characters in the novel. See Student Handout: Characters and Teacher Resource: Characters.
4. Distribute Student Handout: Patterns in *Woman at Point Zero*. Ask students to work independently, in small groups, or as a whole class in order to trace some of the reoccurring patterns in the novel. This exercise should lead to a discussion of the overall themes of the novel. For example, in Part IV of the handout, students may see that Firdaus develops a pattern of unveiling psychological masks with each one of her negative interactions. She learns that money is a source of power and that neither prostitution, nor a virtuous life, gain her respect. She also determines that marriage is a form of prostitution.
5. Ask students to discuss the patterns they have identified in the novel and to decide whether or not they agree with Firdaus's point of view.
6. Distribute Student Handout: A Frame Story of the Life of an American Woman and assist students in identifying background information they will need in order to interview their subject. Assist students in obtaining research materials on gender inequities in the United States. Require as much or as little research for this assignment as appropriate.
7. Ask students to develop the questions they will ask the oldest or most interesting woman they know. Students may be able to make connections between Islamic and western women.

Assessment:
Writing Assignment: Frame story on the life of a woman in the United States.
- The suggested due date for this assignment is approximately one to two weeks after students have completed reading *Woman at Point Zero*.
- The teacher may determine how much background research on gender inequities is required for the assignment.
- Checkpoints may be scheduled where students can share their research, interviews, and various drafts of their frame stories.

Student Handout
"Women and Islam" by Nawal El Saadawi

According to Nawal El Saadawi, ancient societies allowed women many freedoms. However, as the monotheistic religions of Judaism, Christianity, and Islam evolved, patriarchal values based on the division of society into classes of landowners and slaves caused women's rights to erode. Saadawi claims that women are inferior to men in all three monotheistic systems.

Literally the term Islam means "submission to God's will." Islam, also referred to as the Moslem or Muslim faith, holds Allah as the supreme deity. The chief prophet and founder of the religion is Muhammad, who lived from 570 to 632 AD. The *Qur'an,* or Koran, is considered the primary source of Islamic jurisprudence and theology along with the teachings of Muhammad and religious leaders. However, the teachings often provide ambiguous instructions pertaining to the lives of women.

In Pre-Islamic and early Islamic societies, many tribes were matriarchal, and desert women mixed freely with men in the economic sphere. These women did not wear veils, were free to choose their husbands, and in some cases practiced polyandry. In the early phases of Islam, polyandry was abolished, but women retained their rights to choose their husbands and to request divorce.

The question of polygamy is ambiguous; Muhammad himself married several wives after his first wife died. As continuous wars killed many men and supplied large numbers of women prisoners and slaves, polygamy became a common practice. However, monogamy remained the moral code for women.

Some of the prominent women in early Islamic society include the wives of the Prophet. His first wife, Khadija was involved in a monogamous marriage with Muhammad for twenty years. She was socially and economically independent because she earned her own living through trade. After her death, however, the Prophet practiced polygamy.

'Aisha, his eighteen year old wife, was a warrior and involved in politics as well as cultural and literary activities. The Prophet's other wives, Nessiba Bint Ka'ab and Um Sulaym Bint Malhan were also warriors.

In early Islamic societies, authority belonged to the supreme ruler or *caliph*, the political and religious leader or the *imam*, and the husband as the head of the family. Political and religious positions were limited to men. Nevertheless, women resisted male authority and succeeded in opposing the unilateral use of the male gender in the Koran. They defended their rights to sexual pleasure and were entitled to divorce. Women retained the rights to inheritance and dowry, which was a form of security against possible divorce, separation, or the death of the husband. A woman had a right to keep what she earned, choose her own husband, and separate from him if she wished.

Furthermore, according to Saadawi, the Koran does not instruct women to wear the veil. However, the text does instruct them not to wear makeup and ornaments, and to cover all parts of the body except the face and the palms of the hands. Historical studies indicate that the wearing of the veil is related to Eve, a source of sin, who must feel shame for her corrupt nature and cover her body.

Finally, Saadawi claims that during the time of the third Muslim caliph in the eighth century AD, Arab women were plunged into a "long night of feudal oppression and foreign domination in which women were condemned to toil, to hide behind the veil, to quiver in the prison of a harem fenced in by high walls, iron bars, windowless rooms and ever-present eunuchs on guard with their swords" (p. 79). Saadawi believes that women have been severely oppressed by so-called Islamic jurisprudence.

<u>Source</u>: "Women in Islam." *The Nawal El Saadawi Reader*. New York: Zed Books Ltd., 1997. 73 -84.

Student Handout
"Some Problems of Contemporary Arab Women"
by Nawal El Saadawi

Nawal El Saadawi claims that many contemporary laws and statues pertaining to Arab women are in conflict with Islamic teaching and reflect the beliefs of religious men through different periods of Muslim history. Arab women did not lose their independence suddenly; rather, it was a gradual process related to social and economic changes. Fundamental principles of social justice, freedom, and equality were buried under the growing authority of men over women and the growing prosperity of the new ruling classes over the poor majority. For example, the religious thinkers who followed Muhammad subjected women to new laws imposing marriage upon them and depriving them of their right to divorce.

Saadawi identifies tradition, which perpetrates female circumcision and the veil, as one of the most pervasive problems facing contemporary Arab women. Female circumcision is practiced mainly in Egypt, Sudan, and Yemen. In Egypt, most girls undergo a ritual before puberty whereby the labia minora or clitoris is cut resulting in loss of sexual pleasure during intercourse. Saadawi claims that this tradition is neither Muslim nor Arab, but comes from pre-Islamic and non-Arab societies.

In terms of wearing the veil, poor women who work outside the home do not often wear veils. However, middle and upper class women are often required to wear veils; usually these women are not allowed to work outside the home because this is considered a humiliation. At the beginning of twentieth century, most middle and upper class Arab women were confined to the home. Women were allowed to leave only if severe illness required hospitalization. In such a case, a woman would hide her body and face behind a heavy veil and be accompanied by a male.

Subservience to men is another major problem for Arab women. Women often have no right to choose their husbands and are often regulated to severe work in the homes of their in-laws. Women are subject to their husbands' beatings and the addition of new wives through polygamy. A woman generally has little recourse to divorce, but her husband will divorce her if she grows old or infertile, gives birth only to females, disobeys him, or rebels in any way.

Poverty and insufficient health care are other problems. Many Arab women are peasants who work full-time in the fields. Health care is minimal; women are often malnourished and suffer from repeated pregnancies. In Egypt, the abortion rate is estimated to be one in four pregnancies, and the infant mortality rate is 10%.

Finally, Arab women do not have equal access to education. In the rural areas, boys attend school while girls work in the fields, help with the household chores, and care for the younger siblings and elders in the family. As soon as a young girl reaches puberty, she is given away in marriage. Often marriages are consummated with old men and girls twelve to fourteen years old.

Saadawi claims that women are extremely vulnerable in Islamic society and are exposed to three forms of oppression: national, economic, and sexual. She believes the patriarchal class system, which manifests itself as world capitalism and imperialism, is the original cause of these injustices and claims that freedom for Arab women will be found in political power. She states: "Their only hope lies in political organization and a patient, long-enduring struggle to change and abolish the structures that keep women victims of the crudest, most cruel and sometimes most sophisticated forms of oppression and exploitation" (p. 91).

Source: "Some Problems of Contemporary Arab Women." *The Nawal El Saadawi Reader*. New York: Zed Books Ltd, 1997. 85-92.

Teacher Resource
Historical Highlights of Egypt

Phase I   **Farming in Ancient Egypt**
1. 18,500 - 6,000 BC - Barley, sorghum, and wheat are cultivated in ancient Egypt
2. 5,000 - 4,000 BC - Permanent settlements of farmers are established in Nile Valley
3. 4,000 BC - Tools appear, pottery, basketry, stone and leatherwork develop
4. 3,500 BC - Hieroglyphics, a practical form of writing, appears

Phase II   **Ancient Egyptian Dynasties**
1. 3,150 BC - Upper and Lower Egypt unite creating first dynasty
2. 2,700 - 2,200 BC - Old Kingdom Dynasties
3. 2,100 - 1,600 BC - Middle Kingdom Dynasties and Intermediate Periods
4. 1,500 - 1,100 BC - New Kingdom Dynasties
5. 1,000 - 300 BC - Late Period Dynasties

Phase III   **Greek and Roman Invasion**
1. 200 BC - Greek invasion
2. 100 BC - Foundation of Ptolemaic dynasty; ancestors of Cleopatra
3. 30 BC - Roman Conquest of Egypt
4. 200 AD - Christianity penetrates urban centers

Phase IV   **Islam in Egypt**
1. 632 AD - Prophet Muhammad dies after uniting all Arabs of Arabia under Islam
2. 642 AD - Arabs conquer lower Nile region and expel Byzantine power from Egypt
3. 732 AD - Islamic rule extends throughout northern Africa
4. 969 AD - Fatimids control Egypt; declare independence from rule of Bagdhad

Phase V   **Arab Migration in Northern Africa**
1. 900 - Arab pastoral nomads migrate from Arabia into northern Africa
2. 1050-1070 - 250,000 Bedouin move westward from Egypt into the Maghrib
3. 1200's - Berber nomads move eastwards from the Maghrib* into Egypt
4. 1300's - Local populations of the Maghrib and Egypt speak Arabic

Phase VI   **Ottoman and European Control**
1. 1453- 1500 - Ottoman Empire stretches over northern Africa
2. 1800 - Egypt is autonomous province of Ottoman empire
3. 1850 - Egypt becomes part of "informal" European empire
4. 1882 - Britain occupies Egypt

Phase VII   **The Twentieth Century**
1. 1914 – 1944 - token independence; Britain controls Egyptian defense and foreign affairs
2. 1952 - Monarchy ended; President Nasser promotes anti-imperialist sentiments
3. 1970 - Anwar al-Sadat reopens Egypt to foreign investment
4. 1979 – 1981 - Sadat ends war with Israel; he is target of discontent and assassinated

* Arabs refer to the whole coastal region of North Africa west of Egypt as al-Maghrib, Maghrib, or Maghreb, meaning "the West."

Student Handout:
The Author and Her Work

Nawal El Saadawi was born in the village of Kafr Tahla on the banks of the Nile River in 1931. Her father served as the General Controller of Education for the Province of Menoufia in the Delta region, and her mother attended French schools. At the age of six, Saadawi was circumcised in the Egyptian tradition, an experience that haunted her throughout her life.

Saadawi was one of nine children, and she studied in Egyptian Arabic through primary and secondary school. At the age of thirteen, she wrote her first novel entitled *Memoirs of a Female Child named Su'ad*. After high school, she was one of fifty women selected among hundreds of men to study medicine at the University of Cairo. She practiced thoracic medicine and psychiatry and worked in rural areas where she witnessed the inequalities suffered by women. She later served as Egypt's Director of Public Heath, editor of *Health Magazine*, and Assistant General Secretary in the Egyptian Medical Association.

In 1972, however, Saadawi was removed from her positions in the Ministry of Health after the publication of *Women and Sex*, in which she challenged political and theological authorities and directly addressed the inequities of gender. From 1973-1976, she researched women and neurosis, and from 1979 through 1980 she served as the United Nations Advisor for the Women's Program in Africa and the Middle East. She continued to write fiction and non-fiction, focusing on the situation of women. In 1975, Saadawi published a novel entitled *Woman at Point Zero*, which was inspired by a psychiatric interview with a prostitute facing the death sentence for murder. Her work entitled *The Hidden Face of Eve*, a personal account of women in the Islamic world, gained her international attention in 1980, and the Western world became familiar with Saadawi through her accounts of her own

circumcision. However, her books were banned in Egypt and other Arab countries.

In 1981, Anwar Sadat imprisoned Saadawi for her activities, an ordeal which she recounts in *Memoirs from the Women's Prison* (1986). Her incarceration also inspired a novel entitled *The Fall of the Imam* (1988), which provoked conservative Islamic groups to add her to their death lists. Nevertheless, Saadawi, founded the Arab Women's Solidarity Association in 1982, which was granted status as an Arab non-governmental organization within the Economic and Social Council of the United Nations in 1985 and dismantled by the Egyptian government in 1991. At the 1983 International Women's Conference, Saadawi also led a systematic review of female circumcision in the Middle East and Africa.

The Algerian writer Assia Djebar has translated many of Saadawi's literary works from the Arabic into French. However, Saadawi's novels did not appear in English until the 80's. Many of her works are now available in English translation, including *The Circling Song* (1989), a story about the conflicts of military violence, sex, and class, *God Dies by the Nile* (1985), a tragic political allegory, and *The Innocence of the Devil* (1994), which redefines the relationship between good and evil.

Saadawi's writing deals with traumas women experience in the Arab world and the suppression of the individual by economics, society, and tradition. However, her work cannot be dismissed as simply "Western feminism," and a foreign import into Egypt. Rather, her novels are rooted in the realities of the Arab woman and based on her own experience.

Currently, Saadawi lectures in Europe and the United States; under the shadow of death threats, her visits to Egypt are brief. Tirelessly, however, she continues to stand for the equality of Muslim women in domestic, economic, and political life.

Student Handout
A Selected Bibliography of Nawal El Saadawi's Works
Translated into English

The Cirling Song. Atlantic Highlands, NJ: Zed Books Ltd., 1989.

A Daughter of Isis: The Autobiography of Nawal El Saadawi. Trans. Sherif Hetata. New York: Zed Books Ltd., 1999.

Death of an Ex-Minister. Trans. Shirley Eber. London: Methuen, 1987.

The Fall of the Imam. Trans. Sherif Hetata. London: Minerva, 1988.

God Dies by the Nile. Trans. Sherif Hetata. London: Zed Books Ltd., 1985.

The Hidden Face of Eve: Women in the Arab World. Trans. Sherif Hetata. Atlantic Highlands, NJ: Zed Books Ltd., 1980.

The Innocence of the Devil. Trans. Sherif Hetata. Berkeley: University of California Press, 1994.

Memoirs of a Woman Doctor. Trans. Catherine Cobham. San Francisco: City Lights Books, 1989.

Memoirs from the Women's Prison. Trans. Marilyn Booth. 1986. Berkeley: University of California Press, 1994.

My Travels around the World. Trans. Shirley Eber. London: Methuen, 1987.

The Nawal El Saadawi Reader. New York: Zed Books Ltd., 1997.

Searching. Trans. Shirley Eber. Atlantic Highlands, NJ: Zed Books Ltd., 1991.

She Has No Place in Paradise. Trans. Shirley Eber. London: Zed Books Ltd., 1989.

Two Women in One. Trans. Osman Nusairi and Jana Gough. London: al-Saqi Books, 1985.

Woman at Point Zero. Trans. Sherif Hetata. London: Zed Books Ltd., 1983.

Women and Sex. Jerusalem: Guy Printing Press, 1974.

Student Handout
Characters in *Woman at Point Zero*

Narrator   _____

Firdaus   _____

Father   _____

Mother   _____

Mohammadain   _____

Uncle   _____

Uncle's wife   _____

Wafeya   _____

Miss Iqbal   _____

Sheikh Mahmoud   _____

Bayoumi   _____

Sharifa   _____

Fawzy   _____

Policeman   _____

Di'aa   _____

Fatheya   _____

Ibrahim   _____

Marzouk   _____

Arabian prince   _____

Teacher Resource
Characters in *Woman at Point Zero*

Narrator	female psychiatrist who interviews Firdaus and narrates the frame story
Firdaus	prisoner on death row who tells the internal story
Father	supposedly a religious man who cares little for his children
Mother	woman who has Firdaus circumcised
Mohammadain	Firdaus's childhood friend
Uncle	relative who both molests and assists Firdaus
Uncle's wife	cruel woman who arranges Firdaus's marriage to Shiekh Mahmoud
Wafeya	friend who accuses Firdaus of being in love with Miss Iqbal
Miss Iqbal	teacher who befriends Firdaus in the school garden
Sheikh Mahmoud	Firdaus's elderly abusive husband
Bayoumi	owner of a coffee house who befriends and exploits Firdaus
Sharifa	madame who befriends and exploits Firdaus
Fawzy	client who wants to marry Firdaus to save her from prostitution
Policeman	threatens to arrest Firdaus if she will not sleep with him
Di'aa	friend who tells Firdaus she can never be respectable as a prostitute
Fatheya	friend who accuses Firdaus of being in love with Ibrahim
Ibrahim	revolutionary whom Firdaus loves
Marzouk	pimp who tries to take a major share of Firdaus's profits
Arabian prince	client who thinks Firdaus must be a princess

Student Handout
Women in Ancient Egypt

According to the Egyptologist Barbara Watterson, ancient Egyptian women primarily worked as wives and mothers responsible for the household. Women were allowed certain freedoms, however, and in some cases exerted influence beyond the home. Women were generally accorded legal rights equal to those of men from the same social class and likewise expected to celebrate life after death.

Ancient Egyptian art, such as sculptures in temples and tombs, depicts women as creamy yellow, whereas the flesh of their male counterparts is red or brown indicating that women had less exposure to the sun. Some reliefs depict a wife smaller in scale than her husband and kneeling at his feet. The statue of the great woman Sennuwy dated 1950 BC is an exception, however, as she is seated alone with her hands on her knees. Overall, women are depicted as slim and youthful in Egyptian art, and sexuality is expressed in relationship to fertility.

Ancient Egyptian literature provides varied images of women. Egyptian love poetry describes the ideal woman as slim, feminine, beautiful, pale-skinned, with small firm breasts, a graceful neck, and blue-black shinning hair. The effect of love on women is a consistent theme in the ancient love poems. A second genus, the "Wisdom and Instruction Texts," reveal both positive and negative attitudes toward women. Mothers are beyond reproach, wives are either faithful helpmates or unfaithful nags, and the harlot is dangerous. Finally, secular narratives boast male heroes and portray women in secondary roles such as doting mothers, faithful wives, or wicked temptresses.

Women are also important figures in ancient Egyptian religion. For example, Isis, the most popular goddess in Egypt, is the faithful companion of Osiris, the great judge of death and the afterlife. On the other hand, she is also understood as a scheming magician. Artistic, literary, and religious sources indicate that ancient Egyptians held stereotypes of women ranging from the goddess to the shrew.

Ancient women were engaged in the textile industry and professions such as the priesthood and midwifery. Some women worked as wet nurses, mourners, dancers, and musicians. Although there is little evidence of prostitution, some sources indicate that professional singers and dancers may have sold sexual favors.

However, unlike most ancient civilizations, women enjoyed the same legal rights as men. A women had the right to inherit, buy, and sell property. Furthermore, women were not secluded, did not wear the veil, and had opportunities for meeting and falling in love with men. Nevertheless, sources indicate that most marriages were arranged in order to enhance social status; overall, marriages were monogamous. The Wisdom Literature never advises a man to beat his wife or force her to be obedient. However, men were permitted to have concubines. Divorce was private, and a woman could divorce her husband.

Finally, some ancient Egyptian women held positions of great political power. The first queen regnant was the lovely Nitocris who came to the throne at a time of political instability in 2180 BC. Sobekneferu was the last ruler of the Twelfth Dynasty in 1790 BC, and the great Queen Hatshepsut ruled Egypt in 1490 BC. She concentrated on the arts in an era of peace, and built new monuments, temples, and a large tomb in the Valley of Kings. Finally, the famous Cleopatra VII, born in 69 BC, formed a union with Caesar who was assassinated in 44 BC. The powerful queen spoke many languages, was considered a goddess by many of her Egyptian subjects, and sought to unite the east with the west.

Source: Watterson, B. *Women in Ancient Egypt*. New York: St. Martin's Press, 1991.

Student Handout
Patterns in *Woman at Point Zero*

Identify and analyze the following patterns in Firdaus' life. Indicate other patterns if possible.

Pattern #1　　　　　　　**Firdaus' Eyes and the Eyes of Others**
Reference #1　Pages _____
Description　　_____
Meaning　　　_____
Reference #2　Pages _____
Description　　_____
Meaning　　　_____
Reference #3　Pages _____
Description　　_____
Meaning　　　_____

Pattern #2　　　　　　　**Firdaus Meets Seemingly Helpful People Who Exploit Her**
Reference #1　Pages _____
Description　　_____
Meaning　　　_____
Reference #2　Pages _____
Description　　_____
Meaning　　　_____
Reference #3　Pages _____
Description　　_____
Meaning　　　_____

Pattern #3　　　　　　　**Firdaus Flees to the Street for Safety and Comfort**
Reference #1　Pages _____
Description　　_____
Meaning　　　_____
Reference #2　Pages _____
Description　　_____
Meaning　　　_____
Reference #3　Pages _____
Description　　_____
Meaning　　　_____

Pattern #4　　　　　　　**Firdaus Unveils Psychological Masks**
Reference #1　Pages _____
Description　　_____
Meaning　　　_____
Reference #2　Pages _____
Description　　_____
Meaning　　　_____
Reference #3　Pages _____
Description　　_____
Meaning　　　_____

Student Handout
A Frame Story of the Life of an American Woman

Background
As we have discussed, *Woman at Point Zero* is a frame story. The novel is mainly concerned with Firdaus' first person account of her own life. However, her story is framed at the beginning and end by the female psychiatrist who interviews Firdaus shortly before her death.

Contacting Your Subject
Request an interview with a woman who can tell a story about her struggles or triumphs. Consider interviewing the oldest woman you know or the strongest woman you know. Contact your subject and indicate her name and the time and place of your interview on the line below.

_____
Subject's name   Interview date   Interview place

Research
Research a topic that relates to the woman you will interview. You may use a variety of sources including magazine and newspaper articles and information on-line. Look for facts, statistics, or anecdotes. Ideas you may wish to consider include: unequal wages for men and women; domestic violence; homelessness and poverty for women; women in professions; women in politics; and women in the media.
List the three sources you are using for your research on the lines below:
Source #1_____
Source #2_____
Source #3_____

The Interview
Interview the woman you have contacted by asking questions related to her life and informed by your research. Use a tape recorder or take notes as you strive to record the woman's life accurately and get a sense of her voice and character. List some of your interview questions below:
1. _____
2. _____
3. _____
4. _____
5. _____
6. _____
7. _____

Your Frame Story
Write up your interview as a frame story. Your story must include the following three parts:
1. an introduction written by you, the narrator in "your voice." In this section, you should describe your feelings about the woman prior to the interview.
2. the woman's story in her "own voice" written by you the narrator.
3. a concluding section by you, the narrator written in "your voice." In this section, you articulate your impressions about the woman. For example, you might write about how you were affected by this woman's story and how she enable you to further understand the realities of women in the world today. If you wish, you may make connections between Islamic and western women in this section.

Reading Resource
Summary and Analysis

Author's Preface

<u>Summary</u>: Nawal El Saadawi conducted extensive research on neuroses in Egyptian women and published most of her research in *Women and Neurosis in Egypt* in 1976. She wrote *Woman at Point Zero* after meeting a woman named Firdaus in Qanatir Prison. Firdaus had been sentenced to death for killing a man, and she agreed to tell El Saadawi her story. The author says that Firdaus was a woman set apart, especially in "her absolute refusal to live and her absolute fearlessness of death" (p. iii). Her story inspired El Saadawi to challenge those forces that deprive human beings of the right to live fully.

<u>Analysis</u>: Nawal El Saadwai was drawn to conduct research in prisons because so many Egyptian intellectuals had been incarcerated for political offenses. Her husband was imprisoned for thirteen years for working with a left-wing opposition party, and she was imprisoned by Anwar Sadat in 1981. The preface was added to the novel when *Woman at Point Zero* was published in English in 1983. This introduction provides a realistic context for a story that seems far-fetched in the extreme hardship and violence faced by the protagonist Firdaus.

Chapter 1 (pages 1-7)

<u>Summary</u>: The narrator, a female psychiatrist, is recounting the story of a woman she met in Qanatir Prison while researching female inmates. The woman named Firdaus is unlike any other: she will not eat or sleep; she will not talk to legal assistants; and she refuses to sign the appeal made by the prison warder to the President requesting that her sentence be commuted to life imprisonment. Initially, Firdaus denies the narrator an interview, causing her to think of Firdaus constantly and lose confidence in her own importance. But just as the psychiatrist convinces herself not to take the rejection personally, the warder informs her that Firdaus requests a meeting. She describes Firdaus as having "eyes that killed, like a knife, probing, cutting deep down inside, their look steady, unwavering" (p. 6). Firdaus instructs the psychiatrist to sit on the cell floor and begins her story in a dream-like voice.

<u>Analysis</u>: The narrator in *Woman at Point Zero* appears to be El Saadawi herself, yet the extreme emotional tone transforms the author/narrator into a fictional character. She is affected by Firdaus as a rejected lover might be, for she doubts herself when Firdaus ignores her inquiries and becomes excited when Firdaus finally agrees to meet her. Although this emotional response might suggest lesbian attraction between the two women, it is more probable that the narrator's intense response to Firdaus is designed to impress the reader with the power of Firdaus's person.

Chapter 2 (pages 11-51)

<u>Summary</u>: Firdaus begins by instructing the narrator not to interrupt her since her execution is scheduled for that evening. Her anticipated death makes her feel superior to everyone else, "including kings, princes, and rulers" (p. 11). She announces that every man she has ever known has filled her with the one desire: "to lift my hand and bring it smashing down on his face" (p. 11). As a woman and as a prostitute, she was trained to hide her violent feelings, but now she firmly embraces a retaliatory position.

Firdaus explains that her father was a poor, illiterate peasant who appeared to be a holy man that invoked the name of Allah and respected the Imam. However, he beat his wife, cheated his neighbors, and pretended piety at the mosque. One day, Firdaus questions her father's paternity, which prompts her mother to beat her and have her circumcised. Previous to this, Firdaus had played bride and groom with a little boy named Mohammadain during which she would experience "a sensation of sharp pleasure" (p. 14). After her circumcision, however, she is no longer allowed to play in the fields and is forced to work around the compound. Here, an uncle molests her, and she no longer feels sexual pleasure. Her circumcision makes her feel "as though a part of me, of my being, was gone and would never return" (p. 15). Ironically, Firdaus admires her uncle and wishes she could attend classes with him in Cairo. He explains that schooling is for men, and she fears she will never escape village life. Firdaus questions her relationship with her mother. Thinking back, she recalls a mother's eyes like "two rings of intense white around two circles of intense black" (p. 17), but that maternal memory is soon replaced by images of another woman whose eyes were "dull, impervious to the light, like two extinguished lamps" (p. 18).

Firdaus had many brothers and sisters; some would creep off into the corners and die. Her father would beat her mother if a son died but not if a daughter died. He also never failed to eat supper, even when there was no food for the children. This reaffirms Firdaus's conviction that he was not really her father. After her father dies, Firdaus's uncle sends her to elementary school, and after her mother dies, her uncle takes her to Cairo. She is amazed by the electric lights in his house but dismayed by the mirrors that filled her with a deep hatred for the way she looks. She attends school in Cairo while also caring for her uncle's house. During the cold winter nights, she curls up in his arms like a baby. One night he takes her to a film featuring a couple dancing and kissing, and these images make Firdaus ashamed of the intimacy she shares with her uncle. Even so, her uncle continues to press himself on her.

Finally, her uncle's advances cease when he gets a job at the Ministry of Works and marries. However, he seems to be fearful of his wife because she comes from a higher social class; although he treats her politely, there is little respect. Firdaus continues to do the housework until her uncle hires a servant girl and sends her to boarding school. He never visits Firdaus or invites her home on weekends; however, despite this neglect, Firdaus loves school where she exchanges secrets with her close friend Wafeya. In some ways, she feels different from the other girls; while they talk about love and men, she contemplates becoming a doctor, an engineer, a judge, or a head of state; while her friends read romances, she reads about politics. She discovers that most rulers are men with "a never-ending appetite for money, sex, and unlimited power" (p. 27). While the Islamic leaders assume pious poses in the newspapers, Firdaus knows that they do not fear Allah, and they believe the poor should defend the rich.

When bored with reading, Firdaus sits alone on the playground. One night, Miss Iqbal joins her. Without warning, Firdaus bursts into tears; she cannot explain why, and Miss Iqbal begins to cry as well. Looking into her eyes, Firdaus sees "two rings of pure white, surrounding two circles of intense black" (p. 29). Firdaus takes her teacher's hand, and the touch makes her tremble with deep distant desire. Afterwards, Wafeya accuses Firdaus of being in love with Miss Iqbal, but the teacher seems to have forgotten the event. She treats Firdaus as she does all the other students until the day of the certificate ceremony. Firdaus must collect her award for scoring second in the school and seventh in the country on the national exam, and since her uncle is not present, Miss Iqbal leads Firdaus to the platform and signs as her guardian.

At the end of the school year, her uncle takes Firdaus home. She walks with heavy steps, wishing she could see Miss Iqbal again and dreading the thought of living back in the house where there is little room for her now that her uncle has children of his own. That night she hears her uncle and aunt discussing her future. They agree they could not send her to college because of the expense and because it would be inappropriate for a man of religion to send his niece off to mix in the company of men. Her aunt proposes that they marry her off to Sheikh Mahmoud, despite his advanced age and the obvious deformity on his face. Her uncle agrees, especially when hearing of the two hundred pound dowry the Sheikh might be willing to pay. The next morning, Firdaus packs her meager belongings and runs away. A new world is opening up for her, like a third eye in her head. As she observes people running in different directions, she feels like an infant being projected onto a new environment. But suddenly, she senses two eyes following her, pursuing her body with a cold intent. Overcome with terror, she rushes back to her uncle's house.

Firdaus is soon married to Sheikh Mahmoud. He is over sixty years old and has a large swelling below his lip with a hole in the middle, which often runs with pus. He watches her as she eats, and one day he beats her after discovering leftover scraps of food in the garbage bin. After one particularly bad beating, Firdaus returns to her uncle's home, but she is told that that all men beat their wives, especially religious men because the precepts of Islam permit such punishment. Once back in her husband's home, she endures his abuse until he hits her with a heavy stick and causes blood to run from her nose and ears. She runs away again and ends up in a coffee house. The owner, Bayoumi, befriends her and invites her into his two-room flat. He begins touching her like her uncle, reminding her again of her lost pleasure. She stays with him throughout the winter and the following summer. When she finally asks for permission to get a job, he slaps her violently. Afterwards, he begins locking her in the flat. One night she discovers that the man making love to her is not Bayoumi but rather one of his friends. She is similarly abused by many of his friends until a neighbor sees her weeping and helps her escape. She is back on the street again; by now the street has become the only place in which she finds refuge.

Analysis: Ironically, Firdaus' name means *Paradise*.[1] However, her life on earth is the antithesis of paradise, and the harshness with which she views the world is hardly a heavenly attitude. Firdaus opens her story with a violent declaration against all men, causing the narrator and the reader to wonder what has transpired in her life to foster such bitterness. Circumcision shatters Firdaus' childhood. This slicing of the clitoris occurs immediately after she questions her father's paternity and patriarchal control. After experiencing this trauma, Firdaus begins to question whether she really is her mother's child. It is uncertain whether Firdaus's mother died and was replaced by a cruel stepmother or whether her mother's eyes change after she orders her daughter's circumcision. In either case, Firdaus longs to reconnect with the loving person behind those eyes either in the figure of a male lover or in a surrogate mother like Miss Iqbal. Her deep desire to recreate this primal bond is echoed throughout the novel in her longing to rediscover the sexual intimacy that was burgeoning before her circumcision. The physical procedure of circumcision not only permanently effects Firdaus's sexuality, but it also becomes a metaphor for the experiences Firdaus faces throughout the novel, for she is circumcised by poverty, lack of education, and a religion that condones male dominance. For example, Firdaus's father eats while his children go hungry; she is not allowed to go to college, and she is forced to marry a religious man who is both disgusting and abusive.

The reader should also note that El Saadawi herself was forced to undergo circumcision and writes extensively about the psychological effect upon women in *The Nawal El Saadawi Reader* (1997) and *A Daughter of Isis: The Autobiography of Nawal El Saadawi* (1999).

Chapter 2 (pages 51-103)

Summary: While wandering the streets, Firdaus is befriended by Sharifa, a female pimp who recognizes her as an abused woman. She offers Firdaus a luxurious apartment and pampers her with fine clothes and perfumes. Sharifa's philosophy is that to endure existence, a person must be harder than life itself. Under Sharifa's tutelage, Firdaus comes to understand her past and to see the beauty of her own body. And as she begins to sell her body for profit, she learns that a woman must determine her own value and must set a high price for herself. Firdaus sinks into the luxury of this life, though she is confused as to why she feels pain instead of pleasure with her clients. Sharifa tells her to look for comforts only in the material goods that such a lifestyle provides. But

---

[1] Fedwa Malti-Douglas. *Men, Women, and God(s): Nawal El Saadawi and Arab Feminist Poetics*. Berkeley: University of California Press, 1995.

soon enough Firdaus can no longer take pleasure in this way of life. She is locked in her room day and night and every hour another man comes in. She comes to understand the severity of her circumstances when one of her clients, Fawzy, makes her realize that Sharifa has been exploiting her. He announces his intentions to marry Firdaus, but Sharifa argues that he is incapable of love. Because they are former lovers, Sharifa and Fawzy's argument quickly turns from fighting into frenzied passion. Feeling the need to escape, Firdaus flees to the streets once more.

This time Firdaus feels no fear. A policeman approaches her and insists she come to his house. Because he threatens to arrest her for being a prostitute and promises to pay her a full pound, she acquiesces. Afterwards, he refuses her the money. She continues on her way in the darkness of a rainy night, and a man helps her into his car and into his home. The next morning he gives her a ten pound note for services rendered. Firdaus says, "It was as if he had lifted a veil from my eyes, and I was seeing for the first time" (p. 64). The ten pound note gives her a sense of unprecedented control. She notices that the waiter, in a movement of respectful humility, avoids looking at the money as she pulls it out to pay her bill. She is seized with wonder that money could be regarded as illicit and forbidden like the thrill of a sacrilegious pleasure, but she also recalls that she too had always looked in the other direction when a man was counting his money.

From that day onward, Firdaus ceases to bend her head or look away. When a man approaches her, she refuses him if she does not want to go with him. She demands high prices for her services and is paid well. She gets her own apartment and engages a cook and a personal secretary. While her bank account is mounting, she has free time to relax, enjoy cultural events, and discuss politics with close friends. One friend, Di'aa, comes to her house for talk rather than sex. He shocks her by saying that she is not a respectable person because of her profession. Her self-esteem changes completely, and she has no respite from the torment of those words.

Because another veil has been torn from her eyes, Firdaus becomes a new woman again. She is willing to sacrifice all, even her life, to become a respectable woman. She takes a secretarial position in a large industrial company, rents a small, simple room, and rides a crowded bus to work each day. She identifies herself with the working class and when any of the higher officials make advances towards her, she rebuffs them with the reply, "The price of my body is much higher than the price that can be paid for it with a pay rise" (p. 75). But after working for three years, she begins to realize that she had been more respected and highly valued as a prostitute than as a secretary. She does not fear losing her job and becoming a prostitute like other female employees because she knows that a prostitute's job would actually be better than her own position. Nevertheless, she enjoys her job despite her awareness that she is paying a high cost for something of little value.

One evening, while sitting in the garden outside the office, Firdaus is approached by Ibrahim, who is a revolutionary. When he asks her why she is crying, she can't explain, causing him to cry as well. She says, looking into his face, "I could see two rings of pure white surrounding two circles of intense black looking out at me" (p. 78). They hold hands, and she says, "the feel of our hands touching was strange, sudden" (p. 78). After this exchange, he does not take any special notice of her, and her friend Fatheya accuses her of being in love with Ibrahim. She joins the revolutionary committee and works for it day and night in order to be near him. He admires her zeal, energy, and conviction and makes advances towards her, saying he had been thinking of her ever since their first meeting. They share their pasts with each other and sleep together in a warm embrace. Love makes the world beautiful for Firdaus, but her joy is short-lived for she soon discovers that he is engaged to the chairman's daughter. She suffers pain and humiliation and realizes that her efforts to become respectable and to gain love are in vain. She concludes that her virtue is "as a kind of stupidity, or simple-mindedness, to be despised even more than depravity or vice" (p. 86).

Now Firdaus wants only the truth, no matter how harsh. She comes to the conclusion that "A successful prostitute was better than a misled saint" (p. 86). Being totally unbound to anyone, Firdaus experiences a tranquillity and independence in her renewed life of prostitution. Eventually, Ibrahim becomes one of her clients, and she realizes that he never really loved her but had come to her every night because it was free. Some of the men who visit her try to help her escape her life, but she refuses, figuring that as a prostitute with her own free will, she is better off than most women. One important personality from a foreign state sends for her, but she rebuffs him, making him even more intent on gaining a victory over her. He argues that it is her sacred national duty to respond to his request, but she again refuses and is put in prison for a brief period. She hires a lawyer for a large sum of money and the court decides she is an honorable woman after all.

By this point she has no doubts about her own integrity. Now she uses her money to get whatever she wants: servants for her home, lawyers to defend her honor, doctors to give her an abortion, journalists to write something about her. One day a pimp named Marzouk asks her to marry him, but she has no interest in marriage. Then he insists on sharing her profits, promising her protection and threatening her harm if she refuses. She goes to the police but discovers he is better connected than she is. He forces a share of her profits, confiscating the larger part for himself and taking her freedom away. When she attempts to leave him, he hits her. When she slaps him in return, he goes for a knife in his pocket, but she grabs the knife and plunges it into his neck, his chest, his belly, and almost every part of his body.

Firdaus walks onto the street again, proud of having destroyed many masks. She walks with the footsteps of a woman "who believed in herself, knew where she was going, and could see her goal" (p. 96). An Arab prince passes by and offers her three thousand pounds. When he actually does pay her this outrageous amount of money after sex, she is so infuriated with him and with all men that she rips the money into little pieces. She explains that this tore "the last remaining veil from before my eyes, to reveal the whole enigma which had puzzled me throughout, the true enigma of my life" (p. 98). The prince thinks she must be a princess to be so careless with money, but she insists she has just killed a man. To prove her potential for violence, she slaps him and chastises him for spending the thousands he had taken from his starving people on prostitutes. He screams in fright, bringing in the police, and she denies their accusations that she is a criminal, saying, "To be a criminal one must be a man" (p. 100). Firdaus is then led off to prison and kept in a room where the windows and doors are always shut. They are afraid to let her live because she challenges them so much. She sees herself as triumphing over life and death because she no longer has a fear of death. She refuses to make an appeal because she does not see her murder as a crime, and she knows she will keep on killing. While waiting for her execution, she feels pride for the murderous act which has enabled her to destroy fear and discover truth.

Analysis: Sharifa means "Honorable One,"[2] and in some ways the meaning is appropriate since this woman is the first to teach Firdaus that her numerous misfortunes reflect a pattern of patriarchal abuse. She tells Firdaus, "They're all the same, all sons of dogs, running around under various names. Mahmoud, Hassanein, Fawzy, Sabri, Ibrahim, Awadain, Bayoumi" (p. 52). But Sharifa is also dishonorable in exploiting Firdaus for profit, and in that way, she continues the pattern of female-induced abuse established by Firdaus's mother and her uncle's wife. In escaping Sharifa and Fawzy, Firdaus is again on the streets, which are her only safe haven. Another pattern is developing in Firdaus's story: when she returns to the streets, she is immediately rescued by a savior, such as the policeman who demands sex from her and the client who pays her ten pounds. These saviors, however, soon become abusers. After being saved and abused, Firdaus flees to the streets again.

---

[2] Fedwa Malti-Douglas. *Men, Women, and God(s): Nawal El Saadawi and Arab Feminist Poetics*. Berkeley: University of California Press, 1995.

As Firdaus establishes autonomy from her mother, teachers, and Sharifa, she removes veils from her vision and moves toward the harsh but enlightening truth. The first veil is removed when she receives the ten pounds. She eats a plentiful meal at a restaurant, proving her own ability to gain control over her life, and realizes that sex and power are connected in the same way that food and power are intertwined. A second veil is lifted when a friend tells Firdaus that sex and power cannot gain her respect. She reevaluates her life and takes up a humble job where she rebuffs all the advances made by men in power above her. She eventually falls in love with the revolutionary Ibrahim. Her early interactions with him replicate her exchange with Miss Iqbal and are again reminiscent of her ties with her mother. As with her childhood and adolescent bonds, this relationship is futile; it causes her to shed any illusions about virtue and marriage. "All women are prostitutes of one kind or another," she says, "Because I was intelligent I preferred to be a free prostitute, rather than an enslaved wife" (p. 91). In suggesting that marriage promises more cruel suffering for woman than prostitution, Firdaus challenges the sanctity of marriage and offers a discomforting insight into the personal compromises asked of women when they become wives. Firdaus's final mask is stripped away when she kills Marzouk, the pimp. In stabbing him multiple times all over his body, she is clearly reversing the male act of penetration through which she has been victimized. As she walks onto the street after the murder, she is no longer fleeing. This murder is her first truly independent act, and she is now in control of her own body. She can now rip up the three thousand pounds given to her by the lustful prince. Believing that the only way to avoid the abuse of men is to commit violence against them, she can destroy all of her connections to the men of her past, including her father, her uncle, and her clients.

Chapter 3 (pages 107-108)

Summary: As Firdaus comes to the end of her story, the narrator feels like someone moving in sleep. The police enter the cell and take Firdaus away. The narrator never sees her again, but Firdaus's voice continues to resonate with her, "vibrating in my head, in the cell, in the prison, in the streets, in the whole world, shaking everything, spreading fear wherever it went, the fear of the truth which kills, the power of truth, as savage, and as simple, and as awesome as death, yet as simple and as gentle as the child that has not yet learnt to lie" (p. 107). The narrator realizes that Firdaus had to die because the world is constructed on lies. She leaves the prison, feeling great shame about her own lies and fears and realizes that Firdaus has more courage in life than she has.

Analysis: Firdaus's story has universal application, for she emerges as a female picaresque or "every-woman" of sorts. Her self-description early on in her story affirms the notion that she represents women across the board. She states, "Only my make-up, my hair and my expensive shoes were 'upper class.' With my secondary school certificate and suppressed desires I belonged to the 'middle class.' By birth I was lower class" (p. 12).

Firdaus certainly ends up speaking for the narrator, even though the two women come originally from opposite social classes. Despite her status as a psychiatrist, the narrator concludes that her own life is no better than a prostitute's and in fact may be even less admirable. El Saadawi casts doubt on the psychiatrist's profession by suggesting that truth lay in the understanding of harsh realities rather than in science and wisdom. Because the narrator is silent at the end, she becomes part of the general group of women who share the common experience of victimization. She is no longer a distanced observer. The narrator has become as caught up in the story as El Saadawi. Given the frames around the internal story, the reader is also invited to view Firdaus with great admiration, despite her murderous deed, and to take notice of the "savage and dangerous" (p. 100) truth that her words convey.

Finally, in his analysis, Kenneth Payne states, "Notwithstanding the frequent stridency of her feminism, El Saadawi presents us with a picaresque heroine who finally surmounts the limitations of the genre stereotype, and who becomes the voice of 'the savage, primitive truths of life' (p. 102). If the picaresque tradition really is in a state of continuing evolution and diversification, as most authorities seems to agree, then Nawal El Saadawi's feminist version should certainly be recognized as one expression of it. *Woman at Point Zero* is evidence of the enduring attraction of the picaresque motif to the modern literary imagination, and of its appeal in particular to those, like El Saadawi, who are concerned with the real struggle between the dissenting individual and a repressive society."[3]

---

[3] Kenneth Payne. "*Woman at Point Zero*: Nawal El Saadawi's Feminist Picaresque" in *Southern Humanities Review*, Winter 1992, vol. XXVI, No. 1, p. 17.

List of Works Consulted

Al-Ali, Nadje Sadig. *Gender Writing/Writing Gender: The Representation of Women in a Selection of Modern Egyptian Literature*. Cairo: American University in Cairo Press, 1993.

Boullata, Issa J. *Trends and Issues in Contemporary Arab Thought*. Albany: State University of New York Press, 1990.

Bruner, Charlotte H., ed. *The Heinemann Book of African Women's Writing*. Portsmouth, NH: 1993.

Killam, Douglas. ed. *The Companion to African Literatures*. Bloomington & Indianapolis: Indiana University Press, 2000.

Malti-Douglas, Fedwa. *Men, Women, and God(s): Nawal El Saadawi and Arab Feminist Poetics*. Berkeley: University of California Press, 1995.

Newman, Elana. "Ethical Issues in Teaching about Violence against Women." *Women's Studies Quarterly* XXVII.1-2 (Spring/Summer 1999): 197-202.

Nnaemeka, Obioma, ed. *Sisterhood: Feminisms & Power: From Africa to the Diaspora*. New Jersey: Africa World Press, 1998.

Payne, Kenneth. "*Woman at Point Zero*: Nawal El Saadawi's Feminist Picaresque." *Southern Humanities Review* XXVI.1 (Winter 1992): 11-18.

Saadawi, Nawal El. "Islamic Fundamentalism and Women." *The Nawal El Saadawi Reader*. New York: Zed Books, 1997. 93-99.

---. "Some Problems of Contemporary Arab Women." *The Nawal El Saadawi Reader*. New York: Zed Books, 1997. 85-92.

---. "Women and Islam." *The Nawal El Saadawi Reader*. New York: Zed Books, 1997. 73-92.

Schulman, Barbara. "The Unsettling Subject of Violence in Women's Lives: Encouraging Notes from the Classroom Front." *Women's Studies Quarterly* XXVII.1-2 (Spring/Summer 1999): 167-184.

Watterson, Barbara. *Women in Ancient Egypt*. New York: St. Martin's Press, 1991.

CHAPTER SIX

———

Song of Lawino **and** *Song of Ocol*
Songs of Satire from Uganda
by Okot p'Bitek

Okot p'Bitek is a biting satirist who sparked a literary revolution in East Africa soon after Uganda gained her independence. He is best known for the traditional African woman's lament in *Song of Lawino* and her westernized husband's response in *Song of Ocol*. *Song of Lawino,* which was originally written in Acholi and later translated into English, was published in 1966. *Song of Ocol* was written as a response to Lawino's lament and was published in 1970. These two songs were later republished in a single volume. The narratives reflect the traditional song stories of the Acholi people and raise issues concerning the conflict of culture. Both songs dramatize the tension between the values and lifestyles of traditional Acholi people and the new educated elite who seek to imitate western civilization. The husband and wife heighten the tension as they articulate their differences. Lawino berates her husband Ocol for uprooting the pumpkin, or the traditions of the Acholi people; Ocol responds with disdain.

Song of Lawino and *Song of Ocol* by Okot p'Bitek are excellent examples of satire and present the clash of cultures as European powers colonize the peoples of Uganda. Lawino represents the Acholi people who inhabit the northern region of Uganda. Ocol, on the other hand, champions the culture of the Europeans. The Acholi are related to the Luo people of the southern Sudan and developed a culture closely related to other Luo groups in East Africa.

Because *Song of Ocol* is a response to the first narrative, it cannot stand on its own. The songs provide opportunities for students to experience biting satire and dramatize both sides of a culture clash. The author invites his audience to experience the traditional Acholi song story and empathize with Lawino, the symbol of traditional African life. These songs are recommended for middle school or high school students as well as college students and may be incorporated in units on satire, proverbs, or poetry as well as units on colonialism in East Africa.

Lessons

Lesson One   Introduction
                Background on Traditional Acholi Song Stories
                The Author and His Work
                Reading Assignment: *Song of Lawino*

Lesson Two   *Song of Lawino*
                Literary Techniques and African Proverbs
                Reading Assignment: *Song of Ocol*

Lesson Three   *Song of Ocol*
                Dramatization

Lesson One Introduction
Background on Traditional Acholi Song Stories
The Author and His Work

Objectives:
1. Students will identify East Africa by locating Kenya, Tanzania, Uganda, Burundi, and Rwanda on a map.
2. Students will locate Acholiland in northern Uganda on a map.
3. Students will identify salient geographical features of East Africa by locating:
   - Snow-capped Mt. Kilamanjaro on the equator,
   - the Serengeti Plain in Tanzania and Kenya, and
   - Lake Victoria, the source of the Nile River.
4. Students will become familiar with the author Okot p'Bitek and the Acholi song story.
5. Students will define satire and satirical techniques.

Materials:
1. Classroom World Map
2. Student Handout: Map of Africa, Chapter Two: Africa Overview of the Continent
3. Teacher Resource: Historical Highlights of the Acholi People
4. Student Handout: Traditional Acholi Songs and Dances
5. Student Handout: The Author and His Work
6. Student Handout: A Selected Bibliography of Okot p'Bitek's Works

Procedure:
1. Begin with satirical remarks concerning issues important to the students, such as class elections, sports, or social events, or begin with satirical remarks concerning current domestic and international political issues. Use simple satirical techniques such as exaggeration and simile to poke fun at the president and vice-president of the United States, the governor, etc.
2. Distribute Student Handout: Map of Africa. Using a wall map, locate Kenya, Tanzania, Uganda, Burundi, and Rwanda in East Africa. Introduce northern Uganda as the home of the Acholi people.
3. Explain that the Acholi people are related to a large people group known as the Luo and migrated to northern Uganda from southern Sudan.
4. Locate Lake Victoria in East Africa. Explain that in the 19th century, David Livingstone and Henry Stanley discovered that Lake Victoria is the source of the Nile. The Nile River therefore flows from south to north.
5. Inform students of important events and periods in the history of the Acholi people of Uganda. Refer to Teacher Resource: Historical Highlights of the Acholi People.
6. Distribute Student Handout: Traditional Acholi Songs and Dances. Review the literary techniques of the ancient song story tradition. Introduce the concept of satire; the students may learn satirical techniques for the first time, or relate the Acholi techniques to literary techniques studied previously. Review the importance of songs as social criticism for the Acholi people.
7. Distribute Student Handout: The Author and His Work and Student Handout: A Selected Bibliography of Okot p'Bitek's Works and emphasize the importance of songs, stories, and dances for Okot p'Bitek.
8. Explain that *Song of Lawino* and *Song of Ocol* are really a conversation between husband and wife focusing on the clash of cultures in Uganda in the 20th century.
9. Begin reading/dramatizing Section One of *Song of Lawino* orally.

Assessment:
1. Ask students to define satire.
2. Ask students to define a satirical technique used by the Acholi people.
3. Based upon the reading so far, why has Lawino's husband rejected her?

Reading Assignment:
Song of Lawino

Thought Questions:
1. Identify one satirical device Okot p'Bitek uses in *Song of Lawino*.
2. Identify the target of the satirical device and explain the message.
3. How does Lawino compare herself to Clementine?
4. How do you feel about Lawino as she pleads with Ocol to come back to his senses and recognize the value of traditional life?
5. How do you feel about Lawino as she pleads with Ocol to love her again?
6. Based upon your knowledge of African life, does Lawino accurately represent the woman of East Africa or is she a caricature, a gross exaggeration of the true African woman?
7. Identify one proverb in the song. What do you think that proverb means in the context of African life?
8. Create one question for Lawino about an aspect of Acholi life that you do not understand.

Lesson Two
Song of Lawino
Literary Techniques and African Proverbs

Objectives:
1. Students will analyze the literary techniques and satirical devices used in *Song of Lawino*.
2. Students will interpret African proverbs.
3. Students will begin to recreate the voice of Lawino and her lament.

Materials:
1. Student Handout: Literary Techniques in *Song of Lawino*
2. Student Handout: The Pumpkin in the Old Homestead Must Not Be Uprooted
3. Reading Resource: Summary and Analysis: *Song of Lawino*

Procedure:
1. Discuss the thought questions for *Song of Lawino*. Refer to <u>Summary and Analysis: *Song of Lawino*</u>.
2. Review the theme of *Song of Lawino* and emphasize that Lawino berates Ocol for uprooting the traditions of the Acholi people. According to Lawino, how has he betrayed his community and disgraced his ancestors?
3. Distribute <u>Student Handout: Literary Techniques in *Song of Lawino*</u>. Put students into small groups and ask them to review the examples of literary techniques used in the song. Ask students to find one other example of each of these literary techniques used in the song. Then, students should help Lawino berate Ocol by creating one original example for each technique.
4. Ask students to share the examples of the literary techniques they have found.
5. Ask students to share their original examples of literary techniques designed to help Lawino.
6. Distribute <u>Student Handout: The Pumpkin in the Old Homestead Must Not Be Uprooted</u>. Ask students to interpret the African proverbs listed and to create one original proverb helping Lawino make her point to the Acholi community. Students may write other original proverbs about issues at school, at home, or in their community.
7. Introduce *Song of Ocol* by reading/dramatizing the first few pages orally. Refer to <u>Summary and Analysis: *Song of Ocol*</u>.

Assessment:
Ask students to imagine Ocol's response to his traditional wife, Lawino, and create a response to her lament using one of the literary techniques they have studied.

Reading Assignment:
Song of Ocol

Thought Questions:
1. Do you think Ocol has truly lost his manhood in a forest of white men's books, or is he pursuing a better life?
2. Ocol not only detests Lawino, who can neither read nor write, but he despises Africa and all that is African. Why does he betray his people and despise himself?
3. As a proud rich neo-colonial elite, what responsibility does Ocol take for improving the economic plight of the rural peasants?
4. Where do you think the author, Okot p'Bitek, an educated, westernized Acholi writing shortly after Uganda gained independence, stands in the debate between Lawino and Ocol?

Lesson Three
Song of Ocol
Dramatization of Story Songs

Objectives:
1. Students will attempt to defend Ocol and his interest in neo-colonial life in Uganda.
2. Students will dramatize the conflict between Lawino and Ocol.
3. Students will assess the portraits of Lawino and Ocol presented by Okot p'Bitek.

Materials:
1. Any kind of hat worn in western civilization
2. Any kind of colorful cloth
3. Reading Resource: Summary and Analysis: *Song of Ocol*
4. Student Handout: Dramatization of *Song of Lawino* and *Song of Ocol*

Procedure:
1. Discuss the thought questions for *Song of Ocol*. Refer to <u>Summary and Analysis: *Song of Ocol*</u>.
2. Review the theme of *Song of Ocol* and plead his case. Emphasize that Ocol has not betrayed Lawino and Acholi customs; he is simply taking advantage of the opportunities offered by western education and civilization.
3. Ask for two student volunteers, one female and one male. Ask the female to wrap the colorful cloth around her waist and impersonate Lawino. Ask the male to wear the western style hat and impersonate Ocol. Ask the students to improvise as they dramatize sections of the songs. Students may choose to read directly from the songs or make up new sections of the songs as they go along employing as many literary techniques as possible.
4. Distribute <u>Student Handout: Dramatization of *Song of Lawino* and *Song of Ocol*</u>. Divide the students into groups. Have each group choose either Creative Writing Project # 1 or Creative Writing Project # 2 and continue the *Song of Lawino*, the *Song of Ocol* or write a song story satirizing a public figure, such as a politician, a Hollywood star, or a famous athlete.

Assessment:
Have students from each group perform their song stories. They may use Ocol's hat and Lawino's colorful cloth and/or other props.

Optional Writing Assignment:
Ask students to respond to the following questions:
- Do you think Lawino is a strong figure? Or, do you think Lawino is a portrait of a pathetic, stupid wife scorned by her progressive husband? Support your position with examples and illustrations from the text.
- Do you think Ocol is a strong figure or is he an arrogant imitation of the European oppressor? Support your position with examples and illustrations from the text.

Teacher Resource
Historical Highlights of the Acholi People

Phase I   **14ᵗʰ - 18ᵗʰ Century: Migrations and Monarchies**

1. 1300's - Highly centralized African nations emerge in southern Uganda
2. 1300's - Bunyoro kingdom develops in west central Uganda
3. 1400's - Luo groups of southern Sudan migrate into northern Uganda and become Acholi
4. 1600's - The powerful kingdom of Buganda emerges in southern Uganda

Phase II   **19ᵗʰ Century: Trade; Exploration; Missionaries**

1. 1820's - Arabs seek ivory and slaves; they call Luo migrants from southern Sudan Acholi
2. Sir Samuel Baker attempts to curtail slave trade in Acholiland
3. David Livingstone and Henry Stanley discover Lake Victoria as the source of the Nile
4. Anglicans set up two missions in Buganda; Roman Catholics follow

Phase III   **End of 19ᵗʰ Century: Colonialism**

1. 1890 - Britain and Germany terminate Anglo-German competition in East Africa
2. 1894 - Uganda is declared a British protectorate
3. 1895 - Britain implements indirect rule through cooperation of Buganda kingdom
4. 1898-1901 - military campaigns push northward into Acholiland from Buganda

Phase IV   **1900 - 1950: Christianity**

1. 1904 - Anglicans set up temporary Christian reading houses in Acholiland
2. 1913 - Anglicans set up permanent station and dispatch teachers throughout Acholiland
3. 1914 - Roman Catholics set up reading houses in Acholiland
4. 1950 - Many Acholi fight in Britain's army against Mau Mau in Kenya

Phase V   **1950's - 1960's: Political Consciousness and Independence**

1. 1952 - Educated Protestants in Buganda form Uganda National Congress
2. 1955 - Buganda ends demands for separate Bugandan independence
3. 1955 - Conservative intellectuals in Buganda form Progressive Party
4. 1956 - Catholics from Buganda and Acholiland form Democratic Party
5. 1960 - Milton Obote forms Uganda Peoples Congress in a deeply divided Uganda
6. 1961 - Elections are boycotted by Buganda
7. 1962 - Milton Obote leads peoples of Uganda to tenuous independence from Britain

Source: Girling, F. K. *The Acholi of Uganda*. London: H.M. Stationery Office, 1960.

Student Handout
Traditional Acholi Songs and Dances

Storytelling is valued as an important art by the Acholi people of Uganda in East Africa. Performing stories through dance and telling stories through song were crucial didactic methods of retelling history, defining social norms, instilling moral values, and venting individual differences. Traditional dances ranged from formal communal celebrations dramatizing the power of the chiefdom to trysts between groups of lovers. Stories ranged from the family folklore shared around the evening fire to critical oral songs performed by professional singers in conjunction with a specific audience.

Traditionally, the Acholi retold their history and defined social norms through a variety of different dances. The *otole* songs and dances involved the whole community and were performed during elaborate political occasions; by reenacting past battles and retelling the exploits of war, the *otole* dance cemented relationships between two chiefdoms. Likewise, the *bwole* dance, which was often performed at coronations, further celebrated the power of the chief and his lineage. The *orak* dance was a popular dance between young people from neighboring clans who gathered together in the hopes of meeting a future spouse. Other songs and dances celebrated the hunt, prepared warriors for battle, and commemorated the dead through funeral dirges.

In addition to this dramatic communal story dancing, stories were performed regularly before responsive and participatory audiences. An evening in the family compound often began with children's stories; gradually the tales became longer and more complicated addressing profound problems in the society. Often the storyteller proposed changes in the character and behavior of his audience and directed his lessons toward specific individuals. Although the basic tale may have been told many times before, each performance allowed the individual storyteller to recreate a unique story specific to a particular time, place, and situation.

In addition, professional singers performed oral songs and often accompanied themselves on musical instruments. These singers often integrated traditional myths into their songs and used a variety of techniques to point out undesirable traits in their listeners. The *carolok*, or proverb, was often used to allude to fact and give authority to the story's argument. The *calo*, or simile, created images that expressed exaggerated feelings ranging from admiration to disgust. Moreover, the singer often employed an apostrophe, whereby the audience was addressed and invited to respond. Often the apostrophe introduced dramatic confrontations between the singer and audience and provided a dramatic framework for the narrative. All these storytelling techniques underscored the social and moral norms that governed society. The dramatic interactive nature of the oral song emphasized responsibility to the society and allowed the individual and group to respond to the singer's criticism. Consequently, each story song was unique. Although a singer began with a basic story line, as he interacted with the audience, the performance took on a life of its own.

Source: Okumu, Charles. "The Form of Okot p'Bitek's Poetry: Literary Borrowing from Acoli Oral Traditions." *Research in African Literatures* 23.3 (Fall 1992): 54-66.

Student Handout
The Author and His Work

Okot p'Bitek was born in Uganda in 1931. His father, Opii Jebedyo, and his mother, Lacwaa Cerina, were members of the Patiko and Palaro chiefdoms in northern Acholiland and kept the traditional Acholi folklore alive although they were involved in the missionary activity of the Anglican Church Mission Society. Opii often performed story songs around the evening fire, and Lacwaa, an accomplished composer and singer, inspired her son's love of traditional oral literature.

As a bright and creative student, p'Bitek enjoyed a prestigious education. He attended Gulu High School and Kings College Budo, where he wrote and produced an opera in English titled "Acan" about a poor slave boy who could not afford to marry his beloved. He then attended a teachers' training course at the Government Training College Mbarara and taught for three years at Sir Samuel Baker's School. There he served as choirmaster and married his first wife, Anek. At the age of twenty-two, p'Bitek published his first novel in Acholi titled *Lak Tar Miyo Kinyero Wi Lobo*, or *Are Your Teeth White? Then Laugh*!

P'Bitek was an outstanding educator with diverse talents. In 1958 he was selected to play on the Ugandan National Football Team and tour Britain. He remained in England as a student and earned a certificate in Education from Bristol University, an L.L.B. degree in law from the University of Wales in Aberystwyth, and a B.Litt. degree at the Institute of Social Anthropology in Oxford. His thesis focused on the social function of myths and proverbs and analyzed the structure, style, and content of traditional Acholi songs.

In 1963, Okot p'Bitek returned to Uganda and joined the staff of the Extra-Mural Department at Makerere University. This position allowed him to expand his research on oral literature. He also instituted the annual Gulu Festival of the Arts and

married his second wife, Auma Kalina Kireng. During this time, p'Bitek wrote a song titled "Wer pa Lawino" in Acholi. The song was performed and discussed throughout the Gulu area, and in 1965 p'Bitek read a small portion of the piece at The East African Cultural Heritage conference held in Nairobi. His song about Lawino was an explosion that opened up the East African literary scene, for the traditional Acholi oral song was uniquely African and not structured after European models. Lawino's message about the value of African culture also challenged writers who looked to Europe for inspiration. P'Bitek published *Song of Lawino* in English in 1966 with the East African Publishing House; it soon became an East African classic.

At this time, p'Bitek was also appointed Director of the Uganda National Theater and Cultural Centre in Kampala. Here he focused on rediscovering the richness of the various indigenous Ugandan cultures. He established a national choir, developed a puppet theater set up a permanent art exhibition, and sponsored regular weekly dance sessions organized by the Heartbeat of African troupe. The activities culminated in a festival, which lasted eight days and coincided with the independence celebrations in October 1967. Over 7,000 people participated in the festival, which included songs, dramas, community dances, children's plays, and traditional games played in nearby villages. Soon after the festival, however, p'Bitek was abruptly dismissed from the center, most probably due to his explicit and extreme criticism of politicians in the post-colonial regime. He then took a position at Nairobi University in Kenya, where he continued to encourage local artists and organized the first Kisumu Art Festival in 1968.

He was later awarded research fellowships at the University of Iowa and the Institute of African Studies in Nairobi and taught at the University of Nairobi until 1978. P'Bitek wrote steadily throughout his career. In 1970, he published *Song of Ocol* in response to Lawino's lament. This was followed by two important scholarly texts: *African Religions and Western Scholarship*, and *Religion of the Central Luo*. In 1971 he published *Song of Malaya* and *Song of Prisoner*, which won the Kenyatta Prize for Literature. *Africa's Cultural Revolution*, a collection of essays he had written and published in various journals over the course of many years, was published in 1973. *Horn of My Love*, a collection of Acholi songs, appeared in 1974, and in 1978, he published *Hare and Hornbill*, a collection of Acholi folktales.

In addition to his work in Africa, p'Bitek also held visiting appointments at both the University of Texas at Austin and the University of Ife in Nigeria. Finally, after Idi Amin was overthrown in 1979, he returned to the Institute of Social Research at Makerere University. In February 1982, he was appointed as the first professor of creative writing in the Department of Literature. Tragically, however, five months later, p'Bitek died at his home in Kampala at the age of fifty-one. Okot p'Bitek's premature death was a shock and tremendous loss for Uganda. His creative voice never ceased singing about Africa's rich cultural heritage, and he insisted that African literature be understood as a living social art. Today his work still challenges storytellers, singers, and writers to prick needles into their audiences and sing songs that will create a just society.

Student Handout
A Selected Bibliography of Okot p'Bitek's Works

Oral Literature and Its Social Background among the Acoli and Lang'o. B. Litt. Thesis, University of Oxford, 1964.

Song of Lawino. Nairobi: East Africa Publishing House, 1966; Cleveland World Meridian Books, 1969. Published with *Song of Ocol* in Portsmouth, NH: Heinemann, 1984.

Song of Ocol. Nairobi: East Africa Publishing House, 1970. Published with *Song of Lawino* in Portsmouth, NH: Heinemann, 1984.

African Religions in Western Scholarship. Nairobi, Kenya: East African Literature Bureau, 1970.Totowa, New Jersey: Rowman and Littlefield, 1972.

Religion of the Central Luo. Nairobi, Kenya: East African Literature Bureau, 1971.

Song of a Prisoner. New York: The Third Press, Joseph Okpaku Publishing Co. Inc., 1971.

Two Songs. Nairobi, Kenya: East African Publishing House, 1971. Nairobi, Kenya: Heinemann, 1988.

Africa's Cultural Revolution. Nairobi, Kenya: Macmillan Books for Africa, 1973.

Horn of My Love. London: Heinemann Educational Books, 1974; New York: Humanities Press, 1974.

Artist, the Ruler: Essays on Art, Culture and Values. Nairobi, Kenya: Heinemann, 1986.

Lak Tar. White Teeth. Nairobi, Kenya: Heinemann, 1989.

Student Handout
Literary Techniques in *Song of Lawino*

Song of Lawino reflects the impact of colonialism. Lawino herself uses many traditional literary techniques of the Acholi song story such as similes and metaphors, traditional images and symbols, repetition, proverbs, lampoons, and apostrophes to plead her case and involve her audience. Ocol does not employ the traditional literary techniques as faithfully as Lawino as he attempts to defend himself and the destruction of traditional Africa.

Simile and Metaphor

The *calo*, or simile, exaggerates feelings ranging from admiration to disgust. Lawino uses a variety of similes and metaphors describing Clementine saying,

> The beautiful one is dead dry
> Like a stump,
> She is meatless
> Like a shell
> On a dry river bed. (p. 40)

Traditional Images

Lawino uses images derived from the traditional homestead and surrounding area to criticize Clementine saying,

> Her lips are red-hot
> like glowing charcoal,
> She resembles the wild cat
> That has dipped its mouth in blood . . . (p. 37)

Traditional Symbols

Lawino also employs symbols representing traditional life such as the horn, bull, and spear to lament her husband's loss of traditional qualities.

- horn - is not only a musical instrument but a ritual object connected with initiation into adulthood. Acholi men blew their horns as a signal of individuality and reputation. Lawino speaks of her own fame when she was the leader of the girls and her name blew like a horn.

- bull - represents bravery and respect, and Lawino combines the symbols of the bull and horn to remind Ocol of the famous ancestry from which he descends.

- spear - symbolizes the essence of manhood in the Acholi culture, for a man is never buried without his spear. Using the spear as a phallic symbol, Lawino ridicules Ocol's impotence and alienation from tradition. She insists that he must ask for a new spear to restore his manhood.

Repetition

Lawino uses repetition of phrases as she describes Ocol in love with Clementine saying:

> You kiss her on the cheek
> As white people do,
> You kiss her open-sore lips
> As white people do,
> You suck the slimy saliva
> From each others mouths
> As white people do. (p. 44)

Proverbs

The *carolok,* or proverb, was often used to allude to fact and give authority to the story's argument. The pumpkin, which refers to Acholi culture and traditional values, is a symbol repeated in the Acholi proverb that ties the entire narrative together. Throughout her song, Lawino cries:

> The pumpkin in the old homestead
> Must not be uprooted! (p. 41)

Lawino presses her point, insisting that neither Clementine nor Ocol can become white westerners with another proverb saying:

> The long-necked and graceful giraffe
> Cannot become a monkey. (p. 56)

Lampoon

The lampoon slings an insult at its target. Lawino ridicules Ocol and uses a lampoon to indict her husband saying:

> You may not feel so,
> But you behave like
> A dog of the white man!
>
> . . . The dogs of white men
> Are well trained
> and they understand English! (p. 115)

Apostrophe

Finally, the apostrophe allows the singer to address the audience and invites a response. Often the apostrophe introduces dramatic confrontations between the singer and audience and provides a dramatic framework for the narrative. Lawino concludes her song with an apostrophe pleading her case with the Acholi community, saying:

> O, my clansmen,
> Let us all cry together!
> Come,
> Let us mourn the death of my
> husband . . . (p. 116)

<u>Source</u>: Heron, G. A. *The Poetry of Okot p'Bitek*. London: Heinemann, 1976.

Student Handout
The Pumpkin in the Old Homestead Must Not Be Uprooted

1. *When two elephants fight, its the grass that suffers*. Gikuyu proverb, Kenya.
    2. *Words are easy; friendship hard*. Ganda proverb, Uganda.
3. *Endurance pierces marble*. Berber proverb, Morocco.
    4. *There is no darkness like ignorance*. Egyptian proverb.
5. *One does not become great by claiming greatness*. Xhosa proverb, Zimbabwe.
    6. *Love paralyzes the joints*. Batswana proverb, Botswana.
7. For *news of the heart, ask the face*. Hausa proverb, Nigeria.
    8. *God will not save one who breaks the ties of friendship*. Guinea.
9. A *coin in cash is better than ten on credit*. Bambara proverb, Senegal.
    10. *One falsehood spoils a thousand truths*. Asante proverb, Ghana.

Student Handout
Dramatization of *Song of Lawino* and *Song of Ocol*

Select Creative Writing Project #1 or #2. Work together with your group to create your own story song. Write the story song together, and select members of your group to perform your story song for the class. Remember the story song is interactive and should involve the entire class or the community.

Creative Writing Project #1
As a group, select Lawino or Ocol. Continue the song of your character and critique the ideas her or she represents. Make sure your satire includes the following literary techniques: similes and metaphors, traditional images and symbols, repetition, proverbs, lampoons, and apostrophes. Identify each literary technique in the margin of your story song.

Creative Writing Project #2
As a group, select a public figure, such as a politician, a Hollywood star, or a famous athlete. Write a story song satirizing this figure. Critique the ideas her or she represents and make sure your satire includes the following literary techniques: similes and metaphors, images and symbols, repetition, proverbs, lampoons, and apostrophes. Identify each literary technique in the margin of your story song.

Reading Resource
Summary and Analysis
Song of Lawino and *Song of Ocol*

Song of Lawino and *Song of Ocol* are two separate narratives written in lyrical verse about distinct fictional characters. The first song is a lament that exposes a traditional Acholi woman's conflict with her westernized husband; the second song is Ocol's response to his wife's bitter complaint. Lawino champions traditional African culture and life while Ocol defends the changes introduced by colonialism.

Song of Lawino: Sections one and two

Summary: In her introduction, Lawino explains how her arrogant husband has rejected her as primitive and inhuman and how he has replaced traditional ways with the modern, progressive, and supposedly civilized ways of the white man. Lawino has been left behind in a deserted homestead; Ocol no longer finds her attractive. Lawino reminds Ocol that he is the son of a chief; instead of hearing complaints, he should be enjoying songs of praise. Then, Lawino focuses on Clementine, the new woman with whom she shares Ocol. Clementine is a beautiful, modern woman who speaks English and aspires to be a white. When she powders her skin, she looks like she has dysentery, and her face is raw from bleaching medications. Lawino compares Tina's lips to red-hot coals and says she looks like she has been struck by lightning. Furthermore, when she sweats, Clementine looks like a guinea fowl! Lawino says Clementine is really old enough to be her mother's age mate, and she can hear her bones rattling. Nevertheless, Lawino is not afraid of a new wife, and she does not disapprove of the customs of other people; she just wants Ocol to stop insulting the family. Lawino concludes the first section by crying, "The pumpkin in the old homestead / Must not be uprooted!" (p. 41).

Analysis: The first two sections of *Song of Lawino* introduce the situation of the narrative. Lawino is a traditional wife who has been abandoned by her husband; he is interested in a modern woman. Clementine is an African woman, who like Ocol, seeks to negate her African nature and make herself white. Lawino uses similes and metaphors to paint the portrait of Clementine. The proverb at the end of this section captures the essence of her argument and is repeated throughout her lament. The pumpkin is a durable vegetable that historically sustained the Acholi people through famine. Planted with great ceremony, its flowers give the homestead the assurance of survival, and it stands as a kind of anchor for the people ensuring stability in society. Lawino will accept a second wife, and she is tolerant of other people's customs; however, she begs her husband to stop the insults and to stop uprooting the pumpkin, for ripping out the roots of tradition will destroy the homestead.

Song of Lawino: Sections three through six

Summary: Lawino celebrates the beautiful dances, songs, costumes, ornaments, and headdresses of the Acholi that boast the health, liveliness, and gracefulness of the human body in the traditional dance arenas. She rejects the obscene European ballroom dances where shameless partners hold one another in public as they kiss and suck each other's saliva. Lawino reminisces about attracting her husband with her dancing as the chief of the girls. Ocol was the son of Bull, and he loved her then; now he despises her because she does not know the western dances. Ocol says she has no ideas, and her hairstyle is old and dirty. He says the Acholi adornments are unhealthy, and she is extremely ugly in her dance costume. But Lawino is a true Acholi; she is proud of her hair and she does not want to look like a white woman. In contrast, Clementine's hair is cooked, boiled, fried, and stretched. Sometimes, she even wears the hair of a dead woman. Lawino compares herself to a graceful long-necked giraffe that cannot become an ugly monkey like

Clementine. Again, Lawino begs Ocol, "Let no one / Uproot the Pumpkin" (p. 56). Lawino continues to defend herself and her way of life, including her traditional methods of grinding grain and cooking on the three-stoned fireplace. Ocol complains that she does not know how to cook white man's food, but she is not comfortable with the primus stove, electric fires, or charcoal stoves; these contraptions are good for cooking tasteless food. She praises her own traditional kitchen with its ground flour, dried carcasses, earthen dishes of honey, grinding stones, drinking gourds, and firewood. Lawino contends that Ocol can eat white man's food if he enjoys it, but wonders why they can't allow each other the freedom to eat what they like.

 <u>Analysis</u>: In sections two through six, Lawino compares concrete elements of Acholi life such as dances, ornaments, hairstyles and food with new European ways. She continues to satirize Clementine by exaggerating the way in which she has tried to make her hair resemble a white woman's hair. The image of the pumpkin again represents the stability of tradition; however, Lawino is still open to new ideas. Lawino seems very level headed as she wonders why she and her husband can't peacefully coexist, practice the customs they enjoy, and eat what they like.

 Song of Lawino: Sections seven through eleven
 <u>Summary</u>: Lawino complains about her husband's time-ticking clock which she cannot read and which she does not need, for she knows when it is time to feed the children and time to harvest the crops. Ocol says she wastes time, and time is money. Time has become his master, but she says time is not split up into seconds and minutes. Ocol says she does not know how to keep track of the months, but Lawino sees the moon, and she knows the planting and harvesting seasons. He says she does not know the birth dates of the children, but she knows that her son was born at the beginning of the Dry Season, her daughter arrived in the middle of the rains, and the baby was born after the small pox outbreak.

 Lawino explains that she believes in Jok and not Christ. She does not understand the Catholics' Mother of the Hunchback and the Clean Ghost. The nuns are always angry, the religion teacher is always drunk, and the priests eye the young girls' breasts. Furthermore, Ocol has given all his children Christian names, including his illegitimate sons. Even though his own Christian name is too difficult for her to pronounce, he wants her to take a Christian name. None of these names have any meaning for Lawino.

 Lawino also complains that the missionaries and the teachers cannot answer her questions about the creation of the world. Where did the Hunchback find the clay for molding the earth? All of the teachers hate questions. Ocol went to the university, but if you ask him a question, he is insulted. He says Acholi is a primitive language. Lawino also explains that her father was a well-known diviner priest, and her mother helped infertile women conceive, but Ocol says the old relatives have diseases and even insults his own mother. He has no confidence in the wisdom of the Acholi and condemns the traditional priests and herbalists. He calls their prayers superstitious and their charms useless. He even threatens to cut down the sacred tree in his father's homestead. Lawino says he must respect his father and mother. If there are unnatural troubles in the homestead, it is because the ancestors are angry. Lawino concludes that none of the western doctors, traditional diviners, or Acholi herbalists can stave off death.

 Finally, Lawino says that even though Ocol is a leader of the Democratic Party, politics will change nothing. Ocol hates his brother who belongs to the Congress Party, but if Ocol dies, his brother will still inherit his property and children, and she will become his brother's second wife. Lawino questions the new politics of independence that promise to unite the Acholi, the Lango, the Madi, the Lugbara, the Alur, the Iteso, the Baganda, the Banyankole, and the Banyoro peoples with the Jo-pa-Dhola and the Toro peoples overnight in one independent and peaceful Uganda. Ocol claims he is the only truthful politician, but she questions how the Democratic party differs from the Congress Party.

Analysis: Lawino moves from satirizing the concrete ideas of hairstyles and food to satirizing more abstract concepts of westernized life such as time, Christianity, mission education, western medicine, and the new politics of independence in these sections. She implies that she understands time and the cycle of life because she is aware of her menstrual cycles. She satirizes Christians who drink human blood from a sacrificial altar and the priests and ministers who, like Ocol, are unable to answer her philosophical questions by claiming that the Acholi language is inadequate for expressing metaphysical concepts. She worships the traditional Acholi Creator God named Jok, and she refers to the Christians' God as the Hunchback. Rubanga is the name of the Christian God in the Luo language. For the Acholi people, this is also the name of the ghost that causes tuberculosis of the spine; hence, the name Hunchback. (See note p. 94.) Lawino also quarrels with Ocol over hygiene and western medicine and finds his disdain for traditional diviners, priests, and healers incomprehensible. She seems to be evenhanded when she says that neither western doctors nor traditional healers can stop death. Finally, Lawino claims that the new independence will not change social norms among the Acholi. Diverse nations cannot be united overnight, and there is really little to distinguish the various political parties that have sprung up.

Song of Lawino: Sections twelve through thirteen

Summary: Finally, Lawino appeals to her clansmen and refers to her husband as a prince of the ancient chiefdom who has lost his mind through western education. He is worthless, for his manhood is destroyed; his testicles have been smashed with heavy books in the colonial oppressor's classroom. Yet, Lawino still holds out hope for Ocol's recovery. Perhaps eating the traditional Malakwang dish may help him. If he removes his dark glasses, perhaps, the scales will fall from his eyes. He is the son of the Bull, a brave and respected leader, and he can still be purified by begging for forgiveness and receiving a new spear symbolizing renewed sexual prowess and strength. Then he will be freed from his emasculation at the hands of the white man. As his first wife, the one who loves him and cares for him like a mother, Lawino begs Ocol to let her dance for him once more and show him the richness of African life. She begs her husband to love her again and to refrain from uprooting the life-giving pumpkin of tradition.

Analysis: Although Lawino's song is addressed to her husband, Ocol, she takes her dilemma to the center of the Acholi compound and appeals to her clansmen. She asks the community and the reader to sympathize with her and affirm her belief in the value of traditional life. She sums up her argument with extended metaphors comparing western education to the impotency of Ocol; she extends, and again refers to the traditional pumpkin in her plea.

Song of Ocol

Summary: Ocol will have none of it! He tells Lawino to shut up, pack her things, and go. He says her song is like rotting buffalo meat, and her pumpkin is rotting too because it is filled with a thousand beetles. Ocol will make a compost heap out of the pumpkin and all the other native vegetables. He will even uproot the trees demarcating the lands of the various Acholi clans. After ordering his houseboy to cleanse his home upon Lawino's departure, he says Africa is nothing but deep unfathomable darkness. In despair, he wonders why he was born black. He vows to destroy all forms of tradition. All ancient taboos will be smashed, all sacred trees will be demolished, and the traditional leaders of Africa will be destroyed. Village poets, musicians, dancers, and storytellers will be disbanded, and teachers of African history will be shunned. African statesmen will be thrown into jail; Ocol will not look back to the blackness of his past.

Everything connected with traditional life must be destroyed. Ocol begs African women to smash their water pots and the chains of slavery, and he rants about the various ethnic groups of East Africa. He disparages all African people ranging from the elders of Karamojong to the mighty warriors of Maasailand, claiming that these ignorant men simply defend barren empires that are closed to progress. He says the new order will not only put the tradition Maasai in western clothes in order to end twenty-five thousand years of nakedness, but it will dynamite their ochre quarries. Furthermore, he promises that as the elder guardians of tradition are arrested, only a select few young people will be invited into the new Africa.

In contrast to these ignorant people, Ocol he has read Econ. at Makerere (p. 138) and spent years in detention planning the revolution. He asks the traditional people how they contributed to *Uhuru*. He claims the leaders need their nice houses in the town and the country and will travel in his Merc. to see his properties. (p. 141) It is not his fault that the primitive people sleep in leaky huts. He is not responsible for their poverty and ignorance, and he reminds the people that no one said the grass would turn to gold in the villages at the time of *Uhuru*. Finally, Ocol asks what *Uhuru* means to primitive people anyway.

Ocol denounces Africa. He vows that every tree sacred to every African ethnic group will be uprooted; he promises that great mountains like Kilimanjaro will be blown up, and the mighty waters of the Nile will be diverted into the Indian Ocean. The traditional village will be swept away by civilization. As he sings the funeral dirge of the old homestead, he says there are two alternatives for the people: enter the new city gate or hang themselves. Ocol salutes the ministers of a new order—the new Head of State, the black bishop, the fat black capitalists, and all the architects and engineers of a modern nation. He questions *Mwalimu* Nyerere's *Ujamaa* and Leopold Senghor's dream of African Socialism. As concrete and steel underpin the new African city, monuments will be erected to honor the butchers of Africa including Leopold of Belgium, and streets will commemorate those great explorers of African life such as David Livingstone and Henry Stanley. No streets will be named after Mansa, the leader of the ancient empire of Mali. Ocol's final wish is that the great chiefs and kings of Africa's ancient nations such as the Kings of Ghana rot in their graves. The proud rulers of Monomatapa and the great Shaka Zulu will be forgotten. He shakes his head and wonders what kind of a poem one could possibly write for these, the vanquished peoples of the earth.

Analysis: Ocol's narrative is shorter and in direct response to Lawino's lament; therefore, it cannot stand on its own. Ocol is a representation of the new post-colonial elite. He has studied Economics at Makerere University and has been rewarded for his involvement in the revolution with multiple properties that he surveys by jumping into his Merc., or his Mercedes. Ocol uses satirical similes to reject Lawino's song. He claims her lament is a solitary cry without a chorus and compares it to the confused death cry of a butchered ram. He compares her song to rotting buffalo meat abandoned by poachers to provide a feast for pests and scavengers like pus-filled maggots, bald-headed vultures, and snarling hyenas. Furthermore, he clearly states that the pumpkin of tradition will not only be uprooted; it will be obliterated! He refers to *Uhuru*, the Swahili word for freedom or independence, and he disparages leaders of modern and ancient African nations. He disdains President Julius Nyerere of Tanzania and his *Ujamaa*, or Tanzanian socialism and Leopold Senghor's dream of a United Africa. He wishes to forget the ancient leaders of Ghana and Mansa Musa of ancient Mali, as well as the Monomatapa rulers of southern Africa and Shaka Zulu of South Africa.

Basically, Ocol rejects Lawino's song about tradition, reveals his disdain of Africa and himself, ridicules the peoples of Africa and their leaders, and looks to other neo-colonial elites for a new way of life. His goal is to negate all that is African.

Overall Analysis:

The character of Lawino may be a ficitionalization of Okot p'Bitek's mother, the great storyteller Lacwaa Cerina. Regardless of whether Lawino was inspired by a real person or not, she has provoked much debate in literary circles. Is Lawino credible? Does she truly represent the women of East Africa, or is she a caricature, a gross exaggeration of the true African woman? Is Lawino a portrait of a pathetic, stupid wife scorned by her progressive husband? Is she blindly clutching the past and offering ridiculous comparisons between Acholi customs and western changes? Are there sections where Lawino appears foolish? How is the reader to understand these sections? Has Okot p'Bitek effectively captured the female voice, or is his song an abomination? What about Ocol who is berated for uprooting the traditions of the Acholi people? By adopting the values of the colonial oppressors and shunning traditional life, has he betrayed his community and disgraced his ancestors? Has Ocol truly lost his manhood in a forest of white men's books, or is he pursuing a better life? How does the reader feel about Lawino as she pleads with Ocol to come back to his senses, to recognize the value of traditional life, and to love her again?

It seems as if both Lawino and Ocol are like caricatures in a melodrama even though each song echoes the traditional Acholi oral song performance. Although Lawino and Ocol defend different ways of life, the reader wonders if they simultaneously deny themselves. Ocol not only detests Lawino, who can neither read nor write, but he despises Africa and all that is African. Tantamount to his betrayal of his people, he despises himself and deplores the very color of his own skin. He praises the colonial imperialists who rape Africa, and he is proud to be a rich neo-colonial elite who takes absolutely no responsibility for improving the economic plight of the rural peasant. Does Lawino likewise simultaneously defend and detest herself and her way of life?

Furthermore, the reader must question whether the exchange between Lawino and Ocol is actually a dialogue between tradition and change. If so, where does the author, Okot p'Bitek, stand in the debate? As an educated, westernized Acholi writing shortly after Uganda gained her independence, which character does he use as his spokesperson—Lawino or Ocol? Does p'Bitek believe that the change represented by Ocol will destroy traditional Acholi life? Does the author wish to live in the homestead with Lawino?

List of Works Consulted

Atkinson, Ronald. *The Roots of Ethnicity: The Origins of the Acholi of Uganda before 1800*. Philadelphia: University of Pennsylvania Press, 1994.

Bodunde, Charles A. "Oral Traditions and Modern Poetry: Okot p'Bitek's *Song of Lawino* and Okigbo's *Labyrinths*." *Orature in African Literature Today*. Ed. E. D. Jones. Trenton, NJ: Africa World Press, 1992. 24-34.

Cook, David and David Rubadiri, eds. *Poems from East Africa*. Portsmouth, NH: Heinemann, 1992.

Duerden, Dennis, ed. "Okot p'Bitek." *African Writers Talking*. New York: Africana Publishing Corporation, 1972. 149-155.

Girling, F. K. *The Acholi of Uganda*. London: H.M. Stationery Office, 1960.

Heron, G. A. *The Poetry of Okot p'Bitek*. London: Heinemann, 1976.

---. "Introduction." *Song of Lawino Song of Ocol*. Okot p'Bitek. London: Heinemann, 1984. 1-33.

Kerr, David. *African Popular Theatre*. Portsmouth, NH: Heinemann, 1995.

Knappert, Jan. *The A-Z of African Proverbs*. London: Karnak House, 1989.

Lindfords, Bernth. "The Songs of Okot p'Bitek." *Popular Literature in Africa*. Trenton, NJ: Africa World Press, 1991. 61-77.

Ngara, Emmanuel. "Cultural Nationalism and Form in Okot p'Bitek." *Ideology and Form in African Poetry*. Portsmouth, NH: Heinemann, 1990. 60-76.

Okumu, Charles. "The Form of Okot p'Bitek's Poetry: Literary Borrowing from Acoli Oral Traditions." *Research in African Literatures* 23.3 (Fall 1992): 54-66.

Ofuani, Ogo. "Old Wine in New Skins? An Exploratory Review of Okot p'Bitek's *White Teeth: A Novel*." *Research in African Literatures* 27.2 (Summer 1996): 185-193.

---. "The Poet as Self-Critic: Repercussions of Textual Revisions in Okot p'Bitek's *Song of Ocol*." *Research in African Literatures* 25.4 (Winter 1994): 159-176.

Senanu, K. D. and T. Vincent, eds. *A Selection of African Poetry*. London: Longman, 1988,

CHAPTER SEVEN

―――

A Grain of Wheat
An East African Novel about Revolution and New Life
by Ngugi wa Thiong'o

A Grain of Wheat by Ngugi wa Thiong'o commemorates the birth of independent Kenya and focuses on national and personal revolution. This complex psychological novel presents the freedom struggle as part of the great cycle of life, and independence is viewed through the prism of the courage, mixed loyalties, treachery, and redemption of five freedom fighters. The psychological complexities of the characters are explored in terms of personal catharsis involving commitment, betrayal, and reconciliation. This movement reflects the birth of the new nation and tentatively heralds the dawn of a new age. The author challenges his readers to experience the profound revolutionary life cycle of birth, life, death, and rebirth and to empathize with the passion of a national freedom struggle in colonial Africa.

Lessons

Lesson One Introduction
East Africa and the History of the Gikuyu People

Objectives:

1. Students will identify East Africa by locating Kenya, Tanzania, Uganda, Burundi, and Rwanda.
2. Students will identify salient geographical features of East Africa by locating:
   - Snow-capped Mt. Kilamanjaro on the equator,
   - Mount Kenya in the area inhabited by the Gikuyu people,
   - the Serengeti Plain in Tanzania and Kenya, and
   - Lake Victoria, the source of the Nile River
3. Students will interpret the mythical origins of the Gikuyu people of Kenya after reading the creation myth of "Gikuyu and Mumbi" orally.
4. Students will outline the history of the African people featured in this novel by identifying the major historical phases of the Gikuyu people.

Materials:

1. Classroom World Map
2. Student Handout: Map of Africa, Chapter Two: Africa Overview of the Continent
3. Student Handout: Gikuyu and Mumbi: The Gikuyu Creation Myth
4. Teacher Resource: Historical Highlights of the Gikuyu People

Procedure:

1. Begin with patriotic music and a symbol of the American Revolution. Use the American flag to begin a discussion of revolution and freedom. Discuss the Americans' motivation for revolting against England in the 18th century. Refer to the Stamp Act and the Boston Tea Party.
2. Explain that *A Grain of Wheat* is about revolution in Kenya, East Africa, in the 20th century. The goals of the Kenyan freedom fighters were the same as the goals of the Americans who fought for independence from England.
3. Using a wall map, compare the size of two continents: Africa and Europe. Compare Africa with the United States. Emphasize that the United States is a *country* that would fit into the *continent* of Africa 3½ times. Africa is made up of over fifty independent countries.
4. Distribute Student Handout: Map of Africa. Ask the students to locate Kenya, Tanzania, Uganda, Burundi, and Rwanda; these countries comprise East Africa. Draw a peak-shaped mountain on the board and ask the students if they can identify a snow-capped mountain on the equator. This is Kilimanjaro, which is located in Tanzania. Introduce Mt. Kenya in Kenya as the sacred mountain of the Gikuyu people.
5. Discuss the Serengeti Plain, the wildlife habitat of the great African lions, giraffes, zebras, elephants, hippos, hyenas, wildebeasts, hippos, impalas, and flamingos.
6. Discuss Lake Victoria, one of the largest lakes in the world and the source of the Nile, the only river in the world that flows north.
7. Explain that the Gikuyu people are one of the largest ethnic groups in Kenya. Other people groups include the Masai, the Luo, and the Turkana, to name a few. The Gikuyu were the major force behind the fight for Kenyan independence. Their main motivation was to regain the land they believed had been given to the founder of their people by God. God is known as *Mungu* in Swahili, and *Murungu* or *Ngai* in the Kikuyu language. Both Gikuyu and Kikuyu are pronounced *Kee-koo-yoo*; Gikuyu refers to the people; Kikuyu refers to the language.

8. Distribute <u>Student Handout: Gikuyu and Mumbi</u>. This myth is part of the oral history and tradition of the people. Have the students read the myth orally, as it would have been told in East Africa. In the discussion, emphasize that Gikuyu and Mumbi are the ancestors of the Gikuyu; ask the students to interpret the myth. Students may compare the myth to other creation stories.

9. Inform students of important events and periods in the history of the Gikuyu people. Refer to <u>Teacher Resource: Historical Highlights of the Gikuyu People</u>.

10. Explain that *A Grain of Wheat* is a novel that takes place during the last five days before the Mau Mau freedom fighters win independence from Britain. The first section of the novel contains flashbacks that introduce the following main characters:

    - Kihika   dead Mau Mau freedom fighter, Kenya's Moses; martyr for the revolution
    - Mumbi   Kihika's sister, married to Gikonyo
    - Gikonyo   a Mau Mau freedom fighter; married to Kihika's sister
    - Karanja   assistant to the Thompsons
    - Mugo   a nervous Mau Mau freedom fighter

Assessment:

Ask students to think about how the Gikuyu creation myth might be related to the freedom struggle.

Reading Assignment:

A Grain of Wheat, Chapters 1-3, pages 1-32.

Thought Questions:

1. Describe Mugo's relationship with his aunt.
2. Why do you think Kihika is considered Kenya's Moses?
3. What is the purpose of the flashback in the second chapter?
4. I Corinthians 15:36 reads: "Thou fool, that which thou sowest is not quickened, except it die. And that which thou sowest, thou sowest not that body that shall be, but bare grain, it may chance of wheat, or of some other grain." How is this scripture passage related to the novel? What does Ngugi imply when he states that a seed must fall to the ground and die before it lives?
5. Create three questions about aspects of the reading that you do not clearly understand.

Lesson Two
The Author, Character, and Plot Development

Objectives:

1. Students will understand the structure of the novel by discussing the use of literary techniques such as flashbacks and monologues.
2. Students will become familiar with the author Ngugi wa Thiong'o by reviewing his life and work.

Materials:

1. Reading Resource: Summary and Analysis: Chapters 1-3
2. Student Handout: The Author and His Work
3. Student Handout: Major and Minor Characters
4. Teacher Resource: Major Characters
5. Teacher Resource: Minor Characters

Procedure:

1. Discuss the questions for chapters 1-3. Refer to <u>Summary and Analysis: Chapters 1-3</u>.
2. Discuss the relationship of the scripture passage from I Corinthians 15:36 to the novel. "Thou fool, that which thou sowest is not quickened, except it die. And that which thou sowest, thou sowest not that body that shall be, but bare grain, it may chance of wheat, or of some other grain." What does Ngugi imply when he states that a seed must fall to the ground and die before it lives?
3. Discuss the issues of martyrdom and sacrifice as well as other historical movements where freedom demanded death. Recall the American Revolution and the great orator Patrick Henry who cried, "Give me Liberty or Give me Death!" Or, discuss the civil rights movement spearheaded by Martin Luther King, Jr., who foretold his own death.
4. Review significant information revealed about each of the five main characters through flashbacks and monologues.
5. Distribute <u>Student Handout: The Author and His Work</u> and discuss the author's life and work. Emphasize the writer's personal and professional freedom struggles.

Assessment:

1. Ask the students to brainstorm a list of ideas indicating why the author has employed the literary techniques of flashbacks and monologues.
2. Distribute <u>Student Handout: Major and Minor Characters</u> and ask students to begin to identify characters. Refer to <u>Teacher Resource: Major Characters and Minor Characters</u>.

Reading Assignment:

A Grain of Wheat, Chapters 4-6, pages 33-69.

Thought Questions:

1. Describe the attitudes of the Thompsons and Dr. Lynd toward the people of East Africa.
2. Describe Dr. Lynd's relationship with her houseboy and dog. What is the significance of Dr. Lynd's vicious dog?
3. At this point in the novel, how are each of the main characters, Mugo, Mumbi, Gikonyo, and Karanja, related to Kihika?

Lesson Three
The Cycle of Life

Objectives:

1. Students will identify and describe the *mbwa kali* culture of the white settlers in Kenya by analyzing the symbolism of Dr. Lynd's dogs.
2. Students will trace the life cycle by identifying the salient elements of childhood, adulthood, elderhood, death, and life after death through the major phases of the traditional Gikuyu life cycle.
3. Students will relate the cycle of life to the independence struggle in Kenya by discussing the preliminary phases of individual freedom fighters as they are born into the revolution, become mature fighters, and in some cases die in order to bring about the new life of freedom.

Materials:

1. Student Handout: Background on the Cycle of Life
2. Student Handout: The Life Cycle Chart
3. Student Handout: Character and Plot Development
4. Teacher Resource: Character and Plot Development
5. Reading Resource: Summary and Analysis: Chapters 4-6

Procedure:

1. Discuss the thought questions for Chapters 4-6 and the *mbwa kali* culture of the white settlers. Refer to Summary and Analysis: Chapters 4-6.
2. Distribute Student Handout: Background on the Cycle of Life. Draw the life cycle on the board and discuss each phase of the traditional Gikuyu life cycle.
3. Through discussion, have students relate the cycle of life to the independence struggle in Kenya by identifying the preliminary phases the various freedom fighters pass through as they are born into the revolution, become mature fighters, and in some cases die in order to bring about the new life of freedom. Use Student Handout: The Life Cycle Chart to facilitate discussion.

Assessment:

Fill in the phases of the life cycle in the Mau Mau struggle for Kihika on Student Handout: Character and Plot Development. Refer to Teacher Resource: Character and Plot Development for possible ideas and interpretations.

Reading Assignment:

A Grain of Wheat, Chapter 7, pages 70-121

Thought Questions:

1. List five facts you have learned about the following characters through flashbacks or monologues.
   - Kihika
   - Gikonyo
   - Mumbi
   - Karanja
2. List five things you would like to know about each of the four characters.

Lesson Four
Characterization and Plot Development

Objectives:

1. Students will begin to analyze the complex relationships between Gikonyo, Karanja, and Mumbi by discussing the significance of the foot race.
2. Students will continue to understand the structure of the novel by discussing the purpose of literary techniques such as flashbacks and monologues.
3. Students will analyze the motives of the main characters, Mugo, Mumbi, Gikonyo, and Karanja in the struggle for independence by dramatizing each character's relationship to Kihika.

Materials:

1. Student Handout: Psychological Complexities: Social and Personal Relationships
2. Teacher Resource: Psychological Complexities: Social and Personal Relationships
3. Student Handout: *Uhuru* Day Speech
4. Reading Resource: Summary and Analysis: Chapter 7

Procedure:

1. Discuss the thought questions for chapter 7. Refer to Summary and Analysis: Chapter 7.
2. Review the discussion of Student Handout: The Life Cycle Chart and I Corinthians 15:36. "Thou fool, that which thou sowest is not quickened, except it die. And that which thou sowest, thou sowest not that body that shall be, but bare grain, it may chance of wheat, or of some other grain." In what ways is Kihika a grain of wheat?
3. Review the life cycle of Kihika in the Mau Mau freedom struggle by referring to the Student Handout: Character and Plot Development. Analyze how the four main living characters were born into the struggle for independence.
4. Divide the class into four or more groups and distribute Student Handout: Psychological Complexities: Social and Personal Relationships. Explain that the main characters Mugo, Mumbi, Gikonyo, and Karanja remember and relate to the famous freedom fighter Kihika, who is deceased. The four main characters also relate to one another. Ask each group to focus on one character: Mugo, Mumbi, Gikonyo, or Karanja. Have students identify at least five quotes in the text that indicate how the character feels about the freedom struggle and Kihika. Ask students to discuss the quotes within their group and list the page numbers of the significant quotes on the lines under their character on the Student Handout: Psychological Complexities: Social and Personal Relationships. Refer to Teacher Resource: Psychological Complexities: Social and Personal Relationships. Note that this resource includes references through the end of the novel.
5. Distribute Student Handout: *Uhuru* Day Speech. Students should develop soliloquies from the various characters' points of view.
6. Allow students to work cooperatively for 15 to 20 minutes.

Assessment:

Ask each group to read their *Uhuru* Day speeches aloud and refer to significant quotes by page numbers if applicable. The class should identify which character has written the speech.

Reading Assignment:

A Grain of Wheat, Chapters 8-11, pages 122-166

Thought Questions:

1. Who is Kenya's Moses? Is it Mugo, Kihika, or Kenyatta? Support your point.
2. Explain the famous brutal beatings at Rira. How are these beatings related to Mugo?
3. Why do you think Mumbi succumbs to Karanja's overtures?
4. At this point in the story, who do you think betrayed Kihika? Prove your point.
5. What are the possible motivations for the traitor who betrayed Kihika?
6. Create three questions about aspects of the reading that you do not clearly understand.

Lesson Five
The Dimensions of Betrayal

Objectives:

1. Students will analyze the love, conflict, commitment, and betrayal experienced by main characters by charting the feelings of Mumbi and Gikonyo for one another; the feelings of Mumbi and Karanja for one another, and the feelings of Mumbi and Mugo for one another.

2. Students will describe the experience of betrayal for Mugo, Mumbi, Gikonyo, and Karanja and predict a resolution to the burden of guilt by suggesting a means of reconciliation or by projecting a symbol of reconciliation for each character.

3. Students will choose a character and begin to build a case for the character's innocence or guilt in betraying a loved one or the freedom movement.

Materials:

1. Student Handout: Psychological Complexities: Social and Personal Relationships
2. Teacher Resource: Psychological Complexities: Social and Personal Relationships
3. Reading Resource: Summary and Analysis: Chapters 8-11

Procedure:

1. Discuss thought questions for Chapters 8-11. Refer to <u>Summary and Analysis: Chapters 8-11.</u>

2. Through discussion, analyze the love, conflict, commitment, and betrayal experienced by the main characters by charting their feelings. Analyze the following:
    *   the feelings of Mumbi and Gikonyo for one another.
    *   the feelings of Mumbi and Karanja for one another
    *   the feelings of Mumbi and Mugo for one another

3. Refer to <u>Student Handout Psychological Complexities: Social and Personal Relationships and Teacher Resource: Psychological Complexities: Social and Personal Relationships</u>. Ask students from various character groups to suggest significant quotes and page numbers that identify how the characters feel about the freedom struggle and one another.

4. Ask students to describe the experience of betrayal for Mugo, Mumbi, Gikonyo, and Karanja and predict a resolution to each character's burden of guilt.

5. Divide students into small groups. Ask them to choose a different character and begin to build a case for the character's innocence or guilt in betraying a loved one or the freedom movement. Focus on Mumbi as the central female figure vis-a-vis the three male characters.

6. Ask students to suggest an ending to the novel that results in reconciliation or a symbol of reconciliation for each character. This may be done as a class, individually, or in small groups.

Assessment:

Ask student groups to orally provide one salient point proving the innocence or guilt of the character for whom they have begun to build a case.

Reading Assignment:

A Grain of Wheat, Chapters 12-13, pages 167-200

Thought Questions:

1. Why does Gikonyo quarrel with Mumbi now? Why is he so upset?
2. Why did Mugo think Kihika was mad, and why did he hate Kihika so desperately?
3. List five things you would like to know about the betrayal of one of the characters.

Lesson Six
Commitment

Objectives:

1. Students will analyze the commitment of each of the four main characters and Kihika by charting their movement through the traditional Gikuyu life cycle as it relates to the freedom struggle.

2. Students will analyze the reasons why each of the main characters failed or died to the struggle by describing the reasons why they betrayed the freedom struggle, someone they loved, or themselves.

3. Students will continue to build a case for one character's innocence or guilt in betraying a loved one or the freedom movement.

Materials:

1. Student Handout: Psychological Complexities: Social and Personal Relationships
2. Teacher Resource: Psychological Complexities: Social and Personal Relationships
3. Student Handout: Character and Plot Development
4. Teacher Resource: Character and Plot Development
5. Reading Resource: Summary and Analysis: Chapters 12-13

Procedure:

1. Discuss the thought questions for Chapters 12-13.

2. Through discussion analyze the movement of each of the four main characters and Kihika by charting their growth through the traditional Gikuyu life cycle. Relate the life cycle to the Mau Mau freedom struggle. Refer to Student Handout: Character and Plot Development and Teacher Resource: Character and Plot Development and Summary and Analysis: Chapters 12-13. Review how each character was born into the struggle and grew. Each character had a death experience: Kihika literally died; Mugo died to the struggle when he betrayed Kihika; Mumbi died to love when she betrayed Gikonyo; Gikonyo died politically and personally when he confessed the oath and heaped disdain upon Mumbi. Perhaps Karanja was never alive in the freedom struggle because he sided with the white settlers. He may be the only character that does not experience rebirth and new life. Have students fill in the Student Handout: Character and Plot Development.

3. Ask the students to write four journal entries from the viewpoints of Mumbi, Mugo, Gikonyo, and Karanja. Each entry should describe: a) each character's commitment to the freedom struggle; b) each character's commitment to those he/she loves; c) each character's commitment to him or her self.

Assessment:

1. Ask students to share their reflections on commitment in groups or with the whole class and continue to debate the innocence or guilt of the main characters in betraying a loved one or the freedom movement.

2. Ask students to suggest symbols of reconciliation for each one of the main characters. How does each symbol relate to the character's journey through death into new life?

Reading Assignment:

A Grain of Wheat, Chapters 14-Harambee, pages 203-247.

Thought Questions:

1. Do you think Mugo should have done what he did at the *Uhuru* celebration? Did he spoil the ceremony and once again put his personal moral dilemma before the freedom struggle? Why? Support your point.

2. Gikonyo has spurned Mumbi since his return. What makes him move toward reconciliation and love?

3. What is the symbolism of the stool Gikonyo plans to carve for Mumbi? Support your point.

4. Do you think Mumbi will return to Gikonyo's home? Why or why not?

5. Do you see Mugo as a hero or a traitor? Support your viewpoint.

6. What questions do you have about the ending of the novel?

Lesson Seven
Reconciliation

Objectives:

1. Students will complete analyzing the rebirth of each of the four main characters and Kihika by charting their movement through the traditional Gikuyu life cycle as it relates to the Mau Mau freedom struggle.
2. Students will analyze the redemptive quality of reconciliation by comparing seeds of new life, such as forgiveness and love, with seeds of destruction, such as guilt and betrayal.
3. Students will put each main character on trial and decide the character's guilt or innocence.
4. Students will choose one main character and review the following:
    *   the character's motivation for participating in the freedom struggle
    *   the failure to meet his or her ideals and the ensuing guilt
    *   the individual's betrayal of the Mau Mau freedom struggle and loved ones
    *   the betrayal of the individual by other characters in the novel
    *   the redemption of failure and guilt through forgiveness and love
    *   the movement from death into new life

Materials:

1. Student Handout: Character and Plot Development
2. Teacher Resource: Character and Plot Development
3. Reading Resource: Summary and Analysis: Chapters 14-Harambee
4. Student Handout: Essay: The Dimensions of Betrayal and Reconciliation

Procedure:

1. Discuss the thought questions for Chapters 14-Harambee.
2. Analyze the movement of each of the four main characters and Kihika from death to rebirth and new life. Relate the life cycle to the Mau Mau freedom struggle and complete Student Handout: Character and Plot Development. Refer to Teacher Resource: Character and Plot Development and Summary and Analysis: Chapters 14-Harambee. Analyze how each character was reborn into new life. Kihika was the grain of wheat; Mugo confesses and acts as the catalyst for others to face their guilt; Mumbi finds strength in her independence, and Gikonyo seeks reconciliation and love. Does Karanja experience rebirth?
3. Ask students to form four groups. Assign each group one of the main characters: Mumbi, Gikonyo, Karanja, and Mugo. Ask each small group to divide in half. One half will prepare the defense of the character, and the other half will prepare the prosecution's case against the character. Allow the students 15 to 20 minutes to prepare their cases.
4. Have each group bring their character to trial. One member of the group may take the character's part. The rest of the class can serve as Wambui, General R., Lt. Konia and the villagers. Ask the class to judge the crimes of each character.

Assessment: Writing Assignment

Ask the students to choose one main character in *A Grain of Wheat* and discuss his or her betrayal of the freedom struggle. Weigh the ideals of the freedom struggle with the character's efforts to meet the demands of the Mau Mau. Analyze the redemptive quality of reconciliation by comparing the seeds of new life such as forgiveness and love with the seeds of destruction such as failure, guilt, and betrayal. Ask students to discuss the points listed in Student Handout: Essay: The Dimensions of Betrayal and Reconciliation and give examples to support their arguments.

Student Handout
Gikuyu and Mumbi: The Gikuyu Creation Myth

According to the oral traditions of the descendants of Gikuyu and Mumbi . . . in the beginning of time, a dense mist covered East Africa and the earth quivered in creation. Then, God, the divider of the universe, descended to his seat upon the dazzling snow-capped mountain known as Mt. Kenya. From that day on, the mountain became God's dwelling place and was revered as sacred.

Then God led Gikuyu, the father of the Gikuyu nation, to the misty peaks of the sacred mountain. Pointing out the beauty of the land lying below God said: "You shall carve your inheritance from this land. It shall belong to you and your children's children. Pass this land from generation to generation until the end of time."

And so it was. The Gikuyu people were given the beautiful land of rivers and ridges, hills, valleys, and forests filled with all God's creatures and all the gifts of nature. As the morning sun broke through the mist, Gikuyu left the mountain top and descended to a grove of sacred fig trees. There he found the most beautiful woman on earth. Taking her to be his wife, he named her Mumbi, the molder of the tribe.

From the sacred Mukuyu grove, Gikuyu took his name. Together, Gikuyu and Mumbi built a home and gave birth to nine daughters who grew to be very beautiful. The daughters of Mumbi prospered as they cultivated the rich earth and produced millet, sugar cane, and yams. In the heat of the midday sun, the daughters of Mumbi led their father's flocks to watering holes to drink from crystal clear streams that ran down the hills and valleys. And in the evening, when the flocks came home from grazing, the sound of pounding pestles filled the air. The voices of the nine beautiful daughters of Mumbi, rich with the melody of grinding grain, floated over the trees and onto the plains.

After many moons had passed, however, the nine beautiful daughters grew into nine beautiful women who rippled with the ripeness of the full moon. Their eyes twinkled like stars in the moonlight, while their breasts stood as proud as the dazzling peaks of Mt. Kenya. The beautiful daughters' enchanting laughter was like a chorus of birds on the plain, and their milky teeth glittered like the snow on Mt. Kilamanjaro. And when Mumbi's beautiful daughters walked, the melody of the beads around their waists beat an enchanting rhythm in the deep forest.

But with the passing of every full moon, the beautiful daughters of Mumbi felt the flow of the rising tide in their wombs. They beseeched their parents: "For many seasons you have cared for us, but we now wish to have homes of our own so that your names may be whispered from generation to generation."

So Gikuyu and Mumbi searched their hearts as they walked the breath of the land. At last, in despair, Gikuyu fell upon his knees. Raising his face to Mt. Kenya, he called upon God to bless his daughters with husbands. God heard Gikuyu's plea and commanded him to make a sacrifice at the foot of the sacred Mugumo tree.

The ancient Mugumo tree stood in the center of the land. No one was permitted to cut down or break any branch from this tree, for God lived nearby. No one was permitted to clear any of the bush around this tree, and any creature who took sanctuary at the foot of the tree was safe in the hands of God.

Gikuyu did as his creator commanded. He bought a lamb, a kid, and nine burning sticks, each stick being the length of one of his daughter's shadows. Sacrificing the lamb and the kid, Gikuyu sprinkled blood and fat onto the trunk of the sacred tree. At the foot of the tree Gikuyu lit a fire with the nine burning sticks, and as the fat of the sacrifice crackled in the fire and the roaring flames rose into the sky, he called out to God saying: "We have come to beseech you for rain and for life. Say now that we may have new life."

As Gikuyu continued to chant this invocation, out of the fire came nine young men whose backs were firm and strong like the trunk of the mugumo tree. When Gikuyu saw the nine men, he lifted his arms in supplication giving thanks and praise to God for answering him.

From his seat of mystery on Mt. Kenya, God's voice rumbled like thunder and the pregnant clouds showered the blessings of rain upon the earth. The nine men were welcomed into Gikuyu's homestead and Mumbi's beautiful daughters wept with joy, for now they would be blessed with many children. A ram was killed for the evening meal while the millet simmered over a wood fire and the men were taken to a nearby stream to wash their tired limbs.

In the heat of the night, as the stars twinkled like a thousand flames, the nine handsome young men and Mumbi's beautiful daughters told tales and sang around the fire. The nine handsome young men could not resist the alluring beauty of Mumbi's daughters or the kindness and generosity of Gikuyu. Early the next morning each young man asked Gikuyu and Mumbi for one of the beautiful daughters in marriage.

Gikuyu blessed the marriages. Each daughter prepared her own home and gave birth to many children. The house of Mumbi and Gikuyu prospered, and its fame spread throughout the hills and valleys of East Africa. When Gikuyu and Mumbi died, each daughter called together all her descendants forming one clan under her own name.

In this way, the nine full clans of the Gikuyu people were formed. These nine clans merged together in unity, kinship, and solidarity. This group was given the ancestral name of the House of Mumbi, and to this day, when the Gikuyu people call upon God, their creator, they turn their faces to the top of the snow-capped mountain, the sacred Mt. Kenya.

Source:
This is the oral history of the Gikuyu people. This version of the myth is adapted from *Nyumba ya Mumbi: the Gikuyu Creation Myth* by Kariuki Gakuo and was published in 1992 by Jacaranda Designs, Ltd. Post Office Box 76691 Nairobi, Kenya. (ISBN 9966-884-72-6)

About the Author:
Kariuki wa Gakuo is among the many Gikuyu people to retell the tale of Gikuyu and Mumbi. He was born in 1964 in Kirinyaga District of Kenya; a graduate of the University of Nairobi, he has a Master's Degree in Oral Literature and enjoys writing poetry, fiction, drama, and short stories. His writings have appeared in many newspapers and magazines including *Viva, New Age*, and the *Daily Nation*. Kariuki is a writer with Jacaranda Designs, Ltd. He also enjoys playing music, traveling, and acting.

Mt. Kenya:
The Gikuyu people call Mt. Kenya *Kirinyaga* because of the dazzling brightness of the snow as it glitters off the black crystal rock. From a distance the mountain looks as if it is covered with black and white stripes. God, the supreme ruler of the universe is also known as *Ngai*, the owner of the stripes of *Kirinyaga*. Mt. Kenya is also known as *Kirimaara*, the spotted mountain.

The Legend:
Some people say that Gikuyu and Mumbi had ten daughters; however, according to Gikuyu custom, counting one's children or wealth is a bad omen that may lead to death. The Gikuyu therefore speak of the nine full clans instead of ten. However, according to the legend, when Gikuyu told his daughters to bring him the ritual sticks, Gikuyu's tenth daughter, Wamuyu, the youngest, failed to do so and therefore did not get a husband. However, later she bore children while still in her father's home and her children became the tenth clan of the Gikuyu people.

Teacher Resource
Historical Highlights of the Gikuyu People

Phase I   15th - 18th Centuries: Gikuyuland

1. Ancestors of the Gikuyu people migrate from the Meru area in northern Kenya to the lands surrounding Mount Kenya.
2. The Gikuyu develop a creation myth which explains the origin of the people and their God-given right to the land.
3. The Gikuyu developed a relatively small-scale agricultural economy like the Kamba and Luo and traded with pastoral groups such as the Masai and Turkana.
4. Mogo wa Kebiro, the national prophet, warns elders of famine and the arrival of strangers with clothes like butterflies and skins like pale frogs. He predicts that they will carry fire sticks and be followed by a huge iron snake.

Phase II   19th Century: The Settlers Arrive

1. The first white men are seen in the Gikuyu lands.
2. The settlers' railway runs from Mombassa to Lake Victoria bring indestructible "iron snakes" into Kenya.
3. In the 1880's Britain lays claim to Kenya as the "magnificent African cake" is carved up by European powers at the Berlin Conference.
4. Famine and small pox decimate the Gikuyu.

Phase III   20th Century: British Colonization

1. The handful of white settlers in Kenya in 1905 swells to 20,000 settlers by 1948.
2. The Gikuyu people are confined to "tribal reserves"; traditional farming methods are destroyed.
3. Gikuyu people who do not work on the reserve are subjected to the pass-like system of registration known as "Kipande."
4. Over six million acres of land including Masai pasture and Kamba and Gikuyu farms are stolen as the settlers develop tea and coffee plantations.

Phase IV   20th Century: Mau Mau and Independence

1. The British destroy the Gikuyu system of social and economic organization, which is dependent upon land tenure. Land tenure refers to the acquisition of land through hunting rights, purchase, or inheritance.
2. In 1951 Gikuyu freedom fighters known as Mau Mau by the British mobilize themselves through oathing ceremonies and initiate armed resistance.
3. The British declare a state of Emergency; 32 Europeans and 13,000 Gikuyu die.
4. Jomo Kenyatta is released from prison and becomes the first president of independent Kenya in 1963.

Source: Furedi, Frank. *The Mau Mau War in Perspective*. London: James Currey and Athens: Ohio University Press, 1991.

Student Handout
The Author and His Work

The son of a Gikuyu farmer, Ngugi wa Thiong'o was born in Kamiriithu, Limuru in 1938. He studied at Kamaandura Maanguuu grammar school and Alliance High School and attended Makerere University in Uganda, where he studied English literature. As a student in 1962, Ngugi wrote his first play, *The Black Hermit*, which was produced for the Uganda National Theater. He also wrote his first two novels while he was an undergraduate. Published in 1964, *Weep Not Child* was the first novel published by an East African writer in English and won awards from the East African Literature Bureau and the Dakar Festival of Negro Arts. Although *The River Between* was published in 1965, it was actually written first and provides the basis for *Weep Not Child*. At first, Ngugi used his Christian name, James Ngugi.

After graduation, Ngugi worked on Nairobi's *Daily Nation* and attended graduate school at the University of Leeds, England. He composed *A Grain of Wheat*, published in 1967 and took a position at Nairobi's University College. He abandoned his Christian name for his traditional Gikuyu name, and became the editor of *Zuka: A Journal of East African Creative Writing*. In 1969, Ngugi resigned in protest of the university's policies concerning students; however, he published *This Time Tomorrow* as well as a variety of essays in *The New African* and *Zuka*.

Ngugi returned to the University of Nairobi and published collected essays in *Homecoming* in 1972, *Secret Lives* in 1975, and *Petals of Blood* in 1977. In 1976, Ngugi wrote *The Trial of Dedan Kimathi*. This work portrayed the tragedy of a Mau Mau hero and was presented during the celebrations commemorating the victory of the Mau Mau freedom fighters; however, finding his work threatening, the government authorities canceled the play after a few performances. Many Kenyans, were enraged.

In 1977, Ngugi wrote *Ngaahika Ndeenda*, or *I Will Marry when I Want*, in Kikuyu. The play featured local peasants and workers as actors and was produced in a theater built by the Kamiriithu community. However, this production was short-lived, for the government felt it was subversive. Ngugi was detained in prison for one year; no charges were levied against him, however, and he was never brought to trial. The overwhelmingly popular response to the play convinced Ngugi of the importance of writing in a language Kenyans could understand.

During his incarceration, Ngugi wrote his prison memoirs and published *Detained: A Writer's Prison Diary*. He also started writing a novel in Kikuyu on carefully hidden sheets of toilet paper. The manuscript was confiscated but eventually published as *Caitaani Mutharaba-ini* in Kikuyu in 1980 and as *Devil on the Cross* in English in 1982. The powerful oral reading of the novel in Kikuyu in neighborhood bars resulted in a surprising realization by both the people and the author. The Kenyans realized that true freedom had never been won, and Ngugi realized that the people could not read any of the work he published in English. His latest novels include *Matigari*, which was published in Kikuyu in 1986 and translated into English in 1987, and *Murogi wa Kagoog*, written in Kikuyu.

Ngugi's theoretical works are written in English. These include *Writers in Politics* (1981), *Decolonizing the Mind* (1986), *Moving the Center* (1993), and *Penpoints, Gunpoints and Dreams* (1998), all of which challenge artists to seek freedom from western cultural dominance. In 1982 Ngugi relocated to the United States. Since 1989, he has taught Comparative Literature and Performance Studies at Yale University and New York University. In 2002, he was made the director of the International Center for Writing and Translation at the University of California in Irvine.

Student Handout
A Selected Bibliography of Ngugi's Work

Weep Not Child. 1964. Portsmouth, NH, Heinemann, 1988.

The River Between. 1965. Portsmouth, NH, Heinemann, 1990.

A Grain of Wheat. 1967. Portsmouth, NH, Heinemann, 1994.

The Black Hermit. Portsmouth, NH, Heinemann, 1968.

The Trial of Dedan Kimathi. With Micere Mugo. 1977. Portsmouth, NH, Heinemann, 1981.

Petals of Blood. 1977. Portsmouth, NH, Heinemann, 1991.

I Will Marry when I Want. With Ngugi wa Mirii and translated from the Kikuyu by the authors. Nairobi, Kenya: Heinemann Educational Books, 1980.

Writers in Politics. London: Heinemann Educational Books, 1981.

Detained: A Writer's Prison Diary. London: Heinemann, 1981.

Devil on the Cross. Trans. Ngugi wa Thiong'o. 1982. Portsmouth, NH: Heinemann, 1987.

Decolonizing the Mind: The Politics of Language in African Literature. 1981. Portsmouth, NH, Heinemann, 1986.

Matigari. Trans. Wangui wa Goro. Portsmouth, NH: Heinemann, 1987.

Moving the Centre: The Struggle for Cultural Freedoms. Portsmouth, NH: Heinemann, 1993.

Student Handout
Major and Minor Characters

Mugo   _____

Gikonyo   _____

Kihika   _____

Mumbi   _____

Karanja   _____

Waitherero   _____
Wambui   _____
Warui   _____
Gitogo   _____
Githua   _____
Lieutenant Koina   _____
General R.   _____
D.O. Robson   _____
Mr. Rogers   _____
Henry Van Dyke   _____
John Thompson   _____
Margery Thompson   _____
Mrs. Dickinson   _____
Dr. Lynd   _____
Richard Burton   _____
Wangari   _____
Waruhiu   _____
Mbugua   _____
Wanjiku   _____
Rev. Jackson Kigondu   _____
Muniu   _____
Wambuku   _____
Njeri   _____
Gatu   _____
Kariuki   _____
Oginda Odinga   _____
Mwaura   _____
Morris Kingori   _____
Wairimu   _____
Njoki   _____

Teacher Resource
Major Characters

Mugo

- despondent character who desires to kill his aunt
- credited with organizing hunger strike at Rira
- revealed to reader as Kihika's traitor
- seeks to isolate himself from the struggle and faces a moral dilemma

Gikonyo

- carpenter and leader in village
- a hard worker who had been in detention
- chairman of the local Mau Mau branch
- loves and marries Mumbi
- troubled over changes in Mumbi his wife
- detained and confessed taking oath
- released from prison
- returns home to unexpected circumstances
- faces his own guilt and desires reconciliation with Mumbi

Kihika

- deceased freedom fighter who came into Mugo's life
- Mumbi's brother; spirit of revolution
- led Mau Mau in forest
- presented as a butcher by some and a hero by others

Mumbi

- beautiful woman; sister of Kihika; wife of Gikonyo
- her name recounts the myth of Mumbi and Gikuyu
- waits for her husband Gikonyo
- gave birth to Karanja's child
- wants to talk to Gikonyo about the child
- acquires a new found independence

Karanja

- appears to be guilty of betraying Kihika
- works at Githima library dusting books
- courted Mumbi and proposed
- contemptuous of Kihika
- fathered Mumbi's child
- became local chief
- resigned as chief after a local scandal

Teacher Resource
Minor Characters

- Waitherero - Mugo's aunt, a drunk who disdains him
- Wambui - a woman who carried secrets for the Mau Mau; she sometimes tied a pistol to her thighs near the groin
- Warui - village elder who carries the history of the Mau Mau
- Gitogo - deaf mute villager
- Githua - comic, cripple villager who was wounded; claims he supplied ammunition to the Mau Mau and was crippled by a white man's bullet; this story is untrue, his truck turned over on his leg and broke it
- Lieutenant Koina - a freedom fighter; revealed as Dr. Lynd's house boy
- General R. - a freedom fighter; quiet man of action; his real name is Muhoya
- D. O. Robson - white settler; district officer shot by Kihika
- Mr. Rogers - agricultural officer and planner crushed by Githima railroad
- Henry Van Dyke - Mrs. Thompson's lover; brought up in South Africa
- John Thompson - Administrative Secretary; former District Officer depth of racism
- Margery Thompson - John Thompson's wife
- Mrs. Dickinson - young librarian
- Dr. Lynd - plant pathologist with fierce dog
- Richard Burton - settler who will sell his land to Gikonyo
- Wangari - Gikonyo's mother
- Waruhiu - Gikonyo's father who ordered mother and son to leave
- Mbugua - Mumbi's father
- Wanjiku - mother of Mumbi and Kihika
- Rev. Jackson Kigondu - traitor who preached against the Mau Mau
- Muniu - Bible school teacher
- Wambuku - Mumbi's friend; pregnant with Kihika's child; she was beaten by home guards in trench and died three months later
- Njeri - Mumbi's friend; loved Kihika and followed him into forest
- Gatu - the good spirit among the prisoners; murdered in prison
- Kariuki - Mumbi and Kihika's younger brother who goes to school
- Oginda Odinga - political activist
- Mwaura - messenger sent to convince Karanja to attend the Independence Day Ceremony
- Morris Kingori - preacher
- Wairimu - Karanja's mother
- Njoki - woman in Wairimu's story about a son who didn't work

Student Handout
Background on The Cycle of Life

The cycle of life, or the force that moves an individual through birth, life, death, and new life, provides a profound cultural and religious worldview for traditional Gikuyu life. Gikuyu society is based on an age-grade system whereby an individual moves through phases related to life and death. The life stages educate the individual and define status, privilege, and responsibility. Ritual sacrifices and prayers, most of which involve communication with the ancestors, mark the major phases of life.

Birth: A child is given a name that reflects his or her relationship to the ancestors. Children perpetuate their grandparents.

Childhood: The child learns obedience and respect. The father places a small wristlet of goatskin on the child signifying that he or she is a full person in the Gikuyu society. When a child is old enough to herd goats, another rite features wristlets that symbolize the bond between the child and the entire nation. The wristlet represents a link in the chain of life, connecting the child with the living and the dead. The ring symbolizes the cycle that links the past with the present. At an early age, the child learns that this sacred link must never be broken. Later, the child reenacts his or her physical birth by being placed between his mother's legs; he is bound to her with a goat's intestine. This symbolic second birth signifies that the child has been born again. This rite prepares the individual to move through the cycle of life.

Initiation: Initiation is the next crucial phase and marks the passage of an individual from childhood into adulthood. This rite includes the surgical circumcision of boys and girls, education, ritual dances, and songs. After initiation, the young adult is considered a fully mature Gikuyu who may marry, found a homestead, bury his parents, inherit property, and participate in rituals. Initiation is an essential link in the life cycle through which the individual is born into adulthood.

Adulthood: Adulthood is marked by marriage, which bestows superior status on an individual. After the first child is born, parents are allowed to take part in ritual ceremonies and to be initiated as elders.

Elderhood: An individual becomes part of the Kiama, or the "Gikuyu Court of Elders," entitled to administer justice. Political authority is delegated to males and females; the elders are revered, for they will soon journey through death and join the ancestors.

Death: Death is a threshold into new life. The departed who are remembered are known as the "living-dead," or the deceased who have achieved immortality by living on in the memory of the living. These ancestors are remembered through the names, songs, stories, dances, and rituals.

The Living-dead: The living-dead are considered people and return to their families to share meals and give advice. They are intermediaries with God, and they are remembered through rituals.

The Dead-dead: Only when the living-dead pass on into the dark and shadowy world of the forgotten do they become the dead-dead. At this point, the soul dies. Therefore, elders who are approaching the threshold of death impress the importance of remembering the ancestors upon young Gikuyu. These elders have a vested interest in training the youth to remember their ancestors well.

Summary: The traditional cycle of Gikuyu life presents life after death as remembrance rather than resurrection, for the relationship between the living and the living-dead is one of reverent remembrance, communication, and communion. Prayer and worship are reserved only for God, whose movement is signaled by thunder and lightning as he travels from one sacred place to another.

Source: Mbiti, John. *African Religion and Philosophy*. London: Heinemann, 1969.

Student Handout
The Life Cycle Chart

After studying the traditional cycle of life, relate the movement of life, death, rebirth, and new life to the independence struggle in Kenya or any other independence struggle. Project the phases of the freedom fighters as they are born into the revolution, become mature fighters, and in some cases die in order to bring about the new life of freedom.

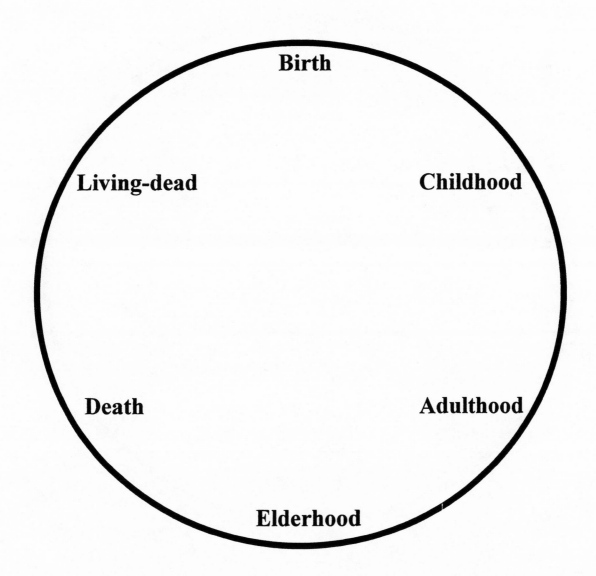

Student Handout
Character and Plot Development

Explain the complexities of human behavior within the Kenyan freedom struggle by analyzing the development of the main characters and plot. Do the characters move through the various stages of the traditional Gikuyu life cycle? Are they born into the freedom struggle? Do they grow, die, and are they finally reborn into new life personally and politically?

Birth
1. Kihika _____
2. Mugo _____
3. Mumbi _____
4. Gikonyo _____

Rebirth
1. Kihika _____
2. Mugo _____
3. Mumbi _____
4. Gikonyo _____

Growth
1. Kihika _____
2. Mugo _____
3. Mumbi _____
4. Gikonyo _____

Death
1. Kihika _____
2. Mugo _____
3. Mumbi _____
4. Gikonyo _____

Teacher Resource
Character and Plot Development

Explain the complexities of human behavior within the Kenyan freedom struggle by analyzing the development of the main characters and plot. Do the characters move through the various stages of the traditional Gikuyu life cycle? Are they born into the freedom struggle? Do they grow, die, and are they finally reborn into new life personally and politically?

Birth
1. Kihika   freedom fighter
2. Mugo   dragged into revolution by Kihika
3. Mumbi   sister of Kihika; wife of Gikonyo
4. Gikonyo   carpenter

Rebirth
1. Kihika   he is a second grain of wheat
2. Mugo   confession to Mumbi
3. Mumbi   reconciliation with Gikonyo
4. Gikonyo   love and forgiveness of Mumbi

Growth
1. Kihika   leader - Kenya's Moses
2. Mugo   freedom fighter
3. Mumbi   supported the home front
4. Gikonyo   freedom fighter – detainee

Death
1. Kihika   dies - he is betrayed and killed by British
2. Mugo   guilt betrayed Kihika
3. Mumbi   Karanja relationship - results in child
4. Gikonyo   confesses that he took the Mau
             Mau oath

Student Handout

Psychological Complexities: Social and Personal Relationships

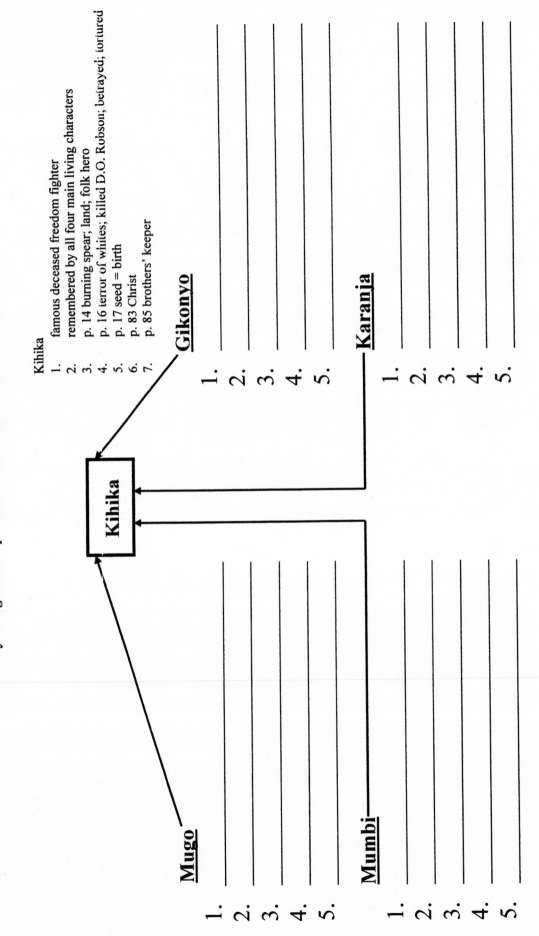

Kihika

1. famous deceased freedom fighter
2. remembered by all four main living characters
3. p. 14 burning spear; land; folk hero
4. p. 16 terror of whites; killed D.O. Robson; betrayed; tortured
5. p. 17 seed = birth
6. p. 83 Christ
7. p. 85 brothers' keeper

Gikonyo

1.
2.
3.
4.
5.

Karanja

1.
2.
3.
4.
5.

Kihika

Mugo

1.
2.
3.
4.
5.

Mumbi

1.
2.
3.
4.
5.

Teacher Resource

Psychological Complexities: Social and Personal Relationships

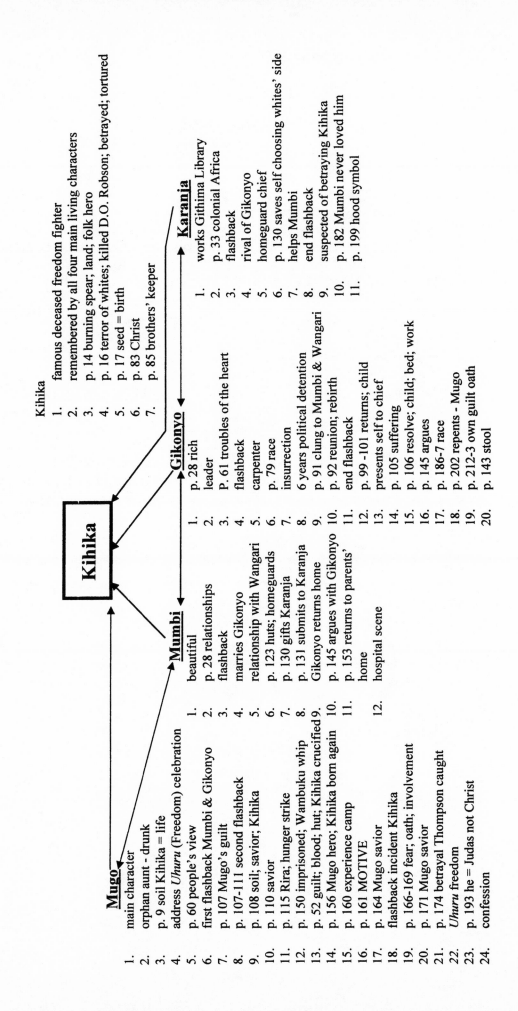

Kihika

1. famous deceased freedom fighter
2. remembered by all four main living characters
3. p. 14 burning spear; land; folk hero
4. p. 16 terror of whites; killed D.O. Robson; betrayed; tortured
5. p. 17 seed = birth
6. p. 83 Christ
7. p. 85 brothers' keeper

Karanja

1. works Githima Library
2. p. 33 colonial Africa
3. flashback
4. rival of Gikonyo
5. homeguard chief
6. p. 130 saves self choosing whites' side
7. helps Mumbi
8. end flashback
9. suspected of betraying Kihika
10. p. 182 Mumbi never loved him
11. p. 199 hood symbol

Gikonyo

1. p. 28 rich
2. leader
3. P. 61 troubles of the heart
4. flashback
5. carpenter
6. p. 79 race
7. insurrection
8. 6 years political detention
9. p. 91 clung to Mumbi & Wangari
10. p. 92 reunion; rebirth
11. end flashback
12. p. 99 -101 returns; child
13. presents self to chief
14. p. 105 suffering
15. p. 106 resolve; child; bed; work
16. p. 145 argues
17. p. 186-7 race
18. p. 202 repents - Mugo
19. p. 212-3 own guilt oath
20. p. 143 stool

Mumbi

1. beautiful
2. p. 28 relationships
3. flashback
4. marries Gikonyo
5. relationship with Wangari
6. p. 123 huts; homeguards
7. p. 130 gifts Karanja
8. p. 131 submits to Karanja
9. Gikonyo returns home
10. p. 145 argues with Gikonyo
11. p. 153 returns to parents' home
12. hospital scene

Mugo

1. main character
2. orphan aunt - drunk
3. p. 9 soil Kihika = life
4. address *Uhuru* (Freedom) celebration
5. p. 60 people's view
6. first flashback Mumbi & Gikonyo
7. p. 107 Mugo's guilt
8. p. 107-111 second flashback
9. p. 108 soil; savior; Kihika
10. p. 110 savior
11. p. 115 Rira; hunger strike
12. p. 150 imprisoned; Wambuku whip
13. p. 52 guilt; blood; hut; Kihika crucified
14. p. 156 Mugo hero; Kihika born again
15. p. 160 experience camp
16. p. 161 MOTIVE
17. p. 164 Mugo savior
18. flashback incident Kihika
19. p. 166-169 fear; oath; involvement
20. p. 171 Mugo savior
21. p. 174 betrayal Thompson caught
22. *Uhuru* freedom
23. p. 193 he = Judas not Christ
24. confession

Student Handout
Uhuru Day Speech

1. Mugo has been asked to write a speech celebrating *Uhuru* or freedom. If your character is Mugo, as a group begin to imagine what you would *really* like to say in that speech. Since this speech is only occurring in the character's mind, you should be completely honest. Your speech will be somewhat like a soliloquy. Try to capture the essence of the character's personality and point of view in the speech. Make sure your speech covers the following:
    - Review Mugo's life history.
    - Explain Mugo's initial reaction to the freedom struggle.
    - Identify Mugo's personal and political motives for supporting or betraying the struggle for independence.
    - Review the life history of Kihika from Mugo's point of view.
    - Provide tentative reasons for Kihika's betrayal and death from Mugo's point of view.
    - Use as many quotes from the text as possible.

2. If your group represents Mumbi, Gikonyo, or Karanja, pretend that you were just about to write an obituary of Kihika when you hear that Mugo has been asked to write a speech celebrating *Uhuru* or freedom. Begin to imagine what *you* would like to say if you could give that speech. Since this speech is only occurring in the character's mind, you should be completely honest. Your speech will be somewhat like a soliloquy. Try to capture the essence of the character's personality and point of view in the speech. Make sure your speech covers the following:
    - Review your life history.
    - Explain your initial reaction to the freedom struggle.
    - Identify your personal and political motives for supporting or betraying the struggle for independence.
    - Review the life history of Kihika from your point of view.
    - Provide tentative reasons for Kihika's betrayal and death from your point of view.
    - Use as many quotes from the text as possible.
    - Be sure to identify your character.

3. One member of your group should be prepared to read your group's soliloquy or *Uhuru* Day speech before the class.

Student Handout
Essay: The Dimensions of Betrayal

Choose one of the following essays.

1. Choose one main character in *A Grain of Wheat* and discuss his or her betrayal of the freedom struggle. Weigh the ideals of the freedom struggle with the character's efforts to meet the demands of the Mau Mau. Analyze the redemptive quality of reconciliation by comparing the seeds of new life such as forgiveness and love with the seeds of destruction such as guilt and betrayal. Discuss the following points in your essay and give examples to support your points:
   - the character's motivation for participating in the freedom struggle
   - the failure to meet his or her ideals and the ensuing guilt
   - the individual's betrayal of the Mau Mau freedom struggle
   - the betrayal of the individual by other characters in the novel
   - the redemption of failure and guilt
   - the movement from death into new life
   - the demands of the freedom struggle on the individual

2. Choose one main character in *A Grain of Wheat* and discuss his or her betrayal of him or her self and loved ones. Weigh the character's ideals with his or her efforts to meet the responsibility of relationships with others. Analyze the redemptive quality of reconciliation by comparing the seeds of new life such as forgiveness and love with the seeds of destruction such as guilt and betrayal. Discuss the following points in your essay and give examples to support your points:
   - the character's motivation for participating in relationships with others
   - the failure to meet his or her ideals and the ensuing guilt
   - the individual's betrayal of loved ones
   - the betrayal of the individual by other characters in the novel
   - the redemption of failure and guilt
   - the movement from death into new life
   - the demands of the freedom struggle on the individual

3. Create your own essay focusing on any relevant point or question. Design a rubric or criteria for exploring the question. Suggested topics include:
   - a comparative analysis of various characters
   - a focus on literary techniques in the novel such as the reoccurring themes of the foot race, and use of flashbacks, monologues, and symbols
   - the psychological effects of guilt and betrayal on the characters in the novel
   - the personal and private betrayals of the characters as premonitions of a larger national betrayal

Reading Resource
Summary and Analysis

Chapter One

Summary: Mugo is introduced as a freedom fighter that has returned home after detention. He spends his day tilling the land given to him by Warui because the government confiscated his own land. Several minor characters are introduced: Githua is a humorous cripple; Gitogo is remembered as the deaf and dumb villager who had been shot by the British. Mugo feels the world has conspired against him; he is an orphan who was left with a distant aunt, Waitherero. She is a drunk and disdains him; he desires to kill her.

Analysis: The Emergency refers to the Mau Mau freedom struggle against British imperialism in Kenya. When Warui, a village elder who holds the history of Mau Mau, says: "These are the days of *Uhuru na Kazi*," he says, "These are the days of Freedom and Work" (p.2). He speaks in Swahili, one of the languages used in Kenya. This is an optimistic view of the situation. The Mau Mau movement emerged in 1946 as Jomo Kenyatta, a Gikuyu nationalist leader founded the Kenyan African Union. Instead of uniting with other ethnic groups in Kenya, the Gikuyu Mau Mau freedom fighters implemented a guerrilla campaign in the forest surrounding their homes. This grassroots struggle culminated in 1952 when the British arrested Kenyatta as the genius of the insurrection and declared a State of Emergency. The Kenyan African Union was banned, and after a controversial trial, Kenyatta was sentenced to eight years in prison.

Chapter Two

Summary: Kihika is identified as the "Burning Spear" of the Mau Mau who broke into the Makee police garrison in the Rift Valley. Kihika freed the prisoners and set the garrison on fire. Known as the "terror of the white man," Kihika was captured alone in the forest. He was tortured as the neck of a bottle was wedged into his anus, and he was finally hanged in public.

Analysis: The character of Kihika, who terrorized the Rift Valley in the heart of the white highlands in Kenya, is developed in this chapter. This chapter also contains an historical flashback. According to the creation myth, God gave the land surrounding Mt. Kenya to the Gikuyu people, and the women who sprang from the nine clans of Mumbi ruled the earth. However, just prior to the arrival of the British, the seer Mugo wa Kibiro predicted that strangers in white skins would take over the Gikuyu lands. The iron snake he describes is the railroad. Waiyaki is an historical freedom fighter that was buried alive by the settlers. He is known as the first grain of wheat that dies, but gives life to many. Kihika is a fictional character that is identified as the second grain of wheat, a martyr of the Mau Mau freedom struggle. The author refers to Harry Thuku, who is a historical leader, and Jomo Kenyatta, who was released by the British to become the first president of Kenya on December 12, 1963. The Swahili proverb *Kikulacho kimo nguoni mwako* means "That which destroys you is within you" (p. 15). This proverb sets the tone for the psychological conflicts experienced by the characters throughout the entire novel.

Chapter Three

Summary: The characters reveal that Kihika had been betrayed in the forest. Lieutenant Koina and General R are Mau Mau freedom fighters who believe Mugo sheltered and helped Kihika the night he was betrayed. The leaders ask Mugo to give a speech at the Independence Day celebration. They suspect Karanja betrayed Kihika.

Analysis: This chapter takes place during present time, four days before *Uhuru* or Independence Day on December 12, 1963. Kihika is revered as Kenya's Moses, the savior of the Gikuyu people, because he killed District Officer Robson. Mugo is hailed as a hero. These characters represent the young Gikuyu men and women who risked their lives in armed struggle against the British. The freedom fighters were supported by hundreds of thousands of Gikuyu in the "homelands." It is estimated that thousands of Gikuyu freedom fighters were murdered in the forest or hanged as criminals by the British.

Chapter Four

Summary: The setting is Githima, a forest between Nairobi and Nakuru inhabited by white settlers. Karanja, a worker in the library encounters Dr. Lynd's vicious dog, and an incident that has plagued Dr. Lynd is revealed. During the Mau Mau revolution, her houseboy, who seemed quite fond of her old dog, opened the door to the Mau Mau who tied and gagged her. They stole money and guns and hacked her beloved dog to pieces before her eyes. John Thompson's past is also revealed. He had been in charge of rehabilitating Mau Mau prisoners, but at his previous post at Rira, he beat prisoners for participating in a hunger strike and eleven detainees died. He was demoted and sent to Githima to serve as the Administrative Secretary.

Analysis: Later in the novel, the reader will learn that Konia, a lieutenant in the Mau Mau movement, is Dr. Lynd's houseboy. The white settlers Dr. Lynd and Thompson are suspicious of Karanja, the librarian, when in fact their house servants are opening them up to the Mau Mau. Dr. Lynd and Mr. Thompson symbolize the *Mbwa Kali* culture of the colonists in Kenya. *Mbwa Kali* is a sign posted on many white settlers' homes. It is Swahili for "Beware of the Vicious Dog." Dr. Lynd has purchased a second vicious dog to protect her from the Kenyan people. Thompson is depressed about turning the colony over to the Kenyan people and returning home to England.

Chapter Five

Summary: Like all the other characters in the novel, John Thompson dwells on the past. He is looking for a replacement for his own position, and his relationship with his wife Margery is strained. Her love affair with Dr. Van Dyke is described.

Analysis: The depth of Thompson's racism is revealed through the manuscript he wrote as an officer in East Africa during the Second World War entitled "Prospero in Africa." This alludes to Shakespeare and indicates that to be English is an attitude of mind. He also refers to Dr. Albert Schweitzer who wrote that the Negro was indeed a child who responded only to authority.

Chapter Six

Summary: The reader learns of Gikonyo's experience in the detention camps and villages. Mugo is revealed as the traitor of Kihika to the reader, but not to the other characters. He is officially asked to give the speech at the Independence Day Ceremony. Some of the villagers are busy preparing for the celebration; others are not sure about independence.

Analysis: The character of Gikonyo is developed as an enterprising, hardworking man who buys grains and vegetables for resale. Mugo is developed as a person who simply cannot love; he is distressed at being asked to sing the praises of Kihika, the man he so treacherously betrayed in the forest. The people who sing *Uhuru bado* are saying "Not yet Freedom" in Swahili. The villagers feel they are not yet free because conditions in the villages have not improved.

Chapter Seven

Summary: Gikonyo begins by telling Mugo of the day he missed the train years ago. The story recounts the race between Karanja and Gikonyo to met the train and to capture the heart of Mumbi. This flashback takes the reader to the railway platform at Rung'ei Trading Center in Thabai Ridge where the train climbs up to Kisumu and Kampala. Karanja wins the race to the train station, but Gikonyo captures Mumbi's heart. Much history is reviewed in this section, for there are flashbacks within the flashback. For example, Gikonyo, the young carpenter displays his skill and love for Mumbi by carving a beautiful wooden handle for her *panga*, or large cutting knife. The background of Kihika, Mumbi's brother is also revealed. As a young boy Kihika attended a Church of Scotland school where he learned the story of Moses. At the conclusion of this flashback, Kihika has moved into the forest to fight for freedom. Gikonyo remains behind, yet he is led into detention for supporting the Mau Mau movement at home.

The second section of the chapter, pages 104-121, is another major flashback to the period of time six years after Gikonyo was detained. At this point, Gikonyo is released from prison and walks the dusty road back home to Thabai. Throughout his detention, he looked forward to his reunion with Mumbi and envisioned giving birth to a new and free Kenya. He remembers how he was driven to the brink of madness when Gatu was hanged; he also remembers when he confessed taking the Mau Mau oath to the British authorities. Although he refused to name anyone involved with the administration of the oath, he carries the burden and guilt of betraying the Mau Mau and knowing that he is not the hero Mumbi thinks he is. Gikonyo arrives home to find Mumbi with a child securely strapped to her back. Mumbi bluntly states that it is Karanja's child. Dazed, he reports his arrival home to the village chief, who is none other than Karanja himself. In desperation, Gikonyo races home to strangle Mumbi.

Analysis: In many ways, chapter seven is the heart of the novel. This chapter is a series of flashbacks from the present to the past. The first flashback is found on pages 70-104. Within this flashback, the reader learns about the foot race and how Gikonyo won Mumbi's heart. There are several flashbacks within this framing flashback. The reader learns that when Kihika attended the missionary school as a child, he clearly understood the God of the Old and New Testament as Ngai, the Creator God of the Gikuyu. Kihika was moved by the story of Moses and related Christianity to his Gikuyu traditions. He claimed that the Bible did not forbid the Gikuyu circumcision of women, and when chastised by his teacher, he escaped from the classroom and ran into the forest. Kihika looks to Ghandi; he also believes that anyone who takes the Gikuyu oath of unity and carries the cross of liberating Kenya is a Christ figure. Kihika clearly identifies land as the mother of the Gikuyu people.

The second major flashback in the chapter alludes to the history of Jomo Kenyatta, Harry Thuku, and a growing awareness of political movements in other nations. The hanging of Gatu in prison represents the death of the good spirit of the revolution. Gikonyo clung to the memory of his mother Wangari and his wife while he was in prison. However, betrayed by Mumbi, Gikonyo enters a new prison when he returns home. Karanja represents the local authority backed by the British regime, yet he is the man with whom Gikonyo had taken an oath to fight the British. Gikonyo's race to strangle Mumbi at the end of the chapter is a dark reflection of the race he ran to win her love at the beginning of the chapter. Gikonyo is confused and distraught by many layers of betrayal and guilt.

Chapter Eight

Summary: Gikonyo continues confessing his guilt to Mugo. He has lost all desire to kill Mumbi and gives himself over to work. He admits his shame at being the first one at Yala Prison to confess the oath. Mugo begins to think of himself as a hero. He remembers how he tried to assist the helpless crippled Githua and his aunt and wonders if he could bury the past and give the speech at the Independence Day Celebration.

Analysis: In this extremely short chapter, Gikonyo's confession simultaneously makes Mugo recoil and reevaluate himself. Mugo begins to fantasize and visualize himself as a hero.

Chapter Nine

Summary: Mugo remembers being taken to Thika detention camp and then to Rira where the Mau Mau wanted to be treated as political prisoners instead of criminals. He gained prestige among his peers by withstanding torture and leading a hunger strike. Mugo visits Mumbi. She remembers her brother Kihika who was hanged on a tree like Christ. She tells Mugo her story about the home guards who burned her family's houses after Kihika captured the police garrison. Karanja helped Mumbi rebuild their homes and supplied them with food. Then he joined the homeguards in support of the British administration. Mumbi withstood the hardships in the village and longed for Gikonyo; she wondered if he were dead. Karanja finally arrived to tell Mumbi that Gikonyo had been released. Full of gratitude, she submitted to Karanja and let him make love to her. Konia and General R arrive during Mumbi's confession. Again, they ask Mugo to speak at the ceremonies, and they call for Kihika's traitor to come forward. They still believe the traitor is Karanja. Mugo says that he is not fit to lead them.

Analysis: While Gikonyo is detained in prison, Karanja helps Mumbi at home. It is not clear why Mumbi let Karanja make love to her. She did not love him. Somehow this gesture may have been a release for Mumbi and a symbol of her gratitude to Karanja for his help. However, Mumbi suffers the consequences of this action, for she becomes pregnant and gives birth to Karanja's child. These circumstances will complicate her life and her relationship with her husband Gikonyo.

Chapter Ten

Summary: Konia and General R. plan to force Karanja to attend the Independence Day Ceremony where he will be tried and perhaps killed. Karanja is increasingly more uncomfortable with the Gikuyu people and more at ease with their rivals, the Luo people. Thompson tells Karanja that he is about to leave the country, and Karanja panics. Mwaura, the messenger, wonders why Thompson didn't shoot Karanja rather than leave him alone and unprotected back in Kenya; this is what most settlers do to their dogs when they leave the country.

Analysis: Karanja has become a symbol of the people who supported the British settlers in Kenya. He is like the *mbwa kali*, the fierce dog that settlers rely on and then shoot when they are forced to flee. Karanja is also betrayed as his protector Mr. Thompson flees. He is wrongly accused of betraying Kihika simply because he has supported the British settlers; no evidence has been produced to indict him.

Chapter Eleven

Summary: The whites hold John Thompson up as a martyr of Rira at their farewell party. He was the official in charge when Mugo lead the hunger strike; as a result eleven prisoners were beaten and murdered. Dr. Lynd has seen her houseboy recently. She is afraid to stay behind, yet refuses to leave her property to the Kenyan people. Like Karanja, the homeguards, the Kenyan police force, are likened to *mbwa kali*, or vicious dogs, needed to protect the white settlers.

Analysis: Mr. Thompson is the official who was in charge of Rira when Mugo lead the hunger strike; as a result eleven prisoners were beaten and murdered. Dr. Lynd plans to leave Kenya only because her life is in jeopardy; she symbolizes the ambivalence and bitterness of many settlers. Likewise, John Thompson refuses to admit defeat; he claims that Africa needs Europe.

Chapter Twelve

Summary: Mumbi and Gikonyo quarrel bitterly, and Mumbi returns to her parents' home. Gikonyo's plans to buy Burton's farm, but he has been betrayed by his representative in parliament, who seeks to enrich himself. Mumbi's story of betrayal has cracked Mugo open. He remembers defending a pregnant woman in the trench who was being beaten by a homeguard. Mumbi has laid Mugo's heart naked. He begins to hallucinate and sees blood dripping from the wall of his hut.

Analysis: As the tension between Mumbi and Gikonyo becomes unbearable, Gikonyo's mother, Wangari, berates him. There has been no communication; Gikonyo has not asked Mumbi what happened, and Mumbi has not explained the situation to Gikonyo as she has explained it to

Mugo. Mugo's guilt seems to be driving him mad. The passing van sings *Aspro ni dawa ya Kweli* or "Aspirin is really the medicine." However, aspirin will not help Mugo's head.

Chapter Thirteen

Summary: The villagers sing of Mugo protecting a pregnant woman in the ditch and believe that he is Kihika born again. Mumbi is not welcomed at her parents' home and is troubled about Karanja being unjustly executed in the name of her brother. She begs Mugo to speak, and Mugo explains what happened years ago. He strangled Kihika by betraying him, and he tries to strangle Mumbi. He retells how Kihika posed as an old man in a World War II army coat. District Officer Robson addressed him saying "Usiogope, Mzee" or "Don't be afraid, Old Man." Kihika murdered Robson and hid in Mugo's hut. In those days, Mugo saw himself as Kenya's Moses and thought Kihika was mad. Kihika attempted to involve Mugo in the struggle and set up a meeting with him in the forest. However, Mugo never took the Mau Mau oath and thought that Kihika would kill him; therefore, he turned Kihika over to John Thompson. He saw this as a great act of moral courage and an end to his nightmare. Thompson accepted Mugo's tip by spitting in his face.

Analysis: The struggle for independence confused Mugo as it confused many of the other characters and the people of Kenya. Although he believed that an *mzungu,* or a white person, is not a man, he just wanted to live his life in peace; he did not want to get involved in the struggle. Believing that Kihika was a butcher, he wanted to keep himself alive for his own mission, not Kihika's mission. Mugo, who once thought of himself as Kenya's Moses, has became Kenya's Judas. Mugo did not want the blood money, nor did he want to know what he had done.

Chapter Fourteen

Summary: Britain's flag, the Union Jack, is lowered over Kenya on December 12, 1963. As part of the celebration, Karanja and Gikonyo compete in a three mile race and reenact their old rivalry for Mumbi's love; General R. and Konia also race. Gikonyo falls and takes Karanja down with him; Mumbi runs to comfort the injured Gikonyo. His arm is broken, and Mumbi follows him to the hospital. Mumbi realizes that Mugo did in fact betray Kihika, and she has written Karanja a note warning him to stay away from the ceremonies. A sense of doom hangs over the day; Kingori the preacher prays, and the people sing the praises of Kihika and Mugo. The crowd clamors for Mugo to speak. Instead of giving a speech that praises Kihika, Mugo confesses that he delivered Kihika into the hands of the white man.

Analysis: There are several important symbols in this chapter. The foot race between Gikonyo and Karanja is a shadow of the foot race in the beginning of the novel when Gikonyo initially won Mumbi's love; in this case, Gikonyo seems to reclaim Mumbi's love. General R, who is also Muhoya, reveals his mother's bondage to a violent husband; as a child Muhoya killed his father. His mother is like the Kenyans who are tied to the slavery of colonialism. As General R. looks out at the people at the Independence Day Ceremony, he sees the traitors of Kenya and the white settlers; he is outraged that the ghosts of the colonial past still haunt Independent Kenya, and he calls for a new Kenya built on the heroic resistance of the Gikuyu people. He reminds the people that Kihika was strangled and hanged at this spot in Rung'ei Market and calls for his betrayer. Mugo steps up and sacrifices himself on the very spot where Kihika was hanged. A sense of doom hangs over the Independence Day Celebration.

Karanja; Mugo; Warui, Wambui; Harambee

Summary:

Karanja: Mumbi tells Karanja she never wants to see him again, and he leaves for Githima on a bus named "Narrow Escape." Karanja had joined the homeguards to save his own life; he confessed the Mau Mau oath and secrets, and he had named men involved in Mau Mau operations.

Mugo: Mumbi is angry because Gikonyo still spurns her; she and Wangari visit him in the hospital. Gikonyo opens up after hearing about Mugo's confession; meanwhile, Mugo returns to his aunt, and she dies. General R. and Konia declare that Mugo must stand trial; Wambui will be the judge, and General R. and Konia will be the only elders present.

Warui, Wambui: Elders and leaders within the freedom struggle say that *Uhuru* was not what they had expected. After Mugo's confession, most people left the ceremony, and only a few elders stayed to pray and perform the ritual sacrifices. Mumbi arrives at Warui and Wambui's hut, and they discuss Mugo's actions and motives.

Harambee: Gikonyo remembers working on an irrigation system in detention camp. On a clear day, he could see the legendary *Kirinyaga*, or Mt. Kenya. While digging the canals, he used to think about carving a stool as a wedding gift for Mumbi from *muiri* wood. Lying in the hospital, the desire to carve the stool returns. Throughout his detention in seven camps, his courage had failed, and he confessed taking the Mau Mau oath. He realizes there is no difference between himself and Karanja and Mugo, those who openly betrayed the Mau Mau freedom fighters. Mugo was the only one with the courage to face his guilt publicly. He thinks about carving the stool again. There will be a thin man with hard lines on his face stretching his right hand to a woman who also has hard lines on her face. A child will join hands with them. When Mumbi arrives at the hospital, he asks her to return to their home to light the fire. She refuses. They need time to open their hearts to one another. Mumbi has acquired a new independence. After she leaves, Gikonyo decides to modify the stool. He will make the woman's figure big with child.

Analysis:

Karanja: Although he did not betray Kihika as the people thought, Karanja has betrayed the people of Kenya by cooperating with the settlers. His naming the Mau Mau freedom fighters while wearing a hood resembles the actions of the Ku Klux Klan in the United States.

Mugo: Mumbi's simple trust had forced Mugo to tell her the truth; his confession has lifted the burden of guilt from Gikonyo's shoulders.

Warui, Wambui: *Uhuru* Day has been a profound disappointment for the Gikuyu people. Some of the new nation's heroes are in fact traitors.

Harambee: Gikonyo realizes that he is also a traitor because he confessed the Mau Mau oath in prison. The stool he dreams of carving for Mumbi is a symbol of new life through reconciliation and love. The man and woman with hard lines on their faces are Gikonyo and Mumbi. The child they embrace is Mumbi and Karanja's child. Gikonyo will make the woman's figure big with child, which indicates that Mumbi will soon carry his child. However, Mumbi's refusal to return to their home to light the fire indicates that she has acquired a new found independence. Mumbi and Gikonyo have lived together in stony silence since his return; they need time to discuss the situation. The stool is a symbol of new life through reconciliation and love for Gikonyo, Mumbi, and the new nation of Kenya.

List of Works Consulted

Cantalupo, Charles, ed. *The World of Ngugi wa Thiong'o*. Trenton, NJ: Africa World Press, 1995.

Cook, David and Michael Okenimkpe. *Ngugi wa Thiong'o: An Exploration of His Writings*. London: Heinemann, 1983.

Davison, Jean, with the women of Mutira. *Voices from Mutira: Lives of Rural Gikuyu Women*. Boulder, CO: Lynne Rienner Publishers, 1989.

Decker, James. "Mugo and the Silence of Oppression." Ed. Charles Cantalupo. *The World of Ngugi wa Thiong'o*. Trenton, NJ: Africa World Press, 1995. 45-57.

Duerden, Dennis and Cosmo Pieterse, eds. "Ngugi wa Thiong'o." *African Writers Talking*. New York: Africana Publishing Corporation, 1972.

Furedi, Frank. *The Mau Mau War in Perspective*. London: James Currey and Athens: Ohio University Press, 1991.

Gikandi, Simon. "The Political Novel: Community, Character and Consciousness in Sembene Ousmane's *God's Bits of Wood*, Alex La Guma's *In the Fog of the Season's End* and Ngugi's *Petals of Blood*." *Reading the African Novel*. London: Heinemann, 1987. 111-148.

Heywood, Christopher, ed. *Perspectives on African Literature*. London: Heinemann, 1975.

Kanogo, Tabitha. *Squatters and the Roots of Mau Mau 1905-63*. London: James Currey, 1987.

Kenyatta, Jomo. *Facing Mt. Kenya*. New York: Vintage Books, 1965.

Killam, G.D. *An Introduction to the Writing of Ngugi*. London: Heinemann, 1980.

Killam, Douglas, ed. *The Companion to African Literatures*. Bloomington & Indianapolis: Indiana University Press, 2000.

Kinyatti, Maina wa, ed. *Kenya's Freedom Struggle: The Dedan Kimathi Papers*. London: Zed Books, 1987.

---. *Thunder from the Mountains: Poems and Songs from the Mau Mau*. Trenton, NJ: Africa World Press, 1990.

Kirwen, Michael C. *The Missionary and the Diviner*. New York: Orbis Books, 1987.

Mbiti, John. *African Religion and Philosophy*. London: Heinemann, 1969.

Nama, Charles. "Daughters of Moombi: Ngugi's Heroines and Traditional Gikuyu Aesthetics."
    Ed. Carole Boyce Davies. *Ngambika: Studies of Women in African Literature*. Trenton, NJ:
    Africa World Press, 1986. 139-149.

Presley, Cora Ann. *Kikuyu Women, the Mau Mau Rebellion, and Social Change in Kenya*.
    Boulder, CO: Westview Press, 1992.

Ray, Benjamin. "Religion and Rebellion." *African Religions: Symbols, Ritual, and Community*.
    Englewood Cliffs, NJ: Prentice Hall, 1976. 154-173.